D0308081

Companion to Japanese Britain and Ireland

In Print
1991

To Janie, Justin and Christina
for putting up with it all

COMPANION TO JAPANESE BRITAIN AND IRELAND

Bowen Pearse

with additional writing by
Christopher McCooey

**Published in the centenary year of
the Japan Society**

1991

© 1991 Bowen Pearse and Christopher McCooey
To be read in conjunction with p xxxi
The poem by Edmund Blunden on pp 140–141 is reproduced by
kind permission of Mrs Claire Blunden.

In Print Publishing Ltd is registered with the Publishers Licensing
Society in the UK and the Copyright Clearance Center in the USA.

British Library Cataloguing in Publication Data: A catalogue record
for this book is available from the British Library.

ISBN 1 873047 10 X

Front cover illustration: Compton Acres, Poole (photograph by
Bowen Pearse)

Back cover illustrations: Soseki Natsume (photograph courtesy of
Soseki Museum in London); 17th century enamelled Japanese jar
(photograph courtesy of the Ashmolean Museum)

Cover design by Russell Townsend
Maps drawn by Andy Prigmore
Typeset by MC Typeset
Printed by Henry Ling

The financial support of The Great Britain–Sasakawa Foundation
towards the production costs of this book is gratefully acknowledged.

First published in 1991 by
In Print Publishing Ltd, 9 Beaufort Terrace, Brighton BN2 2SU,
UK, Tel: (0273) 682836, Fax: (0273) 620958

Foreword

This book is a unique contribution to the history of Anglo–Japanese contacts. As Chairman of the Japan Society, as a British diplomat who served many years in Japan and as an amateur historian I have long been interested in British people who have contributed to relations with Japan. As a result I have visited some of the places in Britain which have connections with Japan. However, until I saw the proofs of this book I had not realized how little I knew about British connections with Japan. I was astonished to see how many museums in Britain have significant collections of Japanese art. I was delighted to learn that there are so many Japanese-style gardens in Britain. I was impressed by the number of places with Japanese associations.

This book is a mine of information for all who want to learn more about people and places with close connections with Japan. I am sure it will be of great value to British and Japanese students and to travellers around Britain.

Sir Hugh Cortazzi

Contents

Foreword v
List of maps x
Introduction xi
Note on the entries xxiii
Addenda xxvi
Acknowledgments xxix
Picture credits xxxi

Chapter 1   London Central   1
Bayswater / Belgravia / Bloomsbury / Chelsea
City / Holborn / Kensington / Knightsbridge
Marylebone / Mayfair / Regent's Park / St James's
South Kensington / Strand / Victoria / Westminster

Chapter 2   London North   26
Camden Town / Edgware / Hampstead
Highgate / Hornsey / West Hampstead

Chapter 3   London East   35
Bethnal Green / Clapton / Greenwich / Limehouse

Chapter 4   London South   43
Battersea / Camberwell / Clapham / Croydon
Lambeth / Lewisham / Sutton / Wandsworth

Chapter 5   London West   50
Ealing / Fulham / Hammersmith / Holland Park
Richmond / Twickenham

Chapter 6   South–east England   58
Birchington / Bournemouth / Brighton
Canterbury / Chatham / Chertsey / Chiddingstone
Dover / Exbury / Faversham / Gillingham
Godalming / Hartley Wintney / Hastings
Hindhead / Maidstone / Merstham / Newport

Poole / Portsmouth / Redhill / Rochester
Rudgwick / Southampton / Southsea / Uckfield
Winchester / Woking

Chapter 7   South-west England   92
Bath / Beer / Bristol / Exeter / Gulval / Newton
Abbot / Ottery-St-Mary / Plymouth / St Ives
Sherborne / Woodford

Chapter 8   Central England   107
Batsford Park / Birmingham / Broadway
Charlton Kings / Milton Keynes / Oxford
Waddesdon Village / Windsor / Woodeaton

Chapter 9   Eastern England   129
Bedford / Cambridge / Cottered / Derby
Hertford / Kettering / Linby / Long Melford
Ware / Wyton

Chapter 10   North-east England   144
Bamburgh / Barnard Castle / Batley
Boroughbridge / Bradford / Doncaster / Durham
Hartlepool / Hull / Leeds / Newcastle upon Tyne
North Shields / Ripon / Rothbury / Scarborough
Scunthorpe / Sheffield / Sunderland / Wallington
York

Chapter 11   North-west England   168
Blackburn / Bury / Carlisle / Chorley / Crewe
Kendal / Knutsford / Lancaster / Liverpool
Manchester / Milnthorpe / Preston / Rivington
Rochdale / Rossendale / St Helens / Warrington

Chapter 12   Wales   194
Aberystwyth / Caenarfon

Chapter 13   Scotland   197
Aberdeen / Alford / Blair Atholl / Bothwell
Bridge of Earn / Cupar / Dollar / Dundee
Dunfermline / Edinburgh / Glasgow / Golspie
Kirkudbright / Mull / Muchalls / Paisley / Stobo

Chapter 14   Northern Ireland   224
Belfast / Florencecourt / Londonderry / Saintfield

Chapter 15   Ireland   231
Bantry / Carrigaline / Cong / Dublin / Enniskerry
Glin / Kildare / County Sligo / Tramore

London bookshops   245
Index   247

List of Maps

Japanese Britain and Ireland xxv
London Central 2–3
London North 27
London East 37
London South 44
London West 51
South-east England 59
South-west England 93
Central England 108
Eastern England 130
North-east England 145
North-west England 169
Wales 195
Scotland 198
Northern Ireland 225
Ireland 232

Introduction

The search for Japan-in-Britain

Some years ago, on a hot late July day in Tokyo, a Japanese friend and I were hurrying to keep an appointment with a professor whom I hoped would be able to help with an article I was writing. As we turned the corner into his street, with a clear view of the professor's garden, I saw something that for a moment stopped me in my tracks. Somehow, for the rest of my life it would sum up for me all the good things that make up Japan, its people and things Japanese.

'It's to create the right mood', my friend said as we watched the professor's maid drenching the *rocks* in his garden, 'For the honoured guest, it is meant to give an illusion of coolness. To create the right mood'.

During my three-year stay, I was to see this mood-creation repeated in almost everything my host-country did. It was in the brush strokes of a scroll, in the way different parts of a garden were put together, each in just the right place. It was in the way that the shapes, textures and hues of fish, fruit, vegetables, laquerware and pottery were arranged in a table setting. It was in the small courtesies of everyday speech and behaviour.

Back in Britain, I wondered how many other travellers had been similarly affected. Had they captured something of this Japan and brought it back with them? Where were the gardens that the rich Victorians and Edwardians had transplanted to the British Isles, with such extravagance and attempted authenticity? Where were the fabulous art collections I had heard so much about, some so rare they cannot now be seen even in Japan?

And the people – Japanese, British, Irish – who had helped shape our four centuries of shared history. There were libraries of fact and fiction about the adventures of Japan's first Englishman, the blue-eyed samurai, William Adams. Pat Barr and others had written with such exuberance and gusto about the colourful adventures of the first foreign expatriates in Meiji Japan (1868–1912). And just as people from Britain and Ireland had gone to Japan, records abounded with accounts of Japanese coming this way, from as early as the 16th century.

There have been artists, adventurers, travellers, diplomats, gardeners, swordsmiths, emperors, princes and kings. What had their passing left behind? They had lived, worked, studied and made love here. Some were born here. Others died here. Where could their legacy still be seen? There were no ready answers.

Over the years in which this book has been in preparation, the number of enquiries has stretched into hundreds, the scope of the research has ranged across England, Wales, Scotland, Ireland, Japan, and the USA. The results of these years of delving and digging have brought some surprises. Whatever happened where, this is the first book that marks the spot.

A gallop through history

On 23 September 1543, at the time of year when typhoons rise out of the China Sea and turn stout ship timbers into kindling, a Portuguese junk struggled desperately to find landfall. The three traders, Antonio da Mota, Francisco Zeimoto and Antonio Peixoto, peered through the deluge of violent rain at the approaching coastline, unable to make out a familiar landmark. They had been travelling from the capital of Siam, heading for the Chinese coast and had lost their way in the storm. At last managing to clamber onto the unknown shore, they found the natives were friendly. 'Whiter than Chinese, with small eyes and scanty beards', was the report the Portuguese bequeathed to history. The friendly natives told them they were in 'Nipongi'.

In fact, the Portuguese had landed at Tanegashima, just off the southern coast of Kyushu. Theirs is the earliest known account of Europeans in Japan. It was the beginning of what is often termed Japan's 'Christian Century', although in truth only a small percentage of Japanese have ever become Christians. The Jesuit saint, Francis Xavier, arrived in August 1549. His often-quoted impression of the natives was: 'The people whom we have met so far are the best who have yet been discovered, and it seems to me that we shall never find among heathens another race equal to the Japanese'.

The other contribution for which the Portuguese will always be remembered was the gun. The traders were armed with the European arquebus, a long-barrelled matchlock. Japanese documents describe how 'some mysterious medicine was put in . . . which lit up like lightning . . . with a noise like thunder'. The Japanese wanted to manufacture their own thunder and the story is told of how the secrets of the gunsmith's art were obtained. The local swordsmith, it seems, had a very pretty 17 year old daughter. The Portuguese had been a long time at sea.

It has generally been considered that the first Japanese to reach the British Isles were a group of about 15 sailors, who arrived in Plymouth on 27 September 1614. There is, however, another claim. In Richard Hakluyt's *The Principal Navigations Voyages Traffiques & Discoveries of the English Nation*, published in 1598–1600, there is an account of two Japanese Christian converts, Christopher, aged 17 and Cosmos, about 20. The boys were aboard a Spanish galleon, the *Santa Anna*. The ship was attacked off the coast of lower California in 1587 by Thomas Cavendish during his voyage of circumnavigation in the *Globe*. The Japanese were well-received in England and became the focus of much attention. It is interesting to note that, at a time when it was not uncommon for the crowned heads of Europe to be illiterate, the boys 'could both wright and reade their own language'.

From the 1540s to the end of the century, the Jesuits in Japan had things much their own way. They were able to propagate a view of a catholic, undivided Europe – without a hint of a pagan past or of alternative protestant beliefs. So when, in April 1600, the priests sighted a Dutch ship in trouble off the coast of what is now Oita they made no effort to help.

This was in fact the famous *Liefde*, carrying Japan's first Englishman, the Gillingham born pilot, William Adams. Adams and his remaining crew of 24 (of whom 18 were so enfeebled they were unable to stand) were the sole survivors of five ships that had last seen the coast of England on 5 July 1598.

The Jesuits did everything they could to discredit the 'heretics'. They were pirates and should be crucified, they told the Japanese authorities. But the shogun, Ieyasu, had no intention of getting involved in Europe's religious squabbles. Adams's skills as a shipwright and his knowledge of the world became so valuable to Ieyasu that for many years he withheld his permission for Adams to return home. As compensation, Adams was made a feudal lord with a large estate, a Japanese wife and the ear of the most powerful man in the country.

The East India Company, hearing of the Englishman's good fortune, sent Captain John Saris to Japan. He arrived in Hirado, near Nagasaki, on 11 June 1613. Adams secured an audience with Ieyasu for Saris and the captain was permitted to open an English trading post near Nagasaki. Ieyasu died in 1616 and his successors were far less tolerant of the presence of foreigners. Adams himself died in 1620, after being in Japan for 22 years. He had never travelled home to Britain to see his English wife and child, even after Iyeasu had given him leave to do so.

The English trading post was unable to compete with the well-established Dutch and it closed two years later, in 1622. The Christian Century was brought to a cruel and terrible end. Overseas travel was forbidden to the Japanese. All foreigners were expelled, save for a handful of Dutch and Chinese traders.

The setting up of strong Tokugawa rule throughout the country had brought an end to Japan's long Age of Battles – centuries of blood-letting between war lords. Now, with a secure internal peace, in an exercise unparalleled in human history, Japan closed the country. For some two and half centuries, there was almost no direct contact between the people of Japan and the outside world.

Politically isolated from the rest of the human race, physically separated from the Asian mainland by over a hundred miles of often dangerous seas, Japanese culture flourished in a world of its own. In a manner of speaking, the Japanese became Japanese. Freed from outside ideas and competition, Japan's artists and craftsmen developed their own unique sphere of specialized workmanship to an extraordinary degree of perfection. With no wars to fight but appearances to keep up, samurai arms and armour became works of art – embellished and decorated and sartorially elegant.

Innovation was added to artistry. Porcelain, which came to Japan through China and Korea, reached a quality in seventeenth century Japan that no European potter could touch. Exports, channelled through the sole European traders, the Dutch at Deshima, found ready and rich European buyers. A recent British Museum exhibition showing some of the finest of these, was called *Porcelain for Palaces* – a title which puts the Japanese product precisely where it belongs!

Aware of the quality of Japanese exports and jealous of the sole trading rights given to the Dutch, other nations attempted to persuade Japan to recommence normal trade. Among the hopefuls were the voyages of the East India Company ship *Return* in 1673, and the Royal Navy frigate *Phaeton* in 1808. But the clam that was Japan remained resolutely clam-like.

By the middle of the nineteenth century, the patience of the Western powers was wearing thin. The industrial revolution had come and almost gone, and the modern world was committed to free trade. The maritime nations were fed up with Japan's brutal treatment of sailors unfortunate enough to be shipwrecked on Japan's shores. And US vessels were in urgent need of a Pacific coaling station.

Japan had spent too long having only itself for company. It was backward, weak and fragmented from within. So when Commodore Perry entered Tokyo Bay on his second (and forewarned) Japan visit in February 1854, with the guns of the US navy trained on the capital of the shogun, it was time for Sleeping Beauty to open her eyes and see how much she had missed.

However, if it was Uncle Sam who planted the wake-up kiss, John Bull was the first to be invited to greater intimacy. Japan's two-and-a-half centuries of withdrawal had been unparalleled in human history. Now her headlong rush from the middle ages to the modern world was to be nothing less than breathtaking.

There were several reasons why Britain became Japan's most favoured suitor. The first Japanese to visit nineteenth century Europe found that the world map over which they travelled was coloured a British-Empire pink. From Hong Kong to Singapore, from Ceylon to India, Aden and Egypt, it was the Union Jack that flew from the flagpoles. The Royal Navy ruled the world's oceans and City of London was the centre of the universe.

But it was perhaps the men on-the-spot who did most to secure an Anglo–Japanese future. Britain's pioneer legation was fortunate in having the services of superb linguists like Ernest Satow and W G Aston. Gaining a remarkably quick mastery of Japanese, these were just the kind of highly educated, cultured young men best able to win the confidence of Japan's leaders in waiting.

The future, our man in Edo was able to assure London, belonged to the monarchists. And when the young Emperor Meiji ascended the chrysanthemum throne in 1867/8, neither he nor his supporters were the kind of men to forget their friends.

Having made the decision to catch up with the West, Japan set about nothing less than to invent a nation. Emissaries were sent abroad to discover who coped best with the modern world – in what departments, why, how and which was right for Japan. The Meiji government adopted the German constitution (including the *Diet* or parliament), and modelled both its army and judiciary on those of Germany. The education system was from France. The navy and the preferred second language came from Britain.

Japan now needed the skilled men to make these systems work. From all over the world, technocrats from every trade and profession were offered contracts in Japan. These were not permanent posts. Like the British colonial service in the 1950s, these teacher–professionals were simply preparing the ground for the natives to take over. In the parlance of the day, they were Japan's 'live machines'. They were the 'honourable foreign menials' who, in a remarkably short time, would transfer a mainly peasant society on the rim of Asia to a power whose statesmen would demand (and get) a place at the top table.

But while men like John Milne were teaching the Japanese to measure earthquakes and Cornwall's Trevithick brothers blasted railway tunnels under Japan's mountain ranges, the Japanese themselves were getting their first glimpse of the outside world. Even before travel restrictions had been officially lifted, Japanese students were being smuggled out of the country to join undergraduates at universities in London and Glasgow. Within less than a decade, the future Admiral Togo was mastering mathematics in Cambridge and practising seamanship on the Thames-moored training ship *Worcester*.

In 1870, the 24 year old Hisanobu Samejima became Japan's first envoy in Europe. From his base in Paris, he represented his country in France, Germany and Britain. Two years later, in 1872, Munenori Terajima set up Japan's first legation in London.

In 1875, the Meiji government authorized the first of a number of shipbuilding programmes that led to full order books all over the British Isles. In Tyneside, on the Clyde, in Belfast and the Mersey, wherever there was space to build a ship, 'the Britain of the East' was being fitted out.

Today, the archives of these cities are crammed with photographs of smiling Japanese crews, of Anglo–Japanese get-togethers, of British-educated admirals coming to inspect and to take delivery of launch after launch. Japanese faces became common on the docksides. Business partners turned into friends and friends became allies.

At the same time, the craze for things Japanese swept across Britain. Shops like Liberty's, which opened in London's Regent Street in 1875, made their name with the first big Japanese shopping bonanza. There were silks, fans, wallpapers, screens, lacquers and Satsumaware.

Japanalia trod the boards in *The Mikado* and *Madam Butterfly*. Japanese art, particularly the woodblock print, had considerable influence on men like Whistler, William Morris and the Scottish architect and designer, Charles Rennie Mackintosh. Like the earlier *chinoiserie*, a new art form came into being, derived from Japanese-inspired Western art – *Japonisme*. The over-romanticized view of the much-read Lafcadio Hearn helped to create the picture of a Japanese fairyland, where anything might just be true.

Round-the-world travellers now included Japan on their itinerary. They brought back crates of Japanese curios – prints, exquisite carvings, swords, armour, *netsuke* and the like. Wealthy individuals amassed large collections which, in later years, became the basis of significant Japanese collections in museums and galleries all over the country.

A number of Japan-struck travellers found something else to go dotty about. One visit to Kyoto and they were ready to charter a yacht and cram it with stone lanterns, Buddhist statues, stepping stones and bright vermillion bridges – and anything else that was going to look fashionably Japanese back in Hertford, Hereford or Hampshire. The originals were not available, of course (the Japanese had grown quite fond of them over the past several centuries), so arrangements were made to ship copies home – with as many

Japanese gardeners as the creation needed and the traveller could afford.

The results of these no-expense-spared gardens began appearing all over the British Isles. Some, like the Japanese gardens at Compton Acres, Poole or the ingenious Tully Gardens in County Kildare made serious attempts to achieve authenticity. Other gardeners simply added a few Japanese touches to what was already there. Perhaps a stone lantern or two here, a tea-house there.

The first of several Anglo–Japanese Alliances came into being in 1902. For many, it was an official seal on friendships already begun. Strategically, it gave both countries additional security against a possible common enemy, Russia. Japan could keep an eye on Britain's interests in the Far East. And Japan (as many saw it) could do what she liked in Korea. The first renewal of the Alliance, during the Russo–Japanese War of 1904–5, seemed a logical step.

In 1911, following the very successful 1910 Japan–British Exhibition at London's White City, the Alliance was again due for renewal. This could by no means be taken for granted. In a lecture given to the Japan Society on 9 October 1978, the Minister Shozo Kadota, having had access to his embassy's records, spoke of the 'Herculean efforts' necessary by the then Ambassador Kato and his staff to obtain the British signature.

Britain's declaration of war against Germany on 28 July 1914 made no demands of Japan through the Alliance, the theatre of war being in Europe. There were in fact British fears that Japan's involvement might give the Japanese a free hand in China while the Western powers were otherwise engaged. Despite these reservations, Britain did ask for Japan's help in protecting Hong Kong and other territories within Japan's sphere of influence.

Japan declared war on Germany on 23 August. Military action was prompt and successful. Within three months, all Germany's Pacific territories north of the equator were in Japanese hands. A number of Japanese men also volunteered to fight alongside their British ally and their efforts are recorded in British war memorials and rolls of honour.

The war brought Japan a number of economic gains and resulted in a rapid expansion of her industries. Between 1914 and 1918, Japanese shipbuilding doubled its output of mercantile marine tonnage. But perhaps the biggest prize from

Japan's point of view was a place at the Versailles Peace Conference, on equal terms with the other allied powers.

In May 1921, the Crown Prince Hirohito made his first overseas tour. Years later, in 1945, in one of the first interviews he ever gave to the press, the Emperor was asked if he could remember the happiest period of his life. Without hesitation, he replied, 'My time in England'.

Hirohito is said to have been immensely impressed with Britain's constitutional monarchy. The dashing young Prince of Wales became an idol he was never to forget. (Half a century later, in 1971, Hirohito loyally made a private visit to the then Duke of Windsor exiled in Paris.)

As a house guest at Buckingham Palace, Hirohito was astonished and delighted by the informality. On the first morning of his stay, King George V strolled unannounced and half-dressed into the Crown Prince's suite. Giving his guest a hearty slap on the back, the king boomed 'Sorry me boy, no geisha here I'm afraid. Her Majesty would never allow it'.

Following the Crown Prince's visit, a replacement of the Anglo–Japanese Alliance was announced on 13 December 1921. It was now to be a four-power pact which included France and the USA. (The final phase of the Anglo–Japanese Alliance was allowed to lapse in August 1923.)

Throughout the 1920s and into the 1930s, Japan moved inexorably into what the Japanese themselves have called the *kurai tanima* – the 'Dark Valley'. It included world revulsion at the Rape of Nanking, Japan's brutal expansionism in China and Manchuria, Japan's walk-out from the League of Nations, and the imposition of US sanctions – culminating in the destruction of the US fleet at Pearl Harbour.

The brilliant tactician, Admiral Isoroku Yamamoto, the man who masterminded the surprise attack, had previously argued against the folly of taking on Britain and the USA. Yamamoto had toured the USA and visited Tyneside in 1923. His name can still be seen in the old Elswick Shipyard Visitors' Book [145]. His fears, ignored by Japan's wartime leaders, were all too well vindicated in August 1945 with the bombing of Hiroshima and Nagasaki and the annihilation of an estimated quarter of a million of his fellow countrymen, women and children. (Japan's *total* war dead was over two million.) This was Japan's first defeat in its millenium or two of history.

Japan's occupation and democratization, its second cataclysmic change in under a century, was initially under the direction of General Douglas MacArthur, the 'American shogun'. He was just the sort of figure to whom the Japanese could relate. If you got up very, very early in the morning, it was whispered, the supreme commander could be seen walking on the waters of the Imperial Palace moat. Japan's ultimate lesson in democracy was, therefore, all the more deeply felt when, on 11 April 1951, the elected US President, Harry S. Truman, gave the 'shogun' his cards.

On 8 September 1951, a peace treaty was signed by Japan and 48 Allied countries, but excluding the Communist powers. A number of political and trade problems remained to be resolved and memories of Japan's barbaric treatment of Allied prisoners of war could not easily be forgotten.

In 1953, the then Crown Prince Akihito attended the Coronation of Queen Elizabeth II. But almost another twenty years would go by before it was considered appropriate to invite his father. In the autumn of 1971, the Emperor Hirohito made a state visit to Britain and was seen by the crowds sharing a carriage with the Queen. But even then, there were controversial comments in the press. The tree, planted by the Emperor in Kew Gardens, was vandalized. (You can, however, see the replacement.)

During the next two decades, considerable progress was made towards reconciliation on all fronts. The post-war generation may have initially shown little interest in Japanese culture, but this, it appeared, was only through lack of opportunity.

In the winter of 1981–82, the *Art of the Edo Period (1600–1867)*, the greatest exhibition of Japanese art ever to leave home base, arrived at the Royal Academy with all the excitement of a pop festival. Impatient queues snaked round the courtyard into Piccadilly and the crush inside resembled the Tokyo underground at rush hour. These were not dutiful academics from university Japanese departments. The man on the Northern Line had heard what was on and he liked what he saw.

Stemming directly from this experience, and as interest in things Japanese continued to increase, a number of museums in the British Isles (including the British Museum, the Victoria & Albert and the National Museum of Ireland) opened new or refurbished Japanese galleries.

Japanese gardens started to come back into favour. A number that had been created around the time of the Anglo–Japanese Alliance, early in the century, were in a very poor state and had their first post-war restoration. During the 1970s and 1980s, new Japanese gardens were being created, some with personal Japanese assistance. Ikebana groups were formed. Quite ordinary garden centres began cultivating, selling and lecturing about bonsai.

Japan had had its own post-war difficulties with labour disputes and poor quality control and applauded Britain's improved economic status and world standing during the Thatcher years. Japanese companies responded to regional incentives with investment in Wales, the North East of England, Milton Keynes, Ireland and other areas. Mrs Thatcher herself visited Japan and was enthusiastically welcomed by the Japanese people. (After a series of embarrassing political and business scandals, there was a joke circulating that Mrs Thatcher would be number-one choice as the next premier of Japan!)

The Japanese presence here continues to increase. It is difficult to remember the 1960s when Japanese electrical equipment was so rare that it was necessary to seek out a specialist supplier who stocked Japanese spare parts. In 1966, when the Hiroko Japanese Restaurant opened in St Christopher's Place in London (after an outlay rumoured to have exceeded £140,000) it was supposedly the only Japanese restaurant in Britain.

Today, visiting a *sushi* bar is required City practice. Japanese restaurants continue to proliferate, instant *ramen* noodle soup is sold in Tesco. *Sake* rice wine is on the shelves of the corner off-licence. In some areas, *natto* (fermented soya beans) can now be purchased from a mobile shop. And *nori* (seaweed) and almost everything else Japanese can be had by mail order.

There are now so many Japanese expatriates here that small Japans-away-from-home have come into existence. A Japanese can work with Japanese colleagues in a Japanese company, seek medical help from Japanese doctors, have his hair done at Japanese hairdressers, play golf at Japanese courses, belong to Japanese-members-only clubs and send his children to Japanese schools.

As this book is going to press, the Japan Festival, the largest of its kind ever mounted here, is just getting into its stride. Costing over fifteen million pounds, there are events in more than 200 venues all over the country. The Albert Hall is putting on a five-day Grand Sumo Tournament. The largest Japanese exhibition ever will be at the V & A. There will be archery on horseback in Hyde Park and numerous performances of traditional and contemporary theatre, music and dance. More than 75 great Japanese films are being shown. And in an effort to see that tomorrow's generations have fewer misconceptions, there will be a nationwide education programme with fifty projects linked to schools.

Whatever would William Adams have made of it all?

Bowen Pearse

Additional note

This is Bowen's book, the product of many months of painstaking sleuthing by letter, by word of mouth, by searching among tombstones, by chivvying curators, by not giving up when the trail went cold.

I was asked to help write some of the entries to meet a tight deadline once the publisher had given the green light.

The material Bowen had uncovered was so well documented, referenced and cross-referenced that my job was comparatively easy – each person, place, and event was waiting for me in its own plastic colour-coded sheath inside a red clip-board box folder arranged by region. Quite simply all I had to do was read through and select the most apposite.

Although writing about Japan and the Japanese is my speciality I have learned a great deal by helping Bowen on this project. Indeed, it is something more than another writing assignment for me. After ten years living in Japan, from 1975 to 1985, like a number of others from Britain who had gone before me and about whom you will read in this book, I returned to my native Kent with a Japanese wife. We have two children, Matthew who is ten at the time of writing and Emi who is seven. The two characters used for writing our daughter's name in Japanese mean 'beautiful' and 'England'. We believe our children are not half-Japanese, half-British, but double – they are Japanese *and* British.

I hope this book will help them, in due course, be proud of the positive contributions each nation has made to influencing the history and enriching the culture of the other.

Christopher McCooey

Note on the entries

This book details and locates a selection of the main Japan connections in Britain and Ireland. It includes Japanese gardens and Japanese collections in museums, art galleries, libraries and archive repositories with important or unusual holdings of Japanese material.

People (Japanese, British and Irish), places, happenings and things with an interesting Japan connection are also described and linked to a particular place. In the case of a person, his or her house may be considered as the *main* entry. The main entry is then cross-referenced to any secondary entries for this person, such as their tomb. All secondary entries are cross-referenced back to the main entry.

There are 238 entries, each listed alphabetically by *place* within one of 15 geographical regions. Of these 15, Greater London is divided into five regions. Each entry has an individual entry number and these numbers are used in cross-referencing, in the index, and in the maps which show for each region the locations of the main places listed.

To get the most out of this guide, there are several other matters which should be borne in mind:

Japanese names. This being the English edition, names are printed as they are in England – given or personal name first, followed by the family or surname. While every effort has been made to achieve accuracy, the use of source materials such as handwritten documents and newspapers of different periods may inevitably lead to some idiosyncratic spelling and name order.

Museums and galleries: the changing scene. Items described could be seen around the time we went to press. However, they may not be on permanent show as displays come and go all the time. If you want to be sure that you see a particular item, most curators are happy to give you a private view if you contact them in advance.

Curator's choice. To give added interest to a number of splendid and eclectic Japanese collections, we asked the curator or keeper to make a personal choice of the item or items he or she coveted most. This is not necessarily the 'best' item in the collection. It can be quite unexpected – fascinating, rare or charming for any reason under the Japanese sun. We hope it makes your visit even more enjoyable.

Telephone numbers and opening times. We have done our best to see that these were correct at the time of going to press. They are, however, subject to change.

An invitation to readers

Japan connections are as infinite as friendship. Find something we've missed and it's a point scored and one more entry for the next edition. Suggestions, comments, and ideas to me please, c/o the publisher, In Print Publishing Ltd, 9 Beaufort Terrace, Brighton BN2 2SU, UK.

Bowen Pearse

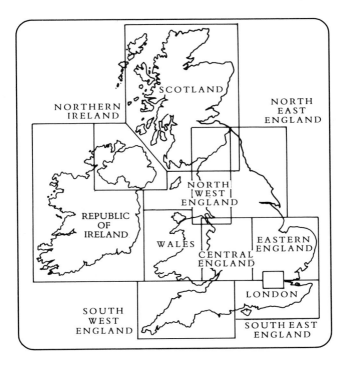

JAPANESE BRITAIN AND IRELAND

Addenda

Because of pressures of deadline, space and other considerations, it was not possible to devote entry space to all the Japan connections in our files for this edition. The publisher and authors wish to apologize for this and to thank all those curators and others who were so cooperative in supplying requested information. The following list of addenda gives the name of each site plus a very brief note of its interest.

LONDON CENTRAL
Museum of Mankind, Burlington Gardens, W1: Mostly Ainu material, available to serious viewers; **Embankment, WC2:** The statue of W.S. Gilbert near Embankment underground station shows the librettist of *The Mikado* holding a Japanese doll.

LONDON NORTH
Hendon Cemetery, Hendon, NW7: Japanese graves; **24 Christchurch Avenue, Kilburn, NW6:** Gunrunner for the Japanese during the Russo–Japan War, Ernst Brevis, lived here. Decorated by the emperor. (Original house extant, now converted into flats.)

LONDON EAST
East London Cemetery, Plaistow, E13: Japanese graves in Chinese section; **William Morris Gallery and Brangwyn Gift, Lloyd Park, Forest Road, Walthamstow, E17:** Examples of the collaboration between the woodcut artist Yoshijiro Urushibara and Frank Brangwyn, working under the patronage of Baron K. Matsukata.

LONDON SOUTH
Lambeth Palace, Lambeth, SE1: Cope and mitre presented by the laymen of the Christian Church of Japan in 1948, worn at the Coronation of Elizabeth II. (Access very restricted.)

LONDON WEST
The Japanese School, 87 Creffield Rd, Acton, W5: The only *Monbusho* – Japanese government Ministry of Education – run school, takes pupils from 9 to 15 years; **Wimbledon, SW19:** Arthur Waley grew up in what was then Hill House, Wimbledon Hill Rd, now Hill Court.

SOUTH-EAST ENGLAND
Brownsea Island, Poole, Dorset: Sika deer; **Teikyo School UK, Fulmer Grange, Framewood Road, Slough, Buckinghamshire:** Opened April 1989, takes pupils 12–17 years.

SOUTH-WEST ENGLAND
Antony House, Antony nr Torpoint, Cornwall: Some Japanese touches in the garden, such as stone lanterns; **Royal Albert Memorial Museum, Exeter, Devon:** A few interesting pieces. Japanese collections have recently been reorganized and records brought up to date. Detailed listing for genuine researchers; **Ilfracombe Museum, Ilfracombe, Devon:** Paintings and carvings; **Dorset College of Agriculture, Kingston Maurward, Dorchester, Dorset:** Historic Japanese garden recently restored; **Salisbury and South Wiltshire Museum, Salisbury, Wiltshire:** Prehistoric Japanese flint implements, part of the Pitt Rivers collection.

CENTRAL ENGLAND
Birmingham Reference Library, Birmingham: Holdings include the Sir Benjamin Stone photographic collection on Meiji Japan and other items; **Cheltenham Art Gallery and Museum, Cheltenham, Gloucestershire:** Small Japanese collection; **Herbert Art Gallery and Museum, Coventry, West Midlands:** Collection includes *c*1600 sword which, in June 1946, was ceremoniously handed over to the mayor from the men of the cruiser *Argonaut*, who had just returned from Hiroshima; **City Museum and Art Gallery, Hanley, Stoke-on-Trent, Staffordshire:** About 150 Japanese ceramics, late 19th to early 20th century; **Hereford City Museum and Art Gallery, Hereford, Herefordshire:** Small collection of Japanese prints, ceramics and costumes; **Warwick District Council Art Gallery and Museum, Leamington Spa, Warwickshire:** A small collection; **Gladstone Pottery Museum, Stoke-on-Trent, Staffordshire:** Jomonware as examples of the earliest pottery, a gift from the Tokyo National Museum; **Minton Factory Museum, Stoke-on-Trent, Staffordshire:** Some *Japonisme*; **Swindon Museum and Art Gallery, Swindon, Wiltshire:** Small collection, the most notable object probably being the suit of armour; **Westonbirt Arboretum, Westonbirt, Gloucestershire:** Rare and notable Japanese species main contribution to outstanding display of autumn colour; **Windsor Safari Park, Windsor, Berkshire:** Sika deer herd; **Aerospace Museum, RAF Cosford, Wolverhampton, West Midlands:** Has display of *kami-kaze* suicide aircraft and probably the last surviving example of *Dinah*, the Mitsubishi Ki-46-III high-speed reconnaissance aircraft, the early versions of which were unarmed.

EASTERN ENGLAND
Albert Sloman Library, University of Essex, Centre for the Study of Contemporary Japan, Colchester, Essex: Japanese

dolls collection; **Cecil Higgins Art Gallery and Museum, Bedford, Bedfordshire:** *Japonisme*; **St Mary's Churchyard, Chadwell St Mary:** Grave of Kadzuo Yamazaki, of the *Kawachi Maru*, died in fire on board ship, 13 July 1899; **Coddenham, Suffolk:** The famous de Saumarez private collection of Japanese art, here and in three other places in the British Isles, viewing by special arrangement with Lord Victor; **Derby Museum, Derby, Derbyshire:** Attractive prints collection and other items, including modern; **Hatfield House, Hatfield, Hertfordshire:** Interesting 16th century lacquer table cabinet inlaid with mother of pearl and some 17th century Imari dishes; **Shitennoji School in the UK, Herringswell near Bury St Edmunds, Suffolk:** Boarding primary and secondary school for Japanese boys and girls, opened April 1986, offshoot of the Shitennoji International Buddhist Schools and University, Osaka); **Ipswich Museum, Ipswich, Suffolk:** Arms and armour, also some interesting Yayoi pottery; **Leicestershire Museum, Leicester:** Small but reasonably good, well catalogued Japanese collection; **Usher Gallery, Lincoln, Lincolnshire:** Small collection including an inscribed 1863 temple bell rescued from a local scrap heap during World War II; **Melton Constable Park, Melton Constable, Norfolk:** Small, privately owned herd of Sika, not open to the public; **Central Museum and Art Gallery, Northampton:** Small collection including swords, armour and ceramics. The museum has lent a number of Japanese items to museums in Japan; **Castle Museum, Norwich, Norfolk:** One or two Japanese items; **Castle Museum, Nottingham, Nottinghamshire:** Part of Sir Frank Bowden's collection of arms and armour, given to the museum in 1921, supplemented with weapons from other sources. An interesting temple bell, *c*1715; **Museum of Costume and Textiles, Nottingham, Nottinghamshire:** Has large embroidered hanging from the Chion-in Temple in Kyoto; **Saffron Walden Museum, Saffron Walden, Essex:** About 50 items including armour and an early spice box; **Burghley House, Stamford, Lincolnshire:** Ceramics and lacquer; **Whipsnade Park Zoo, Whipsnade, Bedfordshire:** Japanese Sika deer, cranes, bears; **Woburn Abbey, Woburn, Bedfordshire:** Interesting Japanese items, some acquired by the family in the 18th century.

WALES

Cardiff: 3-day Welsh tour by the then Crown Prince Akihito and Princess Michiko in 1976; **Amersham International Centre, Whitchurch, Cardiff:** Japanese garden on nuclear site, no access; **Carmarthenshire Record Office – Dyfed Archives, Carmarthen:** Official government reports on Russo–Japanese War and other matters; **Pennar:** Remains of a flourishing shipyard for the Imperial Japanese Navy from the 1870s; **Glynn Vivian Art Gallery and Museum, Swansea, West Glamorgan:** Small collections including prints and screen.

Acknowledgments

No book is produced alone, especially one that attempts to trespass into the remotest corners and pry into undisturbed archives. The uncovering of Japanese Britain and Ireland was really achieved by those best able to know where to look for local secrets – local history librarians, archivists, vicars and curators. I am very much in their debt.

It is perhaps invidious to single out any particular library or information service, but I cannot leave unacknowledged the superbly well informed officers of the Japan Information Service or the librarians of my local Maidstone Reference Library, who have so frequently managed to field all balls bowled at them. I would also like to express my thanks to Satchiko Kimura, librarian at the university library in Kyoto who, when asked questions about Lafcadio Hearn that nobody else seemed to know, sent the text of an entire book with her reply. And for exceptional and painstaking information-gathering along a local trail, I must also include my gratitude to Vera Hodsoll of the Lewes Library.

Many busy people have given me a privileged insight into their personal relationships with Japan. The late Lord Armstrong of Bamburgh wrote to me movingly about his close friendship with the Tokugawas, direct descendants of the medieval shoguns, and of the times they had been his house guests. As liberals and friends of Britain, the Tokugawas had had to tread a delicate path during the fascist military years. In 1953, when the then Crown Prince Akihito stayed with the Armstrongs, the young heir to the throne told his host how much Bamburgh reminded him of home.

Edmund de Rothschild, of the well known banking family, put me in the way of a number of valuable sources. The emperor had awarded him the Order of the Sacred Treasure (1st class) for 'ceaseless endeavours' to secure Anglo–Japanese friendship. Mr de Rothschild told me he believed he was the youngest man ever to receive this honour and only the third foreigner. A passionate gardener, Mr de Rothschild is also extremely proud to have introduced a number of Japanese species into his famous Exbury Gardens.

I would like to thank the Great Britain Sasakawa Foundation and their UK administrator, Donald Warren-Knott, for their support. My thanks too, to Mrs Yu-Ying Brown, head of the Japanese Collections in the British Library, for reading the typescript and for her invaluable comments, pointing out any errors that had crept in (for which I take full responsibility). I am also indebted to Sir Hugh Cortazzi for reading the typescript and for his generosity in writing the foreword.

Vicars and church wardens have seemed tireless in their help, deciphering weathered churchyard inscriptions and extracting vital data from long and cumbersome parish records.

I am most grateful to local researcher John Barnes for his permission to use his recent findings on the childhood of William Adams and for his illustrations. My thanks go too to his namesake, John Barnes, the recently retired headmaster of Yalding Primary School, for information on Edmund Blunden in Yalding. My thanks also to Brian Roddick for the results of his sleuthing and his photographs of the late Ella Christie's Japanese garden in Scotland.

In Japan, my thanks to Richard Trevithick's descendants, Frank Okuno and other family members, for personal information; to the grandson of Lafcadio Hearn, Toki Koizumi, for permission to use photographs from the family album; and to Yutaka Okita for what he found out about Charles Wirgman's Japanese son and for his other searches among the Yokohama archives on my behalf.

I am indebted to John Milne's biographers, L.K. Herbert-Gustar and P.A. Nott, for information and for permission to use their photographs of the great seismologist; to Sammy Ikuo Tsunematsu, founder of the Soseki Museum, for what he told me about Japanese expatriates and for the use of his Soseki and Yoshio Markino pictures; to Maria Conte-Helm for her tips on the north-east she knows so well; to Douglas Cluett, Chairman of the Croydon Airport Preservation Society, for data and photographs pertaining to the record 1937 Tokyo–Croydon flight; to Jeremy and Masayo Passmore, for pointing out aspects of the Japan connection I might otherwise have missed; and to John Nightingale for reading the typescript.

Bowen Pearse

Picture credits

The authors and publishers gratefully acknowledge the valuable assistance and cooperation of the various organizations and individuals who took, supplied, and gave their permission to reproduce the pictures used in this book.

Aberdeen Arts and Museum Department, p 199; Ashmolean Museum, pp 120, 121; Birmingham Museum and Art Gallery, pp 111, 112; Church Missionary Society, p 88; Sir Hugh Cortazzi, pp 227, 228; Alastair Dingwall, pp 4, 8, 16, 33, 36, 39, 40, 49, 54; John Edmondson, pp 17, 246 (bottom); Embassy of Ireland, Tokyo, and Department of Foreign Affairs, Dublin (photograph by Lensmen Ltd), p 237; Gillingham Civic Authority, p 69; L.K. Herbert Gustar and Patrick A. Nott, pp 79, 80; HMSO (Crown Copyright), p 15; *Illustrated London News* (picture out of copyright), p 23; Japan Information and Cultural Centre, pp 127, 139, 153; Toki Koizumi (grandson of Lafcadio Hearn), p 235; Maidstone Museum, pp 73, 74, 75, 76; Manchester Museum, University of Manchester, pp 184, 186; Christopher McCooey, pp 68, 118, 134, 135, 156; John H. Passmore, pp 148, 207; Bowen Pearse, pp 81, 82, 89; Plymouth City Museum and Art Gallery Collection, pp 100–101; Lady Anne Rasch and Mrs David Rasch, p 105; Brian Roddick, pp 203, 204; Royal Museum of Scotland, pp 208, 209; Sheffield City Museum, p 164; M.D. Smith (author of *Leverhulme's Rivington*, Nelson Brothers, Chorley, 1984), p 190; Sutton Heritage Service, pp 46, 47; Heather Swabey, pp 38, 55, 246 (top); Richard Tames (picture out of copyright), p 13; Trustees of the V&A, pp 19, 20; Sammy I. Tsunematsu, Soseki Museum in London, pp 11, 40; Tully Gardens, p 242; University of Glasgow Hunterian Art Gallery, pp 211, 212, 213; University College of Wales, Aberystwyth, p 196.

The colour illustrations are reproduced by permission of: the Ashmolean Museum (Powder-flask and Watanabe screen); Lady Anne Rasch and Mrs David Rasch (Heale House Gardens); Heather Swabey (Oliphant's tomb); the Trustees of the Denys Eyre Bower Bequest, Chiddingstone Castle (The Beckford Cabinet); and the Trustees of the V&A (Hokusai print – photograph by Ian Thomas).

1 | *London Central*

BAYSWATER

(1) Coronet Cinema, 103 Notting Hill Gate, W11

'The Henry Irving and the Ellen Terry of Japan.' This was how the popular magazine, *The Sketch*, of 23 May 1900, hailed the performances of Otojiro Kanakami and his wife, the ex-geisha Sada Yakko, the principal players of the 'full Japanese company' playing at the Coronet Theatre (now the Coronet Cinema). 'The interest in Japanese plays and players grows daily', the paper noted. Sada Yakko's *koto* is in the Pitt Rivers Museum in Oxford [112].

BELGRAVIA

(2) St Michael's Church, Chester Square, SW1

Japan declared war on Germany on 23 August 1914, some three weeks after her partner in the Anglo–Japanese Alliance. Japan's contribution to the Allied cause is commemorated in the War Memorial Chapel of St Michael's Church, at the western end of Chester Square, SW1. The arms, to all 12 World War I allies, including Japan, are set into the perpendicular windows, one above the other, in four columns.

BLOOMSBURY

(3) 36 Gordon Square, WC1

Arthur Waley, scholar, linguist and first translator of Murasaki Shikibu's classic 11th century, *The Tale of Genji*, lived at

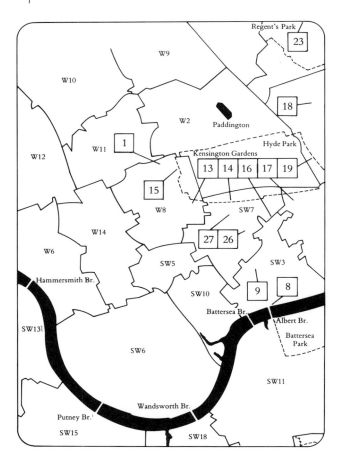

LONDON CENTRAL

number 36 for about 40 years. In 1962, Waley moved to 50 Southwood Lane, Highgate. For main Waley entry see: [35].

(4) 76 Gower Street, WC1

This was one of a number of London addresses of the Japanese writer, Soseki Natsume. For main Soseki entry and Soseki Museum, see: [48].

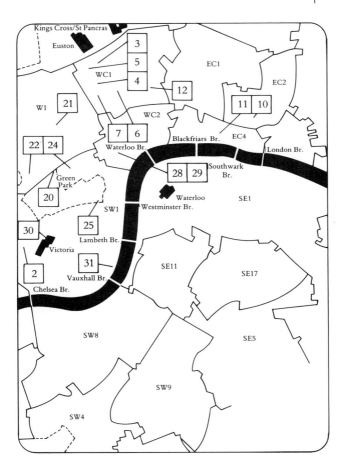

(5) University College, Gower Street, WC1

Professor A.W. Williamson (1824–1904), sometimes described as Japan's first real friend in Britain, lectured at
University College in the latter part of the last century. In
1863, Hirobumi Ito, the future first prime minister of Japan
and other Japanese students stayed with Williamson in his
Hampstead house and attended Williamson's lectures at
University College. Many went on to become celebrated

Japan's contribution to the war effort of the World War I Allies is commemorated in St Michael's church [2]

figures in the modernizing of their country. For main entry for Williamson and Ito, and Ito's journey to Britain, see: [34].

(6) The British Museum, Great Russell Street, WC1 (Tel: 071-636 1555)

On 14 October 1987, to the surprise of passing Londoners, a fully robed Shinto priest, Minoru Taki, ceremoniously evoked the Gods to bless the site of the new Japanese Galleries at the British Museum (North entrance). The Gods were generous. In fact, so important do the Japanese consider the British Museum Japan collections, some 80% of the funding for the new galleries (over £5 million) came from Japan.

The idea for the galleries occurred to Lawrence Smith, Keeper of Japanese Antiquities, in 1982. This was the year of the Great Japan Exhibition at the Royal Academy, the popularity of which seemed to generate the frenzy of the Cup Final. If Japanese art could cause this kind of enthusiasm, then our premier Japanese collections deserved more elbow room.

The outcome has been the Konica, the Main and the Urasenke Galleries, a real tea-house made by Japanese carpenters and a study centre. The official opening was on 6 April 1990, by HIH Prince Fumihito. The aim, as much as possible, has been to create a totally Japanese background. Colours are subdued, with good use of natural wood. The lighting is low, both for effect and because harsh light can damage the old and the fragile. The British Museum's Japanese holdings exceed 24,000 items, comprising every type of material, from every age. Because of a lack of room, however, many have never been shown to the public. The new galleries permit more space for more, better arranged objects; allow a greater number of fresh changes from the museum's own stock; and provide a home for exciting new exhibitions to come from Japan, almost every year.

The British Museum contains a number of Japanese masterpieces, which can no longer be seen in Japan itself. The museum's oldest pieces are *Jomon* pottery, from around 4,000 years ago. These originally came from the collection of Philipp Franz von Siebold, the first European to bring archaeological material from Japan to the West in 1829 and then again in 1861. *Open Monday–Saturday 10am–5pm, Sunday 2.30pm–6pm.*

(7) British Library, Great Russell Street, WC1 (Oriental and India Office Collections, 197 Blackfriars Road, SE1. Tel: 071-412 7000)

This is one of the most important repositories of Japanese books and manuscripts outside Japan. The BL's most outstanding Japanese holding began with a rebellion in the latter part of the Nara Period (710–784). The Empress Shotoku, having suppressed an uprising, did what rulers usually do. She gave thanks to God. And in doing so, seven centuries before the Caxton bible, she created the world's earliest datable printing. It is known as the *Hyakumanto darani* – 'a million Buddhist charms' – printed invocations of thanks. Each was placed inside a small wooden pagoda about nine inches high. The BL has a complete set of the four standard texts and the four variants, although part of this same printing is also held by the Cambridge University Library [121].

Other treasures include the only surviving copy of the . . . *Feiqe (Heike) no monogatari*, from the Japanese Jesuit Mission Press, 1592–93; the BL's oldest book, the *Joyuishiki-ron jukki*, printed at the Kofukuji temple in Nara, c1170–1180; and a fine collection of early examples of Japanese printing (325 works in 1,578 volumes) acquired from that doyen of Japanese bibliographers, the diplomat Sir Ernest Satow [98].

In 1753, the library's foundation stock included the first Japanese books in Europe. These were collected by the German physician and traveller, Engelbert Kaempfer (1651–1716). Kaempfer was responsible for one of the few and perhaps the most interesting breach of Japan's policy of *sakoku* (closed country) – a term he himself is said to have coined. From the early 1640s to the 1850s, a handful of Dutch were the only Europeans allowed in Japan and they were confined to Deshima, Nagasaki. Kaempfer was medical officer there, from 1690 to 1692.

Kaempfer's priceless Japanese books, maps and paintings, now so rare that some are the only ones in existence, were smuggled out of the country under the noses of shogunate officials. The collection formed the source material for Kaempfer's *History of Japan* – for many years, the West's *only* Japanese history. His manuscript for the *History* as well as voluminous notes and sketches are also preserved in The British Library (Western Manuscripts, Bloomsbury).

Other important Japanese collections and individual volumes continued to find their way into what was then the British Museum during the Tokugawa period (1600–1867) but systematic collecting really began after the Meiji Restoration of 1868. This continued until 1905 when the retirement of Sir Robert Douglas left the collections without a Japanese specialist. This was not remedied until 1955, when a great catching-up exercise began.

In the 1960s, with increasing interest in things Japanese, the Japan Library Group was set up with the BL playing a central role. This provides liaison between the principal Japanese collections throughout the country and makes it easier to find what Japanese material is where.

Today, the BL's entire Japanese holdings cover a vast range of material, ancient and modern. The humanities and Social Sciences Division holds over 60,000 monographs, 8,500 periodicals, of which 7000 are official publications, 300 manuscripts and 28 newspapers. In addition to these, the India Office Library and Records, a sister institution with whom the department of Oriental Collections has recently merged to form a single entity in Blackfriars Road, holds some 360 archival documents of the English Factory in Hirado, 1613–23. *Access and opening hours vary. Special exhibitions held. Please telephone.*

CHELSEA

(8) 99/100 Cheyne Walk, SW10

In December 1874, Algernon ('Bertie') Freeman-Mitford (later Lord Redesdale) (1837–1916) married Lady Clementine Ogilvy. They settled down in 99/100 Cheyne Walk. According to the rate books that still exist, Mitford bought 99 Cheyne Walk in his bachelor days, sometime between 1872 and 1875. Then, to provide proper married quarters, he purchased the freehold of number 100 and had the two houses joined together. And this is just how they are today. For main Mitford entry, see: [103].

(9) Sydney Street, SW3

Yoshio Markino (1869–1956), author of the autobiographical *A Japanese Artist in London* and other works, moved here in

One of the homes of Algernon ('Bertie') Freeman-Mitford: Cheyne Walk [8]

about 1903, near Marion Harry Spielmann, the art editor who probably saved his life. The building, now converted into offices and a block of flats, is on the corner of Cable Street. For main Markino entry and his favourite pub, see: [16].

CITY

(10) Guildhall, EC2

When the late Emperor Hirohito visited Britain as Crown Prince, an address of welcome was given here on 11 May 1921. When he returned as Emperor in September 1971, he was given a banquet here by the Lord Mayor.

(11) St Paul's Cathedral, EC4

Sir Harry Parkes (1828–1885), who followed Alcock as Britain's second minister in Japan, from 1865 to 1883, is honoured with a bust in the crypt of St Paul's. For main Parkes entry, the graves of both Sir Harry and Lady Parkes, see: [33].

HOLBORN

(12) 22 Great James Street, WC1

For many years, scholar, linguist and orientalist Arthur Waley (1889–1966) rented number 22 to house his library. A burglary in May 1963 resulted in a serious loss of his journals, manuscripts, notebooks and private papers. For main Waley entry, see: [35].

KENSINGTON

(13) 1 Kensington Court, W8

In 1910, as a result of gross overspending, Algernon ('Bertie') Freeman-Mitford, the First Lord Redesdale, was forced to lease out his beloved Batsford Park in Gloucestershire and rented 1 Kensington Court, on the corner of Kensington High Street. (This is now the Milestone Hotel.) In his early seventies and suffering from increasing deafness, Mitford devoted himself more and more to his writing. Many of his most popular works were written or published in this period. These included his autobiographical *Memories* in 1915 and *Further Memories*, which came out in the year following the author's death in 1917. For main Mitford entry, see: [103].

(14) The Royal Geographical Society, Kensington Gore, SW7

The Royal Geographical Society holds the papers of the Reverend Walter Weston (1861–1940), the so-called Father of Mountaineering in Japan. For main Weston entry, see: [123].

(15) Kensington Palace Gardens, W8

In the garden of the Japanese ambassador's residence here, the Crown Prince Akihito (now Emperor Akihito) planted a cherry tree on 7 June 1953. Another cherry tree was planted in the garden by Prince Aya on 17 June 1990.

KNIGHTSBRIDGE

(16) The Bunch of Grapes, 203 Brompton Road, SW3

One London day early in 1903 a young Japanese artist on the brink of suicide called at the office of Mr M.H. Spielmann, editor of the *Magazine of Art*.

A few years later, Mr Spielmann recalled the meeting. He remembered the young man's battered portfolio under his arm and his clothes rather the worse for wear. He looked tired and pale. But he smiled and bowed.

What Mr Spielmann couldn't see was that the young artist, Yoshio Markino (1869–1956) hadn't eaten for two days. He had already decided that the only honourable way out for the son of a samurai was to take his own life.

Mr Spielmann opened the offered portfolio to reveal first a picture of Marylebone Church on a warm, moist day, bright and luminous. The figures were as simple as a Japanese colour print. The editor was charmed with the combination of artlessness and sincerity. And when he said he would publish the pictures, Mr Spielmann remembered that Markino's eyes 'danced'. Nothing else. His natural dignity seemed to forbid any demonstration of satisfaction.

For Yoshio Markino, this was a turning point. He had arrived from Japan via America in 1897 and worked for a spell with the Japanese naval attaché in London. But after a few months, as warship contracts were fulfilled, the job finished. The British welfare state was half a century away and the artist was soon living from hand to mouth.

Following publication in the *Magazine of Art*, however, commissions began to flow in. Markino also published a number of books. The autobiographical *A Japanese Artist in London* (originally published in 1910, new edition, In Print Publishing, 1991) described his early days of poverty and the kindness of the English people. (He had a particularly soft spot for his landladies – of which there were a great number.) He wrote in quaint, ungrammatical English that won the hearts of his readers with its simple charm and sincerity.

His pictures, so often of London in the mist or fog, were published with the text of many of his books. Reviewing *A Japanese Artist in London*, the Times Literary Supplement of 12 May 1910, described Markino's work as 'drawings of western cities as reflected in an eastern mirror'. His work

The Japanese artist Yoshio Markino, who lived in London from 1897–1942 [16]

sold. He was fêted by London society. He fell in love, usually platonically. He married, also platonically. (The 'marriage' inevitably broke up but quite amicably.) He published the delightfully titled *My Idealed John Bullesses* in 1912.

Markino supported the suffragettes and years later when he was repatriated to Japan in 1942, he left his suitcase in the Japanese embassy containing one of his most prized possessions: Christabel Pankhurst's prison dress. (Alas, by the end of the war, when he tried to recover it, the case had disappeared.)

Between Markino's days of being lionized in Edwardian London and the end of his life in Tokyo after World War II, there were many ups and downs. He continued to paint, to write and even to lecture on philosophy. He had many warm friends. Among them was Douglas Bladen, author of *Queer things about Japan* and editor of *Who's Who*. Markino appeared in *Who's Who* from 1916 to 1949, a period, Markino claimed, that he shared with the emperor and the Japanese ambassador. As his recreation, his entry stated: 'Reading the Ancient Chinese, Latin and Greek Classics in order to forget the modern civilization'.

One of Markino's favourite haunts (when he could afford it) was the pub, the Bunch of Grapes, still open for business today. He became great friends with the landlord, a Mr Lapsey. Yoshio Markino spent some 45 years in London, during which time he changed his address on a great number of occasions. See also: [9, 40].

(17) Sloane Street and Albert Gate area, SW1

On 10 January 1885, to the delight of native Londoners and the dismay of the Japanese business and diplomatic community, an authentic Japanese village was opened in the heart of Knightsbridge by Britain's first minister in Japan, Sir Rutherford Alcock. It was located in the area of Hyde Park's Albert Gate and the top of Sloane Street. The idea came from the Dutchman, Tannaker Buhicrosan, the head of a touring Japanese troupe and married to a Japanese. In a large building called Humphrey's Hall, a number of traditional crafts were displayed.

There were stick carvers, umbrella makers, calligraphers, screen painters and even a tea-house dispensing green tea. The shrine, according to the *Illustrated London News*, was 'devoted to a hideous idol'. For additional entertainment, there were performances of Japanese music, dancing, fencing and wrestling. Admission was one shilling for adults and 6d for children. A lot of the materials such as the low tables had been imported from Japan. But the shops and the goods they produced were only a show. Apparently any idea of a bazaar had been strongly resisted by Tannaker. But the 'almond eyed artisans' were able to give very practical assistance in helping to design authentic costumes, props and scenery for Gilbert and Sullivan's *Mikado*, which opened at the Savoy Theatre, to enormous success on 14 March 1885. For the official Japanese trying to persuade Britain to reverse the

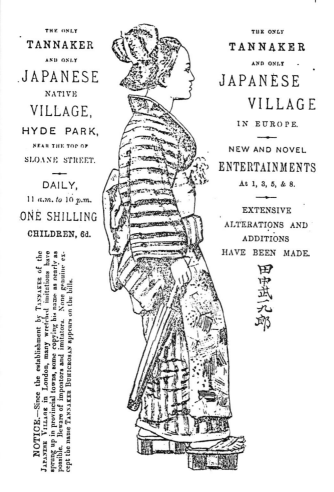

THE ONLY
TANNAKER
AND ONLY
.JAPANESE
NATIVE
VILLAGE,
HYDE PARK,
NEAR THE TOP OF
SLOANE STREET.

DAILY,
11 *a.m. to* 10 *p.m.*
ONE SHILLING
CHILDREN, 6d.

NOTICE.—Since the establishment by TANNAKER of the JAPANESE VILLAGE in London, many wretched imitations have sprung up in provincial towns, some copying his name as nearly as possible. Beware of impostors and imitators. None genuine except the name TANNAKER BUHICROSAN appears on the bills.

THE ONLY
TANNAKER
AND ONLY .
.JAPANESE
VILLAGE
IN EUROPE.

NEW AND NOVEL
ENTERTAINMENTS
At 1, 3, 5, & 8.

EXTENSIVE
ALTERATIONS AND
ADDITIONS
HAVE BEEN MADE.

田中武九郎

'An authentic Japanese village in the heart of Knightsbridge': an advertisement for Tannaker's Japanese village [17]

'unequal treaties' and to take Japan seriously as a civilized modern state, the 'quaint' village and the satire of the *Mikado* were sending out quite the wrong signals. The Japanese embassy even refused to renew the passports of the villagers.

On 2 May, the entire village 'of the flimsiest materials' was destroyed by fire, in no more than about half an hour.

One of the wood carvers lost his life and the financial loss of around £15,000 in 1885 was quite considerable.

In seven months, however, on 2 December 1885, the redoubtable Tannaker was back with a new Japanese village, called 'Japan in London'. The buildings were reported to be more substantial and less combustible and as an added attraction there was a Japanese garden complete with stream and rustic bridge. The idea seems to have caught on elsewhere. In one of Tannaker's advertisements from October 1886, he is warning his public to 'beware of imposters and imitators'. He claims 'many wretched imitations have sprung up in provincial towns'.

However, whether it was the competition, pressure from the Japanese establishment or just the crowds wearying of yet another Japanese novelty, in less than another year, by September 1887, the village had closed and Tannaker and his villagers gone. See also: [155].

MARYLEBONE

(18) The Wallace Collection, Manchester Square, W1 (Tel: 071-935 0687)

There are not many Japanese items in the Wallace Collection except for one outstanding item which is inevitably the 'Curator's choice'. Described as 'unique', it is a 19th century incense burner, shaped as the figure of an elephant, eight inches high. *Monday–Saturday 10am–5pm, Sunday 2pm–5pm.*

MAYFAIR

(19) Park Lane, W1

On 26 August 1858, James Bruce, Earl of Elgin and Kincardine (1811–63), given the full powers of plenipotentiary, signed Britain's first treaty with Japan at Yedo (Tokyo). Lord Elgin's personal secretary was Laurence Oliphant [60], who would be returning to Japan in another capacity later. Elgin was born in Park Lane. His parents had rented a house for the season – 'bow fronted with a terrace on top'. For main Elgin entry, see: [205].

A 19th century bronze incense burner: the 'Curator's choice' from the Wallace Collection [18]

(20) The Japan Information and Cultural Centre, Embassy of Japan, 101/104 Piccadilly, W1 (Tel: 071-465 6500)

In recognition of the London Embassy's increasing work-load, the Embassy moved to its gracious new accommodation in August 1989. Refurbishment of the building cost approximately £11 million. The Information and Cultural Centre provides all manner of assistance in providing information and other resources for cultural and educational purposes in Japan and Britain. *Japan Information Centre office open Monday–Friday 9.30am–1pm, 2.30pm–5.30pm. The Library (which includes the library of the Japan Society) is open Monday–Friday 9.30am–12.45pm, 2.30pm–5pm.*

(21) Liberty's, Regent Street, W1 (Tel: 071-734 1234)

The Japan connection with Liberty's began on the day the shop opened at 218A Regent Street, on 15 May 1875. Of their three pioneer staff, one was a Japanese boy, Kitsui Hara. Japanese goods were novel, cheap and well made and

The London Embassy of Japan in Piccadilly houses the Japan Information and Cultural Centre [20]

the craze for things Japanese was getting under way. Among the first customers was William Morris, one of the founders of the craft movement, who had already said much about the beauty and individuality of Japanese workmanship.

These early days have been described as a Japanese bonanza and Liberty's own success helped to increase demand elsewhere. After the Meiji Restoration of 1868, there were no limits on the amount of Japanese imports and goods of all types came pouring in. On one bank holiday alone, Liberty's completely sold out of all its Japanese sunshades, at one shilling each. New Japanese warehouses were springing up and stores began opening special Oriental departments.

The connections of the Liberty family with Japan stretch back to the early years of the company. In 1889, Arthur and Mrs Lasenby Liberty accompanied the artist Sir Alfred East on a trip to Japan [125].

Like all crazes, it couldn't last forever and Japanese exporters became victims of their own success. Unable to maintain both quality and quantity, standards dropped. As early as

1876, the influential architect and designer, Edward W. Godwin, was complaining that Japanese goods were losing their subtlety and 'rareness', with cruder colours to suit the lowest common denominator of European tastes. Shops that had opened in the boom now closed and Liberty's began casting its net wider to include goods from other Eastern countries. Trade with Japan became more discriminating but the connection was always maintained. Over the years, Liberty's has done much to encourage the craft movement, founded by artists like Shoji Hamada and Bernard Leach [100]. Periodic Japan promotions have maintained their popularity.

The statues outside East India House, the so called *Saints of Liberty's*, are often referred to as Japanese, although this seems to be in some doubt. They may well be Japanese copies of Chinese Lohan, which originated in India as disciples of Buddha.

(22) 15 South Audley Street, W1

Algernon ('Bertie') Freeman-Mitford (later Lord Redesdale), author of *Tales of Old Japan* and other works based on his Japan experiences, was born at 15 South Audley Street, on 24

'The Japan connection with Liberty's began on the day the shop opened at 218A Regent Street, on 15 May 1875': Liberty's Regent Street [21]

February 1837. The house you can see today would appear to be little altered. Bertie was the third son of Henry Revely and his wife, Lady Georgiana Ashburnham. He got his first taste of foreign travel when only three years old when, to save costs, the family moved to the continent where living was cheaper. In 1864, aged nine, Bertie was sent to Eton. For main Mitford entry, his estate and tomb, see: [103].

REGENT'S PARK

(23) Zoological Gardens, NW1

Almost two years before the arrival of the First Japanese Mission [68] on 30 April 1862, a pair of Japanese Sika deer was presented to the London Zoo, by a Mr J. Wilks, on 21 July 1860. The Sika (deified in the Shinto religion) were brought to the UK by Captain D. Rees of the ship *Sir F. Williams*.

About the same time, other Sika deer went to Powers-court in County Wicklow, Ireland [234] and gradually spread to other parts of the British Isles. By now most have interbred with local deer. The Latin name has changed from the 19th century *Rusa japonica Gray* to *Cervus nippon nippon*.

ST JAMES'S

(24) 6A Mason's Yard, SW1

Back in the swinging sixties, there was a girl called Yoko, who seems to have once been a classmate of the present Emperor Akihito. Yoko was into *happenings* – like asking everyone in the audience to, one by one, cut off a piece of her dress with a pair of scissors.

On this particular day, Yoko was setting up her exhibition at the Indica Gallery, 6A Mason's Yard. John walked in and approached a notice saying, 'Hammer a nail in'. Yoko stopped him with the explanation: 'the exhibition doesn't open till tomorrow'.

The gallery owner then advised Yoko that John was a millionaire and should be appeased. Yoko invited John to hammer in the nail for five shillings. John replied he would give her an imaginary five shillings if she would let him hammer in an imaginary nail.

And the rest is in all those millions of words that have been written and said about Yoko Ono and John Lennon. The Indica Gallery disappeared almost as swiftly as it came.

(25) 30 Old Queen Street, SW1

Sir Rutherford Alcock (1809–1897), Britain's first minister in Japan, retired from the foreign service in 1871 and settled in what was then 14 Great Queen Street. His address was renamed and renumbered in July 1893 to become 30 Old Queen Street. For main Alcock entry and his burial place, see: [77].

SOUTH KENSINGTON

(26) Victoria and Albert Museum, Cromwell Road, SW7 (Tel: 071-938 8500)

Museums everywhere seem to be increasing the space devoted to their Japanese collections. On 12 December 1986, The Victoria and Albert Museum (V&A) opened its new £350,000 Toshiba Gallery of Japanese Art and Design.

The new gallery can hold only a fraction of the V&A's vast Japanese collection of over 37,000 objects. There is a good

'One of the finest laquered boxes ever made' – the 'van Diemen box', once owned by Madame de Pompadour: the V&A [26]

'Edo armour was used for precious little fighting' – suit of armour assembled for Lord Akita: the V&A [26]

display of pottery and porcelain in Gallery 143 and textiles in Gallery 98. Material not on show can be seen by appointment. The National Art Library at the V&A has more than 12,000 relevant volumes.

Most of the collection dates from the Momoyama Period (1573–1616) to the first decade or so of the present century. The policy has been made to cover the whole range of

Japanese artistic output. There are certainly individual masterpieces but also quite ordinary craft products.

Former curator, Joe Earle, one of Britain's leading authorities, was asked to make a 'Curator's choice' from this extraordinarily eclectic treasure house. He chose three objects that would, he said, symbolize a major part of the collection. They were of love, war and faith.

By the early 17th century, Japanese lacquerware was probably its most sought after export. Sometime between 1636 and 1639, a celebrated governor of the Dutch East Indies, Anton van Diemen, took delivery of one of the finest large lacquered boxes ever made. The black background was decorated in gold and silver, with scenes from *The Tale of Genji*. Inside the lid was the name of his beloved wife, Maria. The box had at least two subsequent owners – Madame de Pompadour and the English novelist and collector, William Beckford – before becoming a V&A prize exhibit in 1916.

When looking at Edo war apparel, it is important to realize that it would have been involved in precious little actual fighting. These were the long centuries of *Pax Tokugawa*. What really counted was the kind of sartorial dash you'd cut. The V&A's superb example of armour made for Lord Akita would have done its owner proud. Made in 1741 by master armourer Haruta Tamba in the *Domaru* style, it is probably the museum's best example.

Buddhism reached Japan from Korea around the middle of the 6th century and 'Curator's choice' number three is the lovely carved and lacquered wood figure of Amida Nyorai, from the 13th century. Japan's sculptural tradition underwent something of a revival during the Kamakura period (1185–1333) and this is an outstanding example. Note the distinct, though smoothly finished, facial features and the way that the robes fall away naturally.

From September to December 1991 the V&A hosted the 'Visions of Japan' exhibition, the leading exhibition in the 1991 Japan Festival. *Open Monday–Saturday 10am–5.30pm, Sunday 2.30pm–5.50pm.*

(27) Science Museum, Exhibition Road, SW7 (Tel: 071-938 8000)

The Science Museum has no separate Japanese collection as such. Most objects are classed according to subject, which may be Physics, Chemistry, History of Medicine, Printing or even Erotica. Japanese objects are included in these as they are also among the items from the Wellcome Institute for the History of Medicine. John Milne [78], the so-called 'Father of Japanese Seismology' left his collection to the museum.

Being a science museum, everything can be made available for you very scientifically. This includes full computer printouts with all items described and reference numbers given.

Genuine researchers should please address their enquiries to The Keeper, Science Museum, South Kensington, London SW7 5NH.

A major Japanese robotics exhibition was held here as part of the 1991 Japan Festival. *Open Monday–Saturday 10am–6pm, Sunday 11am–6pm.*

STRAND

(28) 198 Strand, WC2

'A fellow of infinite jest.' Charles Wirgman (1832–1891) would have enjoyed his epitaph (in the foreigners' cemetery in Yokohama), put there by his friends. For 30 years he had entertained, informed and amused his fellow expatriates in the fledgling foreign community. He was the first journalist in Japan and the first magazine publisher.

London born Charles Wirgman, artist, journalist and retired army captain, was initially sent to China in 1857, by the then 15 year old *Illustrated London News* (its offices were at 198 Strand, the site currently occupied by the Midland Bank). Wirgman arrived in Japan at the beginning of July 1861 to a baptism of fire. On 5 July he survived an attack on the British legation, simply by hiding under the floor of his room. Despite this savage welcome from the 'expel-the-foreigners' faction, Wirgman felt immensely attracted to Japan and stayed for the rest of his life. He continued to send back many illustrations for publication in the *Illustrated London News*. He was an eye witness, sketch book in hand, of the British bombardment of Shimonoseki. Other pieces recorded daily life in Japan's newly opened treaty ports. In 1883, he founded, wrote and illustrated a local humorous magazine called the *Japan Punch*, which continued at least until 1886.

'A fellow of infinite jest': Charles Wirgman, artist and journalist [28]

Charles Wirgman died in Yokohama of a prolonged mental illness. The Japanese language newspaper, *Mainichi*, for 10 February 1891, carried a death notice for 'my real father' put in by an Ichiro Charlie Ozawa.

(29) The Liddell Hart Centre for Military Archives, University of London King's College, Strand, WC2

The Liddell Hart Centre was set up in 1964, as a repository for private papers on military affairs. Materials relating to Japan include documents on Japanese students attending the college last century and Oriental studies during the 19th and early part of the 20th centuries and war papers. Most of these military documents deal with World War II but there is also a small collection from Sir Ian Hamilton, Military Representative of India with the Japanese Field Army in Manchuria, 1904–05. *Access for bona fide students by application to the librarian.*

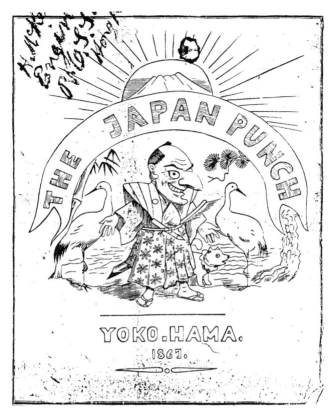

Front cover of Charles Wirgman's Japan Punch [28]

VICTORIA

(30) Victoria Library Archives Department, 160 Buckingham Palace Road, SW1 (Tel: 071–798 2180)

Archives are always a cornucopia of interest and those of the Victoria Library Archives Department are no exception. Liberty's papers are worth a browse. Sir Edward Burne-Jones, in an 1897 letter, deplores Japanese use of Western colours in fabrics. 'Cheapness at the cost of beauty', he snorts. There is also a pictorial record of Mrs Lasenby Liberty's Japan trip published in 1910.

In 1913, a year after the death of the Emperor Meiji, his successor, Taisho, placed a hefty order with the outfitters, Thresher & Glenny Ltd. The order reads, 'to H.I.M. The Mikardo of Japan, Imperial Court, Tokiho (sic)'. Then, 5 doz silk and wool vests, 10 doz white silk and wool trousers, 4 doz white spun silk socks. And so on.

WESTMINSTER

(31) Tate Gallery, Millbank, SW1 (Tel: 071-821 1313)

In 1680, John Michael Wright painted two enigmatic portraits of the Irish Catholic rebel, Sir Neil O'Neil. Each showed him with a suit of samurai armour at his feet. Was a comparison being drawn between England's persecution of Irish Catholics and the Japanese Christian massacres? The Tate Gallery has one of the paintings. The other and perhaps more detailed painting is hung at Dunrobin Castle in Scotland [217]. *Open Monday–Saturday 10am–5.50pm, Sunday 2pm–5.50pm.*

2 | *London North*

CAMDEN TOWN

(32) 91 Agar Grove, NW1

In 1880, when the craze for all things Japanese was sweeping Europe, the Japanese government commissioned the man who was to become known as 'Father of Western architecture in Japan', Josiah Conder (1852–1920), to build a stately pleasure dome. It was to be a kind of Western palace in the heart of Tokyo, a place where upper-class Japanese could properly hold social intercourse with foreigners and do the sort of things that foreigners do.

Japanese historians have named an entire social era after the *Rokumeikan* (the Mansion of the Baying Stag). Here, under ornate chandeliers, Japanese ladies, uncomfortably laced into inflexible, heavy-skirted garments ordered from Berlin, did their best with strange food and strange knives and forks and still stranger foreigners. The Japanese 'new woman' would then attempt the latest dances with the young swells from Europe and America. It was all very puzzling, especially as this was the kind of behaviour ladies had always previously associated with the world of the courtesan and the geisha.

In the end, of course, it had to fail. Many die-hards had been shocked at what they considered lewd behaviour. The Japanese authorities were getting nowhere in persuading Western governments to end extra-territorial rights for foreigners. (Part of the reason for the *Rokumeikan* was to prove to foreigners that the Japanese were 'civilized'.) Worse was to come. According to Pat Barr in her delightful *Deer Cry Pavilion*, there was 'an orgy of ribaldry, bawdy and ridicule'. There would be no more gala masquerades.

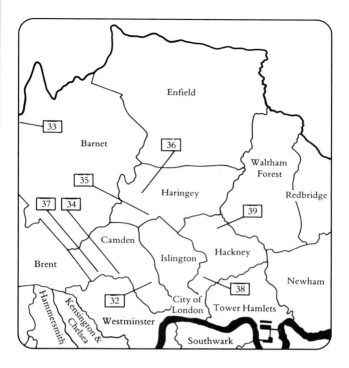

LONDON NORTH

The expatriate architect, Josiah Conder, however, did a lot more than just create 'the mansion of the era'. Of all the foreign architects in Japan then, Conder was probably the most renowned. Academic architectural journals showered praise on the work he carried out for the Japanese government, other foreign governments in Japan and the local elite. His National Exhibition Art Pavilion in Ueno Park, later renamed the Tokyo Imperial Household Museum, has been described as his masterpiece. Conder seems to have been born in the vicinity of Bedford and attended the Bedford Modern School [118]. He passed the University of Cambridge local examinations in 1867, aged 16. At that time, the class list shows him living in Brixton. As a student, Conder was articled to such well known names as William Burgess, one of a number of creative people coming under Japan's spell during the 1860s and 1870s. Conder's later decision to apply for a post in Tokyo was therefore not at all surprising. In 1876, Conder won the coveted Soane Medal for the design of a country house. He was living at 91 St Pauls Road, Camden Square, NW1, then quite a fashionable address. Due to street name changes, that house is now 91 Agar Grove, NW1.

Conder arrived in Japan in January 1877, to practise and to teach. He became professor of architecture at the new Imperial College of Engineering. In 1881, he married Kume-ko Maenam. Conder's books – on architecture, gardening and painting – all show a strong Japanese influence.

Conder was fascinated by Japanese painting and became both a collector and a painter in his own right. Kyosai Kawanabe, often referred to as 'the Hokusai of the Meiji era', taught Conder the authentic Kano style and even gave his pupil the Japanese name of Kyoei. This was a composite of *Kyo* (student of Kyosai) and *ei* (England). Conder died in Japan in 1920, aged 68. His magnificent collection of Japanese art, inherited by his daughter, Helen, was sold and by the 1960s had been dispersed throughout the world. Some particularly fine examples are in the British Museum. See also: [118].

EDGWARE

(33) St Lawrence Church, St Lawrence Close, Edgware

When Sir Harry Parkes (1828–85) became the first foreigner in history to have a private interview with a Japanese emperor, he was doing a great deal more than creating Imperial precedent. Sir Harry's meeting with the new young Emperor Meiji in May 1871 was a personal triumph. It was the culmination of a strategy that was to affect Anglo–Japanese relations for the next half century.

Japan's long seclusion from the rest of the world ended in a two-horse race. The horse backed by France's ebullient minister, M. Leon Roch, was the established shogunate that had ruled Japan for the past two and a half centuries. Parkes, on the other hand, supported by brilliant on-the-ground intelligence and with a tough, realistic shrewdness, sensed that the old order was crumbling. He saw the bright colours of Imperial restoration galloping home and this was where he pledged his country's support. This support by Britain, then the most powerful empire on earth, represented one of a number of factors that finally swept Japanese feudalism into history. After the Meiji Restoration of 1868, Parkes stayed on to see his strategies recompensed. British yards took the bulk of the orders for the new Japanese naval and merchant fleets; British colleges and British instructors trained the new Japanese technocrats; and British railway engineers and British commercial enterprises bore much of the weight of building the new modern Japanese superstructure.

Harry Smith Parkes was born on 24 February 1828, at Birchill's Hall, Bloxwich, near Walsall, Staffordshire. Parkes's parents both died young and the young Harry left school at the age of 13 to join his two older sisters in China. After distinguishing himself as a linguist and diplomat, he was made British minister to Japan and arrived in Nagasaki to take up his appointment on 24 June 1865.

As midwife to the new state and doyen of the corps diplomatique, Sir Harry's name seemed to partner each achievement of the new modern state. Later, an aide was to write that the history of Sir Harry's career in Japan was the history of Japan itself. In a sense, for a short span, perhaps it was. Parkes helped set up Japan's financial system, saw the opening of the first railway, and even introduced the sitings of the country's first lighthouse network [220]. Sir Harry survived the xenophobic fanaticism of the early years when his house was incinerated and he was in constant danger of assassination. Slowly the country calmed and was bound together by good, firm government. Japan was now quite ready to join the rest of the modern world.

In 1883, after 18 of the new Japan's most turbulent years, Sir Harry Parkes was transferred to the Peking legation. In recognition of his services to the new state, Emperor Meiji offered him Japan's most distinguished Order of the Rising Sun (which, as a British minister, he was unable to accept). As a tribute from his own country, however, Parkes became the first member of the Far Eastern corps to be awarded the Order of St Michael and St George.

Sir Harry Parkes survived his Japan appointment by only two years. He died in Peking, aged just 57, on 22 March 1885. His embalmed body was shipped home for burial beside his wife, Fanny, in the churchyard of St Lawrence, Edgware.

Of Sir Harry's many achievements in Japan, there is perhaps one for which every foreigner should be personally grateful. Sir Harry had noticed that in the speeches of the new Japanese parliamentarians, it was not uncommon to hear Europeans referred to as 'barbarians'. He brought this to the attention of the Japanese prime minister and was immediately assured apologetically that such discourtesy must regrettably have gone unnoticed – and would be stopped forthwith. Foreigners, Sir Harry was unequivocally assured, 'are no longer barbarians'. And that's official.

Sir Harry Parkes's first lady deserves a place of her own in Japanese history. Around one o'clock on a raw stormy day in October 1867, Fanny Parkes (c1832–78) became the first woman known to reach the summit of Japan's highest peak, Mt Fuji.

This was more an accident of history than a significant mountaineering feat. Climbers of Fuji-san, as the sacred mountain is known in Japanese, ascend in ten natural stages. Prior to the Meiji Restoration of 1868, women were denied the right to go higher than the eighth stage. The summit, as with most summits in Japan, was for men only. Not feeling subject to such restraints – or perhaps not being aware of them – this beautiful, brown-eyed girl from what is now north London, reached the summit in company with her husband, Harry, and the Irish-born medical pioneer in Japan, Dr William Willis [225]. They seem to have given equally scant heed to seasonal norms. Few Japanese would have considered such a climb in wet, windy October. On the night before reaching the peak, the Parkes party had had little sleep in an insect ridden mountainside cave, through which the wind blew continuously from off the surrounding ice and snow. Sir Harry's predecessor in office, Sir Rutherford Alcock [77], had sensibly conformed with local convention and ascended Fuji during the balmy days of July, in 1860.

Fanny left Japan to make a home for her children in England and died of a chill in Paris, in the autumn of 1878. She is buried with her husband in the same church in which she had been married 22 years before, on New Years Day 1856. The family home, Canons, now the North London Collegiate School, is about five minutes walk from the church.

Fanny was the daughter of Thomas Plumer, son of Sir

Thomas Plumer, Master of the Rolls. Their estate then occupied some 450 acres of what is now north London. Fanny grew up with her family not in the great house, which was occupied by her grand parents, but in the very comfortable estate lodge. All you can see today, however, just south-east of the school, are the adjacent gate pillars, at the beginning of what is now Canons Drive.

Sir Harry and Fanny are buried in a large triple-space grave with very high kerbs and a cross on a pedestal, to the south west of the church tower. There are inscriptions to Harry Smith Parkes, aged 57, and Fanny Hannah Parkes, 47. There are also many other inscriptions to members of the Parkes family and to Fanny's family, the Plumers. In the entrance porch of the church, Fanny is further commemorated on a white marble memorial stone and Harry on a brass plaque inside the church.

For Harry Parkes's birthplace, see: [104]. See also: [11].

HAMPSTEAD

(34) 16 Provost Road, NW3

On 21 November 1863, the young nobleman Prince Hirobumi Ito, Japan's future, first and four times prime minister, gave the decks of the *Pegasus* a final scrub, the brasswork a last spit and polish and prepared to disembark at Gravesend after the worst 130 days of his life. His friends would not have recognized him. Gone was the familiar samurai haircut, lopped off to improve his disguise. Exhausted and emaciated, a contemporary Japanese report described him and his companion as 'looking like hungry crows'.

Ito's friend in travail was the future Marquis Kaoru Inoue. He had fared no better. Unused to any type of menial work, the two young samurai had manned the sails, scrubbed the decks and worked the pumps. Without bedding or even a lavatory, they had survived on no better fare than salt beef, stale biscuits and tea sweetened with red sugar. To avoid paying harbour dues, the ship's master had always anchored off-shore along the route, denying the crew even brief respite on shore.

These were Japan's first overseas students. Although the country's strict seclusion laws were still in force, the shogun-

ate had secretly arranged for Ito and Inoue and three others
to go to England to study and look at the outside world. The
British consul in Yokohama connived to have them referred
to William Keswick of Jardine, Matheson, who in turn
secretly obtained them passages for the first leg of their
journey, to Shanghai. It was in Shanghai that the mistake
occurred. How do you explain your ambition to study the
science of steamship navigation when 'navigation' is the only
relevant English you know? The five were signed on as able
seamen. Ito and Inoue left Shanghai on the *Pegasus*. The
other three, Masaru (Katsu) Inouye, Kinsuke Endo and
Yozo Yamao sailed from Hong Kong on the *White Adder*,
arriving at Gravesend on 18 November 1863.

On reaching London, their world changed. They were
met by Hugh Matheson, head of the shipping company. He
introduced them to Alexander William Williamson, Professor of Chemistry at University College, London. Williamson became their teacher, guardian and friend. Ito and Inoue
lodged with the professor at his home in Hampstead and
were later joined by one of their friends from the *White
Adder*, Yozo Yamao. The house at 16 Provost Road, where
they stayed, can still be seen, more or less as it was.

The boys made friends with other undergraduates at
University College and visited museums, galleries, factories
and dockyards. However, after reading in *The Times* that
there was trouble in their home clan, the Choshu, Ito and
Kaoru Inoue felt obliged to return. They departed from
London for Japan in March 1864, leaving the other three in
Britain until 1868. As a direct result of their studies in
England, Masaru Inoue helped lay the foundations of the
Japanese railways, Yamao developed mining engineering
and Endo introduced European methods of minting. See
also: [5, 75].

HIGHGATE

(35) 50 Southwood Lane; Highgate Cemetery, N6

About 900 years before the birth of Arthur Waley (1889–
1966), there existed in and around the Japanese court of
Heian-Kyo (present Kyoto) a society of elegant, mannered
aesthetes that has probably never been duplicated by any
other culture, at any other time. It is the interpretation of this

Highgate Cemetery, where Arthur Waley, translator of The Tale of Genji, is buried [35]

world, in his classic translation of Murasaki Shikibu's *The Tale of Genji* for which Arthur Waley will be remembered by Japanophiles and others throughout the English-speaking world.

Scholar, poet, linguist and orientalist, Arthur Waley was born in Tunbridge Wells, Kent, as Arthur David Schloss. At the outbreak of World War I, he changed the German sounding Schloss to his mother's maiden name of Waley. He was brought up in Wimbledon, at Hill House, 84 Wimbledon Hill Road (now a block of flats) and educated at Rugby and King's College, Cambridge.

Waley worked for 16 years in the British Museum. It was here, when called upon to index Japanese and Chinese painters, that he began his self-instruction in these languages. He translated a number of Oriental works to great critical acclaim, including the *Pillow Book of Sei Shonagon*, Noh plays and much classical poetry.

Despite this lifelong dedication to Oriental literature, he

never once set foot in Asia. For about 40 years, he lived at 36 Gordon Square [3] and kept many of his books and papers in Great James Street [12]. Waley moved to Highgate in 1962, where he spent his last years at 50 Southwood Lane. He is buried in Highgate Cemetery. A portrait by Michael Ayrton is in King's College, Cambridge; and a pencil drawing by Rex Whistler is in the National Portrait Gallery. See also: [3, 12, 88].

HORNSEY

(36) Priory Park, N8

Here, under a cherry tree, CND hold a commemorative ceremony every 6 August to remember that date in 1945 when the first atomic bomb was dropped on Hiroshima. There is something rather ironic in the repeated peace symbolism given to the planting of cherry trees as symbols of peace. In Japan, the ephemeral nature of the *sakura* (the cherry blossom) has traditionally been associated with the moment of brief glory on the battlefield before death. It was likewise associated with the Japanese *kami-kaze* pilots of World War II.

WEST HAMPSTEAD

(37) 85 Priory Road, NW6

This was one of the many addresses occupied by the writer, Soseki Natsume. For main Soseki entry and Soseki Museum, see: [48].

3 | *London East*

BETHNAL GREEN

(38) Bethnal Green Museum of Childhood, Cambridge Heath Road, E2 (Tel: 081-980 2415)

Traditionally in Japan, a doll is not a toy. It is a work of art, a statue to be protected by a glass case and then admired. There are dolls of paper, wood, porcelain, fabric. There are dolls dressed like a Heian (784–1185) court lady, as a Meiji (1868–1912) bride, as a Gion geisha. Each kimono, each hairstyle is a perfect scaled down model of the original.

There are dolls like their Russian cousins which go one inside the other. There are the jolly, brightly painted *Daruma* dolls. These are round, the Japanese tell you, because the god they represent, Bodhidarma, 'was such a zealous meditator that his arms and legs finally withered away'. There are even phallus-shaped dolls to bring to the temple and pray for fertility. But Japan does have dolls for little girls. Special dolls for a special day. They are called *Hina* and every year in Japan on 3 March, out they come to celebrate *Hina-matsuri* or Girls' Day. *Hina* dolls become family heirlooms and are passed down from mother to daughter. There are fine examples of these at the Bethnal Green Museum of Childhood. Some came with impeccable backgrounds – from the Peeresses School no less (a sort of Tokyo Roedean). Boys traditionally had their festival day on 5 May, when carp flags fly to express the hope that sons, like the vigorous carp, will swim successfully against the stream of life, leaping over all obstacles to success. The Bethnal Green Museum displays include figures of traditional and heroic warriors from Japan's past, commonly associated with the boys' festival. *Open Monday–Thursday and Saturday 10am–6pm.*

'Traditionally in Japan, a doll is not a toy'

CLAPTON

(39) Buccleuch House, Buccleuch Terrace, Clapton, Hackney

Ernest Mason Satow (1843–1929), the brilliant diplomat and linguist, was born here on 30 June 1843, at what was once 10 Buccleuch Terrace. The site is now occupied by Buccleuch House, an old people's home.

Ernest's father was a Swedish merchant who had settled in London. His mother, Margaret Mason, was English. The young Satow was educated at Mill Hill School and University College, London. Stirred by a travel book on Asia, he sat the consular service examination, came top and accepted the post of student interpreter in the new British legation in Japan. For main Satow entry, including his place of burial, see: [98].

GREENWICH

(40) 96 Annandale Road, SE10

The Japanese artist, Yoshio Markino, lived here at number 96, c1898. The house is still standing. For main Markino entry, see: [16].

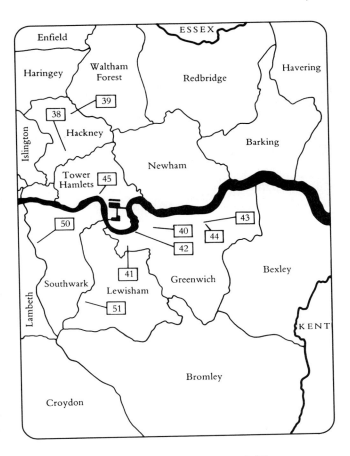

LONDON EAST

(41) The Fan Museum, 12 Crooms Hill, SE10 (Tel: 081-858 7879 or 081-305 1441)

One of the world's finest collections of fans is held at The Fan Museum. Among the 2,000 items are examples of Japanese fans and from time to time special exhibitions are held illustrating the art and craft of Japanese fan-making, which was flourishing in Japan as early as the 10th century. The museum has fans from all over the world and is a research centre and workshop for the conservation and

The Japanese-style garden behind the Fan Museum, Greenwich [41]

manufacture of fans. The museum is located in a pair of fine early Georgian terraced houses with an Orangery and a pool with a water cascade and plant groupings in the Japanese manner. Only a limited number of exhibits are on display at any time, so a phone call before visiting is recommended. *Open Tuesday 2pm–4.30pm, Wednesday–Saturday 11am–4.30pm, Sunday 12am–4.30pm, closed Monday.*

(42) The National Maritime Museum, Romney Road, SE10 (Tel: 081-858 4422)

As the largest of its kind in the world, the National Maritime Museum has a good selection of material relating to Britain and Japan's shared maritime history. There are papers and illustrations concerned with Admiral Togo [65], his training college, the *Worcester*, at Greenhithe, Kent and the Russo–Japanese War of 1904–05. Among the photographic collection are a number of Japanese ships built in British shipyards. There are also five lithographs of Commodore Perry's second Japan visit in 1854, to Tokyo Bay. Much of the material is catalogued. Printed catalogues can also be purchased and photographs ordered. *Open Monday–Saturday 10am–6pm, Sunday 2pm–6pm (5pm in winter).*

(43) Museum of Artillery, Repository Road, Greenhill, Woolwich, SE18 (Tel: 081–316 5402)

On 25 June 1863, the cannon now in the Museum of Artillery attempted to change the course of Japanese history. Britain's first minister in Japan, Sir Rutherford Alcock [77] and the foreign traders who followed in his train, had barely been in the country four years. The power of the shogun had broken down and the emperor was not yet strong enough to replace him. Yet this was the date issued by Imperial edict for all foreigners to be expelled.

In 1863, there were few Japanese who had any knowledge of Western power. Among the few who did were two young Choshu samurai, Hirobumi Ito [34] and Kaoru Inouye [34], who had broken off their studies in London in an attempt to keep these cannon silent. Having lived in the heart of the British Empire, it wasn't difficult to realize that their small backward country, still mostly entrenched in the middle ages, had little chance against the allied powers. Nevertheless, the fanatics had their way and these guns began firing against foreign shipping.

The result was inevitable, but it was not until 5 September 1864 that a joint foreign force of 17 ships, eight of which were British, bombarded the Choshu batteries. By 10 September, all ten batteries had been silenced and brought on board the allied vessels. A total of 65 pieces of ordnance were captured. The Choshu agreed to keep the straits open and indemnities were paid. The path to modernization with Western help – however shakily – had now begun.

'The National Maritime Museum has a good selection of material relating to Britain and Japan's shared maritime history' [42]

Tombstone in Norwood Cemetery designed by the artist Yoshio Markino [16]: these commissions ceased after Markino's angels were thought to look more like dancing girls

The museum has two of the captured Choshu cannon. Both are of bronze, decorated with dragon carvings, with 73.2 inch bore and a calibre of 3.47 inch. There are also a few rifles and some most interesting swords. One sword is of massive proportions with flamboyant decoration. The inscription reads 'made by Fujiwara of Izumo Province, 1661'. *Open Monday–Friday 12am–5pm, Saturday and Sunday 1pm–5pm (4pm in winter).*

(44) Royal Ordnance Factory, Woolwich

For the first Japanese Mission of 1862, the journey from their closed country of knights in armour to the Royal Ordnance Factory at Woolwich must have seemed as fantastic as the exploits of modern science fiction heroes seem to us. Again and again the Japanese asked to be taken back to Woolwich where, according to their escorts, they were like men under a spell.

Following their rousing welcome at Dover on 30 April, the Japanese party were invited to look around while waiting for Alcock [77] to arrive in London on home leave from Japan. They were put up at Claridge's (the old Claridge's on the same site as the present hotel). At the guests' special request, the Japanese flag they had brought with them was hoisted.

The ambassadors were invited to the opening ceremony of the Great Exhibition, where they attracted more public attention than Alcock's collection of Japanese art – the first such display in England. Socially, they were an enormous success and found themselves guests of honour at balls and receptions at the great London homes. In order to fit in as much as possible, the party split up, some travelling north to the heartland of British industry. They visited Newcastle, went down a coal mine at the North Seaton Colliery, and attended a banquet held in their honour in the Liverpool Town Hall.

Alcock finally arrived from Japan and a meeting was arranged with the ambassadors and Earl Russell, Secretary of State for Foreign Affairs. On 6 June, an agreement was signed postponing the opening of the other treaty ports until January 1868. The ambassadors had not got everything they came for. But they had seen the future and knew that it worked.

On 12 June, the ambassadorial party got their 17 tons of luggage ready for home and took the Royal train to Woolwich. Here they prepared to embark on the Dutch man-of-war, *Arturo*. The Japanese had by now been in Britain over a month and their presence caused so much interest that a double line of police was necessary to keep back the crowds of well-wishers. As soon as the party were on board, the Japanese flag could be seen flying from the foretopmast of the *Arturo*.

LIMEHOUSE

(45) Limekiln Dock, Limehouse, E14

'From the age of twelve years old, I was brought up in Limehouse', Gillingham-born William Adams wrote in his own hand, 'being apprentice twelve years to Master Nicholas Diggines'.

The research is probably yet to be done to establish the *precise* location of where Japan's first Englishman learned the trades he later taught the Japanese. It was in the vicinity of Limehouse (now Limekiln) Dock. A map in the Public Record Office, c1573, names the dock and shows the neighbouring houses. Nicolas Diggines (his name had many variants) is recorded as a member of the vestry of St Dunstan, Stepney, representing Limehouse 1594–1621. He was married at Stepney Church in August 1580. For main Adams entry, his birthplace and baptism, see: [71].

4 | *London South*

BATTERSEA

(46) The London Peace Pagoda, Battersea Park, SW11

Pagodas, dedicated specifically to the quest for world peace through inter-faith and inter-cultural harmony, have been constructed by the Japanese Buddhist order, Nipponzan Myohoji, since World War II. There are more than 70 worldwide but the first in Europe was built in Milton Keynes in 1981 [110]. The London Peace Pagoda was the inspiration of the preceptor, or teacher, of the order, the Most Venerable Nichidatsu Fujii, who celebrated his 100th birthday in 1984 and whose order donated the pagoda to the people of London.

The forms of the pagoda may be interpreted as a map of the spiritual life, showing the five elements in ascending order, flowing one into the next. The base represents the earth and stable energy; the white central domed tower the flowing energy of water; the upward energy of fire is represented by the roofs; the saucer dish at the base of the umbrella-shaped crown symbolizes air and free energy; and the jewel drop at the summit represents consciousness and eternal spirit. Around the central tower set in niches are four representations of the Buddha, and two guardian lions face south into the park. The reinforced concrete pagoda was constructed by members of the order and completed in 1985. There was some controversy over the siting of the pagoda on the most conspicuous site in the north part of the park and adjacent to the River Thames. A lakeside location was ruled out for doctrinal reasons. There must never be water on the south side of a Buddhist pagoda. *Nearest underground is Sloane Square and bus services 44, 88 and 137 go to the park.*

CAMBERWELL

(47) 6 Flodden Road, SE5

The writer Soseki Natsume lived here from 6 December 1900 to 24 April 1901. For main Soseki entry and Soseki Museum, see: [48].

CLAPHAM

(48) Soseki Museum, 80B The Chase, SW4 (Tel: 071–720 8718)

The lot of a young Japanese man alone in London around the turn of the century, hard up and speaking little English, was

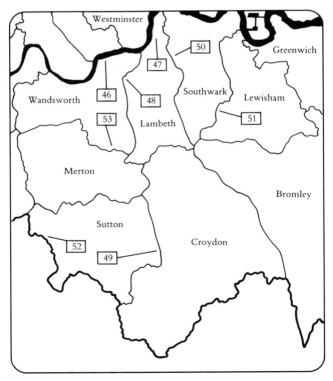

LONDON SOUTH

not a happy one. If you learned he had also been fostered immediately after birth, shunted back to his parents and then back again to his foster home to be eventually adopted, you probably wouldn't be all that surprised to learn that he also suffered from a gastric ulcer, began vomiting blood when he was in his mid forties and died at 50. This is a brief account of the tragic personal life of the writer Soseki Natsume (1867–1916). Yet Soseki's professional career was highly successful and his writings alive with wit and humour. In 1893, he graduated with highest honours from the Imperial University of Tokyo and in 1900 was sent to London as a scholarship student for further studies in English language and literature. On his return to Japan, he became a lecturer at the college from where he had graduated.

In 1907, Soseki joined the highly respected *Asahi Shimbun*, becoming the newspaper's chief literary columnist. Until about 1904, he had become known as a *haiku* poet and writer of short pieces. In 1905 he began fiction writing. His first novel brought him immediate acclaim. Entitled *Rondon To* (The Tower of London), it was a product of his London experience (as was another novel, *Carlyle Museum*). He continued writing (at a prodigious pace) to the end of his short life. His best loved work in English translation is probably *I am a Cat*.

Of his two London years, Soseki later wrote bitterly (and somewhat histrionically) that he had 'led a most miserable life . . . like a dog thrown into the company of wolves'. He was in London between 28 October 1900 and December 1902. He suffered from severe depression, locked himself in his room for days and changed his lodgings five times in the first six months. His final move was to 81 The Chase, SW4. For Soseki's other lodging houses, see: [4, 37, 47, 53].

In March 1984, journalist, art collector, bibliophile, property dealer, travel manager and Soseki aficionado, Sammy Ikuo Tsunematsu, financed and set up the Soseki Museum, directly opposite Soseki's last residence.

The museum contains a mass of Soseki memorabilia, including photographs, books, newspapers and magazines relating mainly to Soseki's life in London. There is also an entire collection of Soseki's writings, critical works on the author and a selection of books on modern Japanese literature. *Open Wednesday 2pm–5pm, Saturday and Sunday 10am–12am, 2pm–5pm.*

CROYDON

(49) Croydon Airport

At 3.26pm, on 9 April 1937, an estimated crowd of 6,000 British and Japanese broke into spontaneous cheering, madly waving Japanese flags as the *Divine Wind* (*kami-kaze* in Japanese) made a perfect landing at the old Croydon Aerodrome. *The Times* and other papers ran full page stories with pictures of the plane, the pilots and the crowds. 'Tokyo to London in 94 hours. Records broken!'

The plane, a Mitsubishi – flying longer and faster – was the 'first Japanese-built aircraft powered by a motor of native design' ever to arrive in Britain. It was sponsored by Japan's leading newspaper, The *Asahi Shimbun*, which claimed the main purpose of the record-breaking flight was to bring warm greetings from the Japanese people to George VI in his coronation year. (It is hard to believe Pearl Harbour was a bare three years away.) The pilot, Maasaki Iinuma, was assisted by his mechanic and wireless operator, Kenji Tsukagoshi, yet nobody seems to have noticed anything different about Kenji Tsukagoshi. In all those column inches, in all those papers, nobody breathed a word that the mechanic was half British.

For the beginning of this sad and largely unreported story, we have to go back to just before the turn of the century. Kenji's father, Kinjiro, was in England studying law. He met a girl called Emily, the daughter of William and Emily Baldwin of 22 Brunswick St (now Deloraine St), Deptford.

The Divine Wind (kami-kaze) landed before a crowd of 6,000 at Croydon Airport in 1937 [49]

Pilot, Maasaki Iinuma (left) and Kenji Tsukagoshi after their record-breaking flight in 1937 [49]

We know that Emily was born on 26 February 1877 (and baptised at St John's Church, Lewisham Way, on 6 June that year). So she would have been in her early twenties when she and Kinjiro fell in love.

They married in Japan on 16 October 1900. There must have been something clandestine about the wedding, for Emily used an assumed name. It was probably Sayler (or possibly Sailor or Seller). The couple had two children, Florence and Kenji. Kenji's father, Kinjiro, became a judge. Then sometime in the period 1907 to 1910, the marriage broke up. Emily returned to England with their two children, but the judge followed her and took his children back with him to Japan. There the story really ends as far as Emily is concerned. There are no further records. Except that in 1914, a Japanese court formally declared Emily dead.

Over half of the old Croydon Aerodrome is still much as it was on that day in 1937 when the *kami-kaze* arrived – with large, windswept grassy areas west of Purley Way. Some of the service buildings, the hotel and the control tower still exist. And if the Croydon Aircraft Preservation Society have their way, there will eventually be an aircraft museum here where Kenji landed. A planning application has been lodged. Should you wish to, Emily's childhood can also be visited. Her house is still there, 22 Deloraine Street, Deptford, SE28.

To see her baptism records, contact St John's Vicarage, St John's Church, St John's Vale, London, SE3 4EA.

LAMBETH

(50) Imperial War Museum, Lambeth Road, SE1 (Tel: 071-416 5000)

The Imperial War Museum has by far the best material, in all media, on the two world wars. Helpful and cooperative staff are a boon to researchers and aficionados. Collections include some fascinating recordings of eye-witness accounts of allied POWs in Japan at the time of the atom bombs. For anything out of the ordinary like this (ie not normal museum displays) do telephone the keeper in advance. *Open daily 10am–6pm.*

LEWISHAM

(51) Horniman Museum and Library, London Road, Forest Hill, SE23 (Tel: 081-699 2339)

The Horniman Museum and Library sets out its displays somewhat similarly to the Pitt Rivers [112] in Oxford – by theme. Therefore, in Japan's case, you will find the following arrangements. Under clothing, shoes, fans, *netsuke* and *inro*; under food preparation, teapots and caddies; under magic and religion, girls' festival items, religious figures and painting, house shrines and carved screens; under masques and drama, masks, puppets. And so on. It gives a whole new slant to comparing Japan to the rest of the world. *Monday– Saturday 10.30am–6pm, Sunday 2pm–6pm.*

SUTTON

(52) St Mary's Churchyard, Church Road, Beddington, Sutton

'First known union between subjects of the two countries'. This curious claim is inscribed on a tombstone near the entrance gateway, on the opposite side of the road to the church. The full inscription reads: 'In memory of Eliza

Teiske Minami, who departed this life July 9th 1902. Aged 53 years. The marriage in 1872 of the above Eliza Teiske Minami, an Englishwoman, with Teiske Minami, a Japanese, was the first known union between subjects of the two countries'. Vandals have daubed paint on the tombstone but it is still legible.

WANDSWORTH

(53) 11 Stella Road, Tooting, Graveney, SW17

The writer, Soseki Natsume lived here from 25 December 1901 to 19 July 1901. For main Soseki entry and Soseki Museum, see: [48].

'A whole new slant to comparing Japan to the rest of the world': Horniman Museum [51]

5 | *London West*

EALING

(54) St Mary's Road, W5

Rutherford Alcock (1809–1897), first British minister in Japan, was not expected to live. His father, an eminent medical practitioner, had his son baptised here at St Mary's Church when he was only one day old. The baptism records (kept in County Hall), show he was christened *John* Rutherford Alcock. The lad was tougher than he looked and became a successful army surgeon and Deputy Inspector of Hospitals, before accepting his first consular appointment in China in 1844 – in Fuchow then Shanghai. For Alcock's grave and main entry, see: [77].

FULHAM

(55) All Saints Church, Church Gate by Putney Bridge, SW6 (Tel: 071-736 6301)

On 27 September 1614 a ship arrived at Plymouth with the first Japanese sailors to come to Britain, a gift of armour from the shogun for James I and 'certain lascivious books and pictures'. The armour can be seen in the Tower of London. The 15 sailors returned home about three years later. The pornography was burnt by the outraged officials.

The man responsible for the sailors and the lewd books and pictures was Captain John Saris (c1580–1646). His memorial slab (with lengthy inscription) can be seen under the choir stalls in All Saints, Fulham Parish Church. Saris first arrived in Japan, as Captain of the East India Company

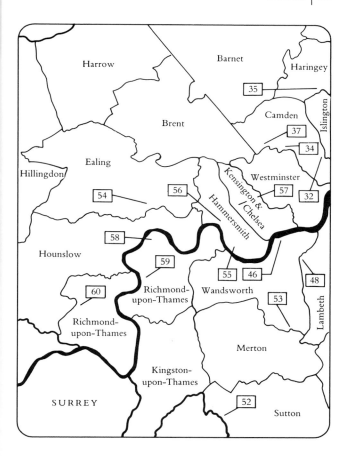

LONDON WEST

ship *Clove*, on 11 June 1613. One of the first reported incidents concerned some young Japanese Christian women who came aboard the ship. Catching sight of the captain's nude pin-up of Venus de Milo, the girls took it to be the Virgin Mary and prostrated themselves before the picture. Saris made contact with William Adams [71] who acted as his interpreter and interceded on Saris's behalf with the Japanese authorities. With Adams's help, Saris obtained permission to establish an English factory at Hirado, under another Englishman, Richard Cocks.

Adams also arranged an audience with the Shogun Ieyasu, when gifts (including the Tower armour) were exchanged. Despite Adams's efforts to be helpful, he and Saris never did get on and the captain's papers are full of criticism. Saris engaged Adams on behalf of the East India Company. Adams refused Saris's first offer of £20 a year and finally settled on £100, a goodly sum in early 17th century Japan.

Saris's voyage home on the *Clove* appears to have been his last. Not only was there the pornography scandal. He was also accused of private trading and was therefore dismissed from the service, but with the recognition that he had navigated a long and difficult voyage on behalf of his employers. The following year, 1615, Saris married Anne Meggs (granddaughter of London Lord Mayor, Sir Thomas Cambell). She died, childless, in 1623, when it seems the couple were living in the region of Thames Street and Botolph Lane. By 1629, the widower had moved to a comfortable retirement in Church Row, Fulham. Saris's house was pulled down in 1750 (and the street name changed to Church Gate in 1937). The site is now occupied by Sir William Powell's Almshouses. See also: [99].

HAMMERSMITH

(56) Hammersmith and Fulham Central Library, Shepherds Bush Road, W6 (Tel: 081-576 5050)

The Hammersmith and Fulham Central Library has a number of items relating to the 1909–10 Japan–British Exhibition at White City. Holdings include the official report as well as a number of albums, news cuttings, photographs, post cards, etc.

HOLLAND PARK

(57) Kyoto Japanese Garden, Holland Park, W11

On 17 September 1991, Crown Prince Naruhito opened London's first real Japanese garden in Holland Park. It is on the site of an 1890s garden, by the Fifth Lord Ilchester and his wife, in the ground of what was then Holland House. The earlier garden, although often described as Japanese, is more

Haiku written by Kyoshi Takahama, Kew Gardens [58]

likely to have been an English garden with the addition of a few Japanese touches, like stone lanterns.

The new Kyoto Japanese Garden, taking approximately the same space of around an acre, was made after consultation with the Kyoto Chamber of Commerce and the Kyoto Garden Association. A simple traditional Japanese design combines the basics of rocks, a lake and waterfalls. Unlike the Victorian creators of Japanese gardens, the mayor did *not* charter a yacht to the homeland to bring back materials and gardeners. The new Kyoto Garden was Japanese designed but mostly British built and made from materials found primarily in Britain. Funding came from both sides. It is hoped that the Kyoto Japanese Garden will long be a happy reminder of the 1991 Japan Festival.

RICHMOND

(58) Royal Botanic Gardens, Kew, Richmond (Tel: 081-940 1171)

Some of the loveliest thoughts ever expressed about the Royal Botanic Gardens are carved in granite, very near to the famous Japanese Gate. They are in the form of a *haiku* written by Kyoshi Takahama (1874–1959), one of the two greatest poets in this genre who have ever lived (the other was Basho Matsuo, 1688–1704).

Mr Takahama visited the gardens here in 1936 and the *haiku* was the result not so much of what he saw but of how he felt. The thought behind the *haiku* was that even sparrows, so often nervous in Japan, were at perfect peace here at Kew. However, it was also the poet's belief that the true meaning of *haiku* ('a sound poem' of 17 syllables in lines of 5,7,5 syllables) could never really be properly understood in translation. The memorial stone, a gift from the Haiku Society of Japan, was unveiled on 10 May 1979, by the poet's daughter, Mrs Haruko Takagi.

Kew's abundant spring and autumn colours remind visitors of Japan. But even more popular with Japanese is the Chokushi-mon, Gate of the Imperial Messenger. It originally formed the gateway to the 1910 Japanese Exhibition at White City and was a gift from the exhibitors. The Chokushi-mon is an exact, scaled-down replica, four-fifths the size, of the gateway to the Nishi Honganji Temple in Kyoto, thought to be the best existing example of Buddhist architecture. The wood carver, Genyemon Wada, followed the original exactly, even using the same close-grained

The Kew Gardens haiku translated [58]

Hinoki wood, from the *Cupressus obtusa*. (At the time of publication, the Chokushi-mon looked to be showing its age and Kew are hoping to be able to raise sufficient funding for restoration.)

The Marianne North Gallery, erected by and named after Marianne North and opened in 1882 is also worth seeing. This Victorian lady artist travelled the world in the latter part of the 19th century, paintbrush in hand. There are some 15 of her Japanese flower and landscape paintings, mostly done during her 1875 visit there. In the afternoon of 6 October 1971, Emperor Hirohito planted a Japanese cedar (*Cryptomeria japonica*) just inside the main gate. Regrettably, this was destroyed by vandals and had to be replaced. *Open all year except Christmas and New Year's Day.*

(59) 3 The Hermitage

It would seem that John Milne, 'Father of Japanese seismology' lodged here around 1874 (at which time the address would have been 3 Hermitage Villas). The houses in the street would appear to be the original 19th century buildings. For main Milne entry, see: [78].

TWICKENHAM

(60) Twickenham Cemetery, Percy Road, Whitton, Richmond-upon-Thames

According to his biographer, Anne Taylor, Laurence Oliphant (1829–88) was one of the most fascinating men of his generation. At various stages during his active and restless life he was a barrister in Ceylon, an MP in Britain, a diplomat in Canada, a government secret agent in Italy, and a war correspondent for *The Times* during the Crimean and Franco–German Wars. He was at all times a shrewd and charming observer of his fellow man and a successful writer. Suggestions of insanity were made from time to time mainly because he was somewhat 'other worldly', believing that the world at large was 'a lunatic asylum'. He believed in a kind of mystical spiritualism and came under the influence of Lake Harris, a self-proclaimed prophet at the head of a religious cult, to whom he signed away all his money.

Oliphant's claim to fame as far as Japan is concerned is that he helped negotiate Britain's first treaty in 1858 as Lord Elgin's private secretary [205] and three years later returned to Japan as chargé d'affaires to the British legation in Edo.

Oliphant's book *Narrative of Lord Elgin's Mission to China and Japan* is particularly important in that it contains a great deal of information contributed by Henry Heusken, the Dutch translator whom the American Ambassador Townsend Harris had lent to the British party to negotiate the treaty with the Bakufu. Heusken was murdered in January 1860; he was only 24 and all that remains of his remarkable knowledge of Japan is in his friend Laurence Oliphant's book.

The British party arrived in Japan from China in August 1858 on board HMS *Furious*. Oliphant was pleasantly surprised: braced for the usual noise, smells, confusion and dirt of a Chinese city, he was enchanted to find broad, clean, gravelled streets and a population friendly and relaxed. He made friends with one of the Japanese appointed to negotiate the treaty, Higo no Kami, who was most anxious to learn English and be selected as one of Japan's first emissaries to go abroad. In the normal round of diplomatic activity presents and meals were exchanged. The Japanese, records Oliphant 'did not jib at European food – ham, champagne, paté de foie gras, curacao and strawberry jam all went down well – and champagne especially well. Mindful of its diplomatic uses, Lord Elgin had thoughtfully brought a plentiful supply'.

The British party had brought with them a yacht to present to the Shogun who was esconced in his palace in Edo and never went out, except on state occasions. 'It was a cruel satire on this unhappy potentate to present him with a yacht', Oliphant wrote, 'one might as well request the Pope's acceptance of a wife'.

The mission was successful and a treaty was secured within a month. But Oliphant was not completely taken in by the charm, courtesy and quaintness of their reception; he had sensed the shock of the encounter with the West and his judgment of the Japanese character was shrewd. 'The people were obedient to their superiors, courageous and honest', he wrote, 'but they were also notoriously vindictive, superstitious, haughty, exceedingly tenacious of their honour and unsparing in their mode of protecting or revenging it'. He thought Britain's relations with Japan would become less amicable as, in effect, they had been forced upon the country. 'The Japanese fancied they saw impending on them the fate of India, and they believed the only alternative was to grant us concessions such as we had already wrung from China', Oliphant concluded.

When Oliphant returned to Japan in 1861 to assist the British Ambassador, Sir Rutherford Alcock [77], his prediction of deteriorating relations with the West had come true – indeed the shock of opening the country had produced a violent dislike of strangers. Higo no Kami, his old friend from the treaty negotiations, had been forced to commit ritual suicide as one of the officials responsible for opening Japan to the detested foreigners. To pass the time, Oliphant and his personal servant Bligh started a collection of rare insects (destined for the British Museum) which was kept, impaled on pins, laid out on the table under the window of Bligh's bedroom.

The British Delegation was accommodated in the temple of Tozenji and one night in July 1861, after everyone had gone to bed, it was attacked by a group of sword-wielding fanatics determined to 'not stand by and see the sacred Empire defiled by foreigners'. In the ensuing melée, Oliphant defended himself with a horsewhip and, although badly cut, managed to drive off the intruders. He would have been murdered but the sword of one of the intruders was deflected from a direct blow, having hit an overhead beam in the dark. Bligh, his servant, escaped being murdered in his bed as the two swordsmen who had entered his bedroom through the window had stepped onto the pins of the insect collection and, in yelling out with the pain, had woken him up.

Oliphant's injury was so severe (he had lost the use of his fingers on one hand by a blow to the wrist) that he was sent back to England to convalesce. He was expected to return to his post in Japan but never actually did so. He died two days before Christmas in 1888 from pleurisy and cancer of the lung at York House, Twickenham where he was staying as a guest of Sir Mountstuart and Lady Grant Duff. He is buried in Twickenham Cemetery. *The Cemetery is open 10am–4.30pm.*

6 | South-east England

BIRCHINGTON

(61) Powell Cotton Museum, Quex Park, Birchington, Kent (Tel: 0843-42168)

'We don't know how good we are till the experts keep telling us', says Derek Howland, curator of the Powell Cotton Museum. Visiting the museum is rather like a treasure hunt that any expert can enter. Apparently, almost every time a Japanese specialist visits the museum – otherwise known for its spectacular African dioramas – another new discovery is made. Like so many small Japanese collections in Britain, the one at the Powell Cotton has never really been completely examined professionally and catalogued. So as knowledge about it is increased, so is its true value.

One of the most important Japanese items so far identified is the large circular 17th century moon-shrine. It seems to have been made from a temple drum and is decorated in gold and coloured lacquer, bearing a rather impressive *mon* (Japanese heraldic crest). From a more recent 1973 donation of teapots, mostly of cast iron, two have been found to be of considerable importance. The *netsuke*, over 300 pieces, in ivory, wood, shell and horn, date from the mid-18th century. They are housed in a particularly splendid red, lacquered chest of compartmented drawers. There are also good examples of *inro*, *tsuba*, swords and armour; and a bow used by a mounted archer. Miscellaneous Japanese items include *cloisonné*, various other pieces of red lacquered furniture and porcelain.

The bulk of the Japanese items were acquired in 1910. They came from the private collection of a Mr R. Pope, who had amassed them over many years residence in the Far East. Mr Pope was in rather frail health and he scurried back to the Eastern sunshine as soon as he could dispose of his treasures.

There is an interesting Japanese carving of the big-game-hunting founder of the Powell Cotton Museum, Mr Powell Cotton himself. This large piece is attributed to the 'carver to the Mikado'. Despite such touches, however – and the apparently outstanding merit of many of the Japanese pieces – regrettably little detail is given to them in the catalogue. This is a lack for which the curator also apologises. He invites you instead to join in the hunt. You never know what new Japanese treasures you might find! *Quex Park is about one mile from the village centre. 1 April–30 September only: Wednesday, Thursday and Sunday, bank holidays and Fridays in August 2.15pm–6pm. 1 October–31 March: Sunday 2.15pm–6pm. Closed winter 1991, reopening April 1992.*

BOURNEMOUTH

(62) Russell-Cotes Art Gallery and Museum, East Cliff, Bournemouth, Dorset (Tel: 0202-551009)

When in March 1915, Sir Merton Russell-Cotes, founder of the museum which now bears his name, had tea with the Japanese ambassador, he may well have wished he hadn't. Sir Merton and Lady Russell-Cotes had visited Japan in 1885 and returned with over 100 crates of what they termed their 'Japanese curios'.

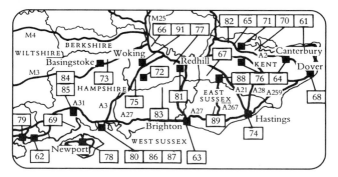

SOUTH-EAST ENGLAND

Now, 30 years later, Ambassador Marquis Katsunosuke Inouye was telling Sir Merton – in the most gracious and indirect manner possible – that items in the Russell-Cotes collection were so priceless and rare, they should never have left Japan! As it happened, nothing more was said, which is to the good fortune of the thousands who every year visit the remarkable Japanese collection at the Russell-Cotes Art Gallery and Museum.

The museum contains many substantial, fine and decorative art collections besides the Japanese. But for Sir Merton, a founder member of the Japan Society, things Japanese were amongst his favourites. (While in Yokohama, he concluded 'from undoubted evidence', that the Japanese were 'a section of the lost tribes of Israel'.)

Of the forbidden treasures alluded to by the ambassador, don't miss the prize silver elephant. It was made in the late 19th century by Komai, probably Japan's greatest metal-smith. The elephant is worked with gold and overlaid with semi-precious stones. Look also for the superb 18th century Buddhist shrine. There are many more objects of great variety, including lacquerwork, stoves, personal chests, rice and sake bowls, and even a set of 18th century black and gold lacquered mail boxes. The list goes on. This is just a taste. Enjoy it! *Monday–Saturday 10am–5pm.*

BRIGHTON

(63) Brighton Art Gallery and Museum, Church Street, Brighton, East Sussex (Tel: 0273-603005)

The Brighton Art Gallery and Museum has a varied collection of around 800 Japanese items. Every now and again, an exhibition is mounted and there is much praise for the prints collection, also the armour and swords. But ring before you come. Most Japanese items seem to be in store most of the time.

CANTERBURY

(64) Royal Museum and Art Gallery, High Street, Canterbury, Kent (Tel: 0227-452747)

The decorative art of the *tsuba* (the sword guard) is unique to Japan. There is a small but interesting *tsuba* collection in the

Royal Museum and Art Gallery. *Monday–Saturday 10am–5pm.*

CHATHAM

(65) Chatham Historic Dockyard, Chatham, Kent (Tel: 0634–812551)

In the naval college near Hiroshima, the Japanese have displayed three locks of hair belonging to the three greatest seamen of all time. One is from Admiral Yamamoto, who masterminded the attack on Pearl Harbour in 1941. Another is from Britain's own Lord Nelson. And the third belonged to the man who carried Nelson's torch to Japan's first modern navy. He was Admiral Heihachiro Togo (1847–1934), 'the Japanese Nelson'.

It was undoubtedly the Battle of Tsushima that won Togo a place in the pantheon of Shinto gods. In May 1905, the newly formed Japanese navy confronted the established might of Imperial Russia and destroyed the Russian fleet. The British observers aboard the Japanese vessels had almost equal reason to cheer. Japan had been an ally since the beginning of the Anglo–Japanese Alliance in 1902. Togo and many of his men were British trained. A good proportion of the Japanese fleet, including Togo's Barrow-built flagship, the *Mikasa*, came from British yards. Even Togo's pre-battle signal to his fleet had the ring of history. 'The destiny of our empire depends upon this action', the flags fluttered, 'Let every man do his utmost'. It was exactly a century since the Battle of Trafalgar.

Togo learned to respect British naval power in 1863 when, as a lad of 16 aboard a small Satsuma war vessel, he attempted to defend Kagoshima against bombardment by the Royal Navy. Other small skirmishes broadened his experience. But Togo was largely ignorant of basic Western seamanship when, with about a dozen other Japanese students, he arrived in Southampton in 1871. The Japanese students were taken straight to London to buy English clothes and see the sights. After a few days, each went his separate way. Togo was sent to a boarding house in Plymouth, to get to know the natives and to learn their language.

At the end of the summer, he continued his education in English and mathematics at the home of the Reverend A.D. Capel, in Cambridge [120]. A serious eye complaint cut short his stay but after a satisfactory operation, Togo joined the Royal Navy Academy at Gosport. In 1873, Togo became a cadet on the Thames Marine Officers training ship, the *Worcester*, moored at Greenhithe until 1968. Until recently, it was possible to visit the nearby Merchant Navy College library at Greenhithe, where a lot of the Togo memorabilia were on display. These were transferred to the Chatham Historic Dockyard in 1989, where they can be seen by appointment. The Togo Collection includes what has come to be known as the 'Togo Cup', a large silver bowl with a motif of chrysanthemums. Togo presented this to his 'beloved *Worcester*' in 1911, when he attended the coronation of George V. Then, in 1932, two years before his death, the Admiral presented the college with his personal ensign.

The 'Togo registers' (comments of 'good', 'satisfactory' and 'excellent' produced praise and promotion from the Meiji government) are now kept at the Marine Society (202 Lambeth Road, London SE1 7JY, Tel: 071-261 9535). They can be seen by appointment.

During Togo's cadetship on the *Worcester* the young Japanese was given the nickname 'Johnnie Chinaman'. (Surprised by Togo's hostile reaction, his puzzled fellow-students asked, 'Why, is there any difference between China and Japan?') Two years into his cadetship, Togo joined his classmates on the small sailing ship, the *Hampshire*, for the gruelling 30,000 mile round trip to Australia and back. A model of the *Hampshire* can also be seen (by appointment) at the Chatham Dockyard Trust.

It wasn't just the English language that Togo had had to master. As a young samurai from a backward medieval state, the whole concept of Western methodology was as foreign as blue eyes and golden hair. Despite this, he passed out second in his class and in 1878 returned to Japan on the Welsh-built *Hiei*, promoted to second lieutenant in the Imperial Japanese Navy.

In later years, Togo returned to Britain on a number of occasions – on personal visits, to inspect Japanese ships being built in British shipyards and to reunions with his old *Worcester* classmates. At Togo's funeral in 1934, Sir John Jellicoe, Admiral of the Fleet, saluted Togo as 'a splendid leader, a gallant sailor and a great gentleman'. *Summer: Wednesday–Sunday and bank holidays 10am–6pm. Winter: Wednesday, Saturday, Sunday and bank holidays 10am–4.30pm.*

CHERTSEY

(66) Thorpe Park, Staines Road, Chertsey, Surrey (Tel: 0932-562633)

An imitation rock and water style Japanese garden has been set in the middle of the much visited fun-for-all-the-family amusement park, Thorpe Park. The garden was made by landscape gardener and British Empire medalist, Philip Bateman, and completed in spring 1982. Not for those wanting to sit and meditate.

CHIDDINGSTONE

(67) Chiddingstone Castle, Chiddingstone, Kent (Tel: 0892-870347)

Some say that this is the last great collection of the common man. It is also in some respects the history of the Japanese antique market over the past one and a half centuries. When Japan's long-sealed doors were finally prised apart in the 1850s and 1860s, both sides seemed transfixed by what they could now see on the other side. Many Japanese, aping everything foreign, turned their backs on their traditional arts and crafts. In turn, these often superb pieces were snapped up by Westerners at bargain prices – to satisfy the new fad for everything Japanese. By the 1920s, however, fashions were again changing. Prices of Japanese objets d'art, cheap to begin with, now plummeted. It was in this buyers' market *par excellence* that collector Denys Bower indulged every penny he could spare from his modest wages as a bank clerk. Bower cared little for the fickleness of changing fashion. But his astute eye for real craftsmanship was to bring him a shogun's ransom. Bower's priceless collections are displayed in the 'country house' he bought to keep them in, Chiddingstone Castle. There are several significant collections as well as the Japanese collection. Most Japanese items are in the North Gothic Hall (arms and armour) and in the three Japanese Rooms, indicated as such. The range is broad as well as of exceptional quality. The earliest objects are the Haniwa clay 'guardians' from the 4th and 5th centuries AD. A number of sword blades, some from master craftsmen such as Sadamune and Muramasa, are also old. But world recognition has really been earned by the castle's Japanese lacquerware. There are over 2,000 items, many of extraordinary beauty and craftsmanship. The greatest single item – undoubtedly the 'Curator's choice' – is the rare Beckford Cabinet, believed to be from the same workshop as the van Diemen Box in the Victoria and Albert Museum in London [26]. Recent research has dated it to 1635–40. It is one of a small group of exported lacquers made around this time which incorporate into their designs motifs from Murasaki Shikibu's *The Tale of Genji*. *Chiddingstone is off the Edenbridge–Tonbridge road (B2027) at Bough Beech. Penshurst Station is two and a half miles away. Open 29 March–31 October, Easter holidays. April, Wednesday, Saturday, Sunday. 1 May–30 September, Wednesday–Sunday. Mid-June–Mid-September and all public holidays as above, also Tuesday. Weekdays 2pm–5.30pm. Sunday and public holidays 11.30am–5.30pm.*

DOVER

(68) Admiralty Pier; HM Customs and Excise Building; Dover Museum, 1203 Maison Dieu House, Ladywell, Dover, Kent
(Tel: 0304-201066)

Dover was not the first landfall for Japanese. That honour belongs to south-west England [99]. However, in 1862, Dover became the welcome port for the First Japanese Mission (also known as The London Protocol). The first Japanese for 248 years chose a clear fine day to arrive. It was 30 April 1862. A fresh south-east breeze made the Channel only slightly choppy. Just after 12.30pm, the French warship, *Le Corse*, carrying the party of some 36 ambassadors, officers, servants, and an interpreter, pulled in alongside Admiralty Pier. An immense crowd jostled to get the first sight of the 'large hats, silken trousers and carved-handled swords'. For their part, the Japanese were as interested in the welcoming crowd as it was in them. The French sailors, being little understood by either side, excitedly called to each other amidst increasing confusion. A small party of British officers came on board to welcome the ambassadors. The officers touched their hats. The Japanese removed theirs. Then, as the party were preparing to disembark, two Frenchmen rushed forward to say their own adieus – embracing the Japanese and kissing the shaven portion of their crowns, exposed by their samurai haircuts. At the landing steps, members of the local corporation, in full regalia, and preceded by the mace, conducted the ambassadors to the Lord Warden Hotel (now HM Customs Customs and Excise Building) where long welcoming addresses were read.

The Japanese Mission, headed by commissioners of foreign affairs Yasunori Takeuchi and Yasunao Matsudaira, had left Japan on 30 January 1862. The mission had two main purposes. The first was to defer opening further treaty ports to Japan until local unrest had subsided. The second was to observe Western power and the Western way of life.

About a mile into the town from the modern ferry terminal buildings, is the early thirteenth century Maison Dieu House, containing both the Town Hall and Dover Museum.

There are only a small number of Japanese items in the museum. The 'Curator's choice' is a notice recalling the arrival in Dover of Prince Fushimi, brother of the Emperor Meiji, on 6 May 1907. The prince was given a tremendous welcome by the corporation of Dover and thousands of well-wishers. In appreciation of this, on 30 May, the Mayor, Mr G.F. Raggett, was awarded the Order of Meiji Number Four and the Order of the Rising Sun. (Following his arrival, Prince Fushimi apparently went on to a very successful British tour.)

EXBURY

(69) Exbury Gardens, Exbury Village, near Southampton, Hampshire

In 1947, the sensation of the Chelsea Flower Show was a small plant from the top of the mountain at Yakushima. It was called *rhododendron yakushimanum*, described in D.G. Leach's sober *Rhododendrons of the World* as 'extraordinary' and (in 1962) 'still very rare'. This and other Japanese plants were first obtained by the large, beautiful and extravagant Exbury Gardens created by the de Rothschild family and begun in 1919. The present owner, Edmund de Rothschild is very proud of his family's many Japan connections. These go back to the last century, with loans from the family bankers to the Japanese government.

Edmund de Rothschild's Japan efforts have not gone unnoticed by the Imperial Palace. In 1973, he was awarded the Order of the Sacred Treasure, first class, only the third foreigner to be so honoured. It was in recognition of the 'great contributions in the monetary field . . . and ceaseless endeavours to . . . promotion of Japanese and British friendship'. *Exbury village is 15 miles south-west of South-ampton. Turn off B3054 between Beaulieu and Dibden Parlieu. Open 2 March–7 July and 7 September to 20/27 October.*

FAVERSHAM

(70) Mount Ephraim, Hernhill, Faversham, Kent (Tel: 0227–750940/751496)

In the years preceeding World War I, it was still *de rigueur* for those of means to include a Japanese garden of sorts in any landscaping plans. At Mount Ephraim, the well known local nurserymen, the Waterers, laid out a seven-acre complex of indigenous gardens, woodlands and lake for the Dawes ship-owning family.

Following the depression years of the 1930s, the gardens were badly neglected and it is only recently that the grandson of the original owners and his wife Mary have done a magnificent job in clearing decades of neglect and over-growth. It is now possible to enjoy the series of pools, stone lanterns and the small bridge that give the Japanese-style garden its pleasant air of authenticity. *From the M2 and the A299, take Hernhill turning at Duke of Kent. Open mid-April to end September daily 2pm–6pm, and bank holidays 11am–6pm.*

GILLINGHAM

(71) Gillingham Parish Church of St Mary Magdalene, The Green, off Church Street; Gillingham Library, High Street (Tel: 0634-281066); William Adams Memorial and Clock, Watling Street, Gillingham, Kent

There has seldom been a character more suited to rip-roaring fiction than William Adams (1564–1620). Born in uncertain circumstances, captain of a supply ship during Drake's defeat of the Spanish Armada, voyager through half the world's seas and almost the sole survivor to reach the unknown 'Japons'. There to be made a prisoner with expectation of imminent crucifixion, then right hand man to the shogun and the first blue-eyed samurai – a lord with power of life and death over 100 villages.

Add to this intelligence and good looks, a wife and family in each country and a mistress or two besides. All human life is there. No wonder Japan's first Englishman has been the subject of countless articles, stories, biographies, novels, films and – in the adaptation of Clavel's best-selling block-buster, *Shogun* – the most successful television mini-series ever made.

The flesh and blood William Adams was born in 1564, the same year as his namesake, Shakespeare. Where precisely in Gillingham has not been established, but recent research has suggested that the Adams family may well have been living on a boat, moored in the Medway (as apparently was Francis Drake's family).

In the Gillingham Parish Church of St Mary Magdalene there is the font where William was baptised on 24 September 1564. The precious ancient registers are no longer kept in the church but the microfilmed copy is in the Gillingham Library. The library also has Adams's original log on microfilm, as well as a specially compiled bibliography, a substantial collection of press cuttings, photographs and other Adams material.

The William Adams Memorial and Clock, unveiled by Ambassador Tsuneo Matsudaira in May 1934, is in Watling Street (near the golf course), now part of the main A2. The 38 Japanese painted maples, horse chestnuts and nettle trees,

'There has seldom been a character more suited to rip-roaring fiction than William Adams' [71]: commemorated in Yokosuka, Japan . . .

gifts from Mitsui, were planted by the company's managing director for Europe, Mr Sozo Ohki, in March 1982.

At the age of 12, the young William began a 12-year apprenticeship to Nicholas Diggines, a shipbuilder at Lime-house [45]. He was taught shipbuilding, astronomy, mathematics and navigation. Historians are divided about Adams's social origins, but it has been pointed out that a number of factors including this education, suggest that he had a fairly comfortable family background. On 20 August

1589, William Adams married Mary Hyn in the parish church of St Dunstan's, Stepney and subsequently had a child by her.

The fateful voyage that was to end in Adams becoming the first Englishman in Japan left England on 5 July 1598. Almost two years later, in April 1600, with four ships lost and most of the crew members either dead or dying, William Adams, pilot of the Dutch ship, *Liefde*, arrived off the coast of Ito.

Adams and those of his crew who had survived spent their first six weeks in prison while the Japanese were deciding what to do with them. The Catholic Jesuits already in Japan, no friends of the British Protestants, did their best to have Adams and his crew crucified. However, the shrewd and

. . . and his home town, Gillingham

wily Ieyasu, the first and perhaps greatest of the Tokugawa shoguns, had no personal quarrel with the newcomers and gave them their freedom. Adams, educated in all the arts of shipping and navigation, became Ieyasu's tutor, adviser, and even shipbuilder. In return, Ieyasu made Adams a samurai with a large estate, 'like unto a lordship in England', Adams described it. He married a Japanese girl and died in Japan at the age of 56, on 16 May 1620. He was buried on his estate, overlooking the harbour of Yokosuka. On 8 February 1982, 362 years on, Yokosuka and Ito (where Adams made first landfall) were officially twinned with the town of his birth.

GODALMING

(72) Hascombe Court, near Godalming, Surrey (Tel: 048632-254)

The Japanese-style water and rock garden at Hascombe Court was built by out-of-work Jarrow miners in the 1930s Depression. This was just one of a number of job-creation schemes by local philanthropist, Sir John Jarvis. The Japanese garden is a small section of much larger gardens covering some 20 acres – designed originally by Gertrude Jekyll and later by Percy Cane. In recent years, decades of neglect have been cleared.

The present owners, Mr and Mrs Poulsen, continue Sir John's tradition by opening the gardens on a number of days every year, in aid of the National Gardens Scheme Charitable Trust, but gone forever are the days when, as High Sheriff of Surrey, Sir John Jarvis would hold garden parties for a thousand or more guests, raising a pound or so from each for his many good causes.

Apparently, his beloved garden was Sir John's last worldly pleasure. On a fine, clear evening on 1 October 1950, he took a last stroll beside the pond, past the Japanese maples, the bamboo clumps, the *Cedar Cryptomeria* and the *japonica spiralis*. (It was a walk he could have done blind-folded, so well did he know his garden.) Then, after a final backward glance, he retired to bed and died peacefully in his sleep early the following morning. He was 74. *Hascombe Court is three and a half miles south of Godalming, off the B2130 between Hascombe and Godalming.*

HARTLEY WINTNEY

(73) St Mary's Church, Hartley Wintney, near Basingstoke, Hampshire

Although there was a Dutch-run sea training school in Nagasaki and the French supervised the construction of a dockyard at Yokosuka after 1864, it was to Britain that Japan turned when it realized it needed a powerful navy.

In 1872, Awa Katsu (also known as Kaishu Katsu) was appointed Minister of the Navy and he set about founding a naval school. Admiral Kawamura was sent to London to persuade the Admiralty to send a 34-man mission to provide systematic education. Archibald Lucius Douglas, then a 31 year old Commander, was approached to become the school's Director and to establish a curriculum for the instruction and other necessary rules and regulations in consultation with the Navy Ministry. He signed a three-year contract at £960 a year; quarters were provided and small sums given for kit, travel expenses and furnishing. He went out to Japan in 1873 with his wife Constance, two children and a nurse.

Douglas served two years of his contract before resigning to return to active duty in order not to be passed over for promotion. He went on to become an Admiral and was knighted and retired in 1907 after 55 years in the navy. He was very highly regarded in Japan for introducing a curriculum based on practical training in seamanship, gunnery, navigation and shipbuilding. He also introduced sports including cricket, football and billiards which became very popular among the Japanese cadets.

Admiral Katsunoshin Yamanashi wrote: 'It may not be an overstatement that the ruling spirit, discipline and manifold faculties of the Japanese Navy were the result of the inestimable work of Commander Douglas and his staff. Besides strictly naval attainments, we received far-reaching teaching of British social customs, liberal thinking and a sense of duty'.

Commander Douglas fostered this spirit of naval ideals by introducing the image of Nelson, so that he became a *kami* or god, and 'What would Nelson have done?' became the foundation of Japanese naval ethics. Years later, when Admiral Togo attended a Trafalgar Day ceremony on HMS *Victory* he burst into tears.

When Douglas left Japan, the Emperor Meiji received him in audience and presented him with the Order of the Rising Sun First Class and commended the commander's work 'being as it is the basis of the development of our Navy'. *The grave is in Section D, Grave 131 D in the churchyard.* For main Togo entry, see: [65].

HASTINGS

(74) Hastings Museum and Art Gallery, John's Place, Cambridge Road, Hastings, East Sussex (Tel: 0424–721202)

When you stand before the suit of fearsome samurai armour in the Hastings Museum and Art Gallery, pause for a spell and listen to what it can tell you. One of its last owners must have put the pieces together. The helmet is actually the oldest part, say early 17th century; the face mask comes from a slightly later period; the breast plate is likely to have been made early last century and the rest probably later still. The decorations on the shoulder plates are Buddhist. The helmet was probably inherited. But the hawk features on the helmet identify the likely owner. This *mon* (crest), the later of two, identifies the Date family (the final 'e' sounds like an English 'ay'). The Date were one of Japan's great families. Great in wealth and great in lineage. The Date family tree can be followed back to the Heian era (801–1185) and the royal line of the Fujiwaras.

There are at least seven other superb objects – in a varied Japanese collection – that qualify for the 'Curator's choice'. These include *tsuba* (sword guards), swords, lacquerware, *inro*, *netsuke* and *okimono*. There's a story in every one of them. *Open Monday–Saturday 10am–1pm, 2pm–5pm. Sunday 3pm–5pm.*

HINDHEAD

(75) Grove School, Hindhead, Surrey

Professor Williamson (1824–1904) host to Hirobumi Ito and other early Japanese students in Hampstead and lecturer at University College, London [34], also owned High Pitfold

Hindhead. The house is much as it was in Williamson's day, and is now an academic block for the senior school, one of the buildings making up the Grove School.

MAIDSTONE

(76) Maidstone Museum and Art Gallery, St Faith's Street, Maidstone, Kent (Tel: 0622-754497)

'By far the most important Japanese collection outside London'. This acclaim by the director of the South-East Area Museums service is what experts have always said of the surprisingly unpublicized treasure house in the Maidstone Museum and Art Gallery. It is not only one of the most important because of its quality. In size alone, it is reckoned to be the third largest in the British Isles. However, the last decade or so has seen increasing recognition. A £1 million rebuilding programme provided additional space for the over 3,000 items in the Japanese collection. The ensuing publicity attracted such luminaries as the V&A's Japan team, who entertained Maidstone's curator with their spontaneous cries of approval and surprise. As if to do justice to these

The 'Curator's choice' from 'the most important Japanese collection outside London' – a black and gold lacquer writing table and matching suzuribako (inkstone box) with moons inlaid in silver: Maidstone Museum [76]

Tsuba of shibuichi (an alloy of copper and gold) inlaid in other metals depicting three of the 47 ronin, probably 18th century: Maidstone Museum [76]

developments, Maidstone has recently initiated a programme of professional overall assessment and cataloguing of the entire Japanese collection – much of it for the first time.

Maidstone has been remarkably fortunate in the generosity of its donors. In 1905, Henry Marsham, son of the third Earl of Romney, did what a lot of other Victorians of independent means were doing and visited Japan. He made himself comfortable in Kyoto's Miyako Hotel, where he spent much of the next three years. He shipped home large quantities of Japanalia, especially pottery and porcelain. Having by now picked up some idea of the aesthetic relationship of fine ceramics to the tea ceremony, Marsham wrote with infinite patience to Maidstone's curator. In a note accompanying a priceless tea jar that his tea master had revered above all things, Marsham would say, 'this is not a cartload of rubbish I am sending you'. Rubbish was the very last thing anyone would have called Marsham's purchases and at his death in 1908, the entire cartload was bequeathed to the museum.

Walter Samuel, eldest son of the first Lord Bearsted, founder of the Shell Oil company, was another collector strongly attracted to Japanese arts and crafts – *and* with the means to back his hobby. Samuel built up a large and varied collection. It included sword fittings, *netsuke*, *inro* and other lacquer work, rare books and over 700 woodblock prints. To give this the space it deserved, his parents had a new wing erected at the museum (it's the kind of beneficence the curator would welcome at any time). The opening ceremony, on 22 April 1924, was attended by a friend of the family, Baron Hayashi, the Japanese ambassador.

With many of the collections in this book, we have asked the curator or one of the senior staff to make a choice of the sort of items that they most particularly covet. With Maidstone's collection, it was more difficult than most. One choice is a rare iron Hoju *tsuba* (sword guard) from around 400AD, with unusual though subdued decoration. Another (for comparison) is a *tsuba* made some 1,400 years later. By the Edo era (1600–1867), *tsuba* could be much more decorative: there's a fine Maidstone example depicting the famous

Late 17th century Nabeshima porcelain dish: Maidstone Museum [76]

Rare iron tsuba, c400 AD: Maidstone Museum [76]

story of the 47 ronin. There are many, many more items of interest – of interest because of their beauty, craftsmanship and rarity. The list would include prints, *netsuke*, swords and armour. However, number one in this 'Curator's choice' is from the museum's large collection of lacquerware. It is a low, rectangular, black writing table (*bundai*). On one corner is a design of grasses in gold low relief. There is also a fine inlaid silver crescent moon. It was probably made between 1800 and 1820. Don't miss it. *Monday–Saturday 10am–5.30pm. Bank holidays 11am–5pm.*

MERSTHAM

(77) St Katharine's Churchyard, Merstham, Surrey

On 6 July 1859 – almost two and a half centuries since the death of William Adams [71] and a year after the Elgin treaty

[205] – the Union Jack was hoisted in the grounds of the Tozenji temple. This was to be Britain's first legation in Japan, a beautiful secluded sprawl of rooms, corridors and outbuildings, near Shinagawa in Edo (Tokyo). It was also cut-off, flimsy, and hard to defend – as Sir Rutherford Alcock (1809–97) would soon discover.

Ealing-born Alcock, fresh from a successful tour of duty in China, must often have wished that he had never left Shanghai. He felt isolated and lonely, missed his friends, and hankered after roast beef. He did, however, make the most of his diplomatic status, and travelled the length and breadth of the country. He climbed Mt Fuji, wrote a book about his experiences (*The Capital of the Tycoon*) and even attempted a (wildly inaccurate) English–Japanese Grammar. Alcock had little trust in the central Bakufu government and only slowly came to realize how restricted its authority had become. Reactionary forces had sworn death to all foreigners and locally-supplied legation guards proved to be totally ineffective. Alcock's chief interpreter was mortally run through with a samurai short sword. On 5 July 1861, in one of a number of attacks on the legation, the newly arrived secretary, Laurence Oliphant [60] was so badly wounded he had to return to England. While Alcock was on home leave, Charles Richardson, a merchant from Shanghai, was cut down in broad daylight on a public highway, by a Satsuma retainer. In the Shimonoseki Straits, another reactionary clan, the Choshu, began firing on foreign ships. Reparations were demanded and also a promise from the Choshu that the straits be kept open, in accordance with the treaties. When the Bakufu proved themselves too weak to fully respond to these demands, Alcock ordered military action against both clans.

The ensuing gunboat diplomacy was remarkably productive. Promises were made and kept and the reparations were paid. The success of the British military action also managed to convince the samurai that they were missing out on a great deal by rejecting the foreigners and the new technology that they brought with them. By 1865, when Alcock happily accepted the post of minister-plenipotentiary in Peking, Britain's power to influence Japanese events had considerably increased. It was left to Alcock's successor, Sir Harry Parkes, to build on this foundation [33].

Sir Rutherford Alcock is buried with his wife in St

Katharine's Churchyard. The grave is on the north side of the church. Walk due north from the base of the tower towards the bank which forms the northern boundary of the church. For Alcock's birth and baptism, see: [54]. *The church is north of Merstham village, proceed south on the A23 London to Brighton road and turn right near Redhill.*

NEWPORT

(78) Shide Hill House, 27 Blackwater Road, Shide, Near Newport, Isle of Wight; Isle of Wight College of Arts and Technology, Newport (Tel: 0983-526631); St Paul's Barton Churchyard, Staplers

'The dragon of the world', the Japanese used to say, 'uncoils itself and the moon and the sun turn blood-red'. This was the traditional, the only and the already-too-late warning of an impending earthquake, when John Milne arrived in Japan in 1876. Over the next 19 years, Milne was to become the driving force behind the country's first scientific study of earthquakes.

Liverpool born John Milne didn't come to Japan to study earthquakes. He had been appointed to teach mining and geology at the New Imperial College of Technology, established in 1873 by Henry Dyer [216]. Milne and Dyer were among the several thousand *oyatoi-gaikokuin* (literally but not pejoratively, 'honourable foreign menials or hirelings') invited by Japan to help it catch up with the rest of the scientific world. On the night of Milne's arrival in Japan in March 1876, something happened to change his life. It also changed Japan. Everything in his fragile wood and paper house suddenly began to move. Unlike most visitors who experience one of Japan's frequent earth tremors, Milne did something about it and went on to become seismology's most important pioneer. With the help of both Japanese and other foreign menials, he invented seismographs, established a seismic survey of Japan with 968 observation stations and in 1880 founded the Seismological Society of Japan. In 1895, after a personal audience with the emperor, an Imperial decoration and a yen pension for life, Milne returned to England. He had married a beautiful Hakodate girl, Tone, and they bought Shide Hill House, on the Isle of Wight. This was an ideal site, Milne had concluded, for setting up his observatory.

John Milne, 'the father of Japanese seismology' [78]

'In Japan, the name of John Milne will never be forgotten': *'Earthquake Milne' and his wife Tone in their garden on the Isle of Wight* [78]

'Earthquake Milne' died in 1913, aged only 63. Among the hundreds of condolences Tone received from all over the world was one from the Japanese ambassador. It was a very simple message. 'In Japan', it read, 'the name of John Milne will never be forgotten'.

Demolition and alterations have left little of the original Shide Hill House. The part that housed Milne's laboratory is now 27 Blackwater Road. A nearby street named after the professor is Milne Way. In 1974, Japan's most prestigious university, the University of Tokyo, remembered its former teacher with 'a living memorial' of cherry tree saplings. They were planted at Shide and also at the Isle of Wight College of Arts and Technology. Each site is marked with a plaque. The then Japanese ambassador, Haruki Mori, who performed the ceremony, laid a wreath on Milne's tombstone in the local St Paul's Barton churchyard, Staplers (a mile east of Newport). The ambassador repeated the tribute paid by his predecessor 60 years earlier.

Two local academics, L.H. Herbert–Gustar and P.A. Nott, have taken an enormous interest in the great man's work and published their Milne biography in 1980. They will be happy to show aficionados Milne's personal collection of magic-lantern slides of Meiji Japan (on application to Vectis Biographies, Pocock's Cottage, Merstone, Isle of Wight, PO30 3DG, Tel: 0983-527351). Milne's notebooks, school and college reports, photographs and other miscellaneous papers are held at the County Record Office. See also: [168, 173, 185].

POOLE

(79) Compton Acres, Canford Cliffs, Poole, Dorset (Tel: 0202-700778)

The Japanese gardens at Compton Acres have all the ingredients to make them among the best and most authentic in the British Isles. The architect was Japanese. The materials were imported from Japan and put in place by Japanese gardeners. The site has all the natural surrounding beauty of sea, sky, hills and woods. And the budget, when the gardens were created, would have been extravagant enough to impress a *zaibatsu*.

Visitors' hazard at Compton Acres [79]

'Among the best and most authentic Japanese gardens in the British Isles': Compton Acres [79]

The Japanese gardens are part of a 15-acre gardens complex overlooking Poole harbour. Each garden is separate and self-contained. The entire showpiece was built in the 1920s by a wealthy philanthropist, Thomas Simpson – as a distraction, it was said, from the boredom of an unhappy marriage. At a time when a gold wedding ring could be bought for around five shillings and a gardener laboured an 11-hour day for not much more, Simpson lavished around £250,000 in an effort to create the best gardens that a very great deal of money could buy.

The best Japanese gardens anywhere may look as haphazard as the mountainous Japanese countryside. In reality, they are planned with the precision of a silicon chip. Water, rocks, earth, sand, and other natural materials are made to imitate nature as if seen through a reducing glass. The symbolism harks back to the ancient gods of nature, Shinto, and mythology. The stream you see gushing through the Japanese gardens at Compton Acres appears at a distance to be issuing from a craggy mountainside. Those stone figures are the guardian deities. The stepping stones over the sunken lake were put there partly to drown the evil spirits that, as everyone knows, are unable to cross water. See the delight on the face of the watching, laughing toad!

The Japanese gardens are also, of course, built to be

enjoyed. The Japanese architect meant visitors to have the best view standing just beside the vivid red tea-house, the gardens' highest point. Do take his advice. The wooden bucket and hoist rope are for the devout to wash their feet in piety (if this does not apply, just reverently admire).

Look for the old, the curious, and the symbolic. The sacred, red crested cranes stand for long life. Strange carved animals lurk in shady corners. There is a rare Japanese sundial and an ancient Buddha. Plantings include a mass of shrubs, trees, cherries, and azaleas.

Compton Acres may not have 'the only completely genuine Japanese gardens in Europe', as the guidebook claims. But there is much charm and beauty, and great efforts have been made to introduce the elements and thought which go to making a true Japanese garden. Another consideration in these days of exhorbitantly high upkeep costs – the gardens are beautifully maintained. *Open 1 March–31 October daily 10.30am–6.30pm (or dusk if earlier).*

PORTSMOUTH

(80) Portsmouth Central Library, Guildford Square, Portsmouth, Hampshire (Tel: 0705-819311)

Portsmouth Central Library has various relevant collections, including photographs and press cuttings concerned with early visits by the Japanese Imperial Navy and the arrival there of the Crown Prince (later Emperor Hirohito) at the start of his 1921 tour of Britain.

REDHILL

(81) 9 Batts Hill, Redhill, Surrey

While the author, Lafcadio Hearn (1850–1904), was at school at St Cuthbert's College, Ushaw [137] between 1863 and 1867, his home address in the school registers was given as Redhill. Before this, he had been raised in Dublin by his great aunt, Mrs Brenane. During the early 1860s, Mrs Brenane came under the influence of a Henry Molyneux, who took out the lease of a house in the growing and fashionable new town, Redhill. The property was Linkfield Lodge, Linkfield Lane, at the foot of Batts Hill.

The house still exists but changed its name in the mid-1930s to Denmark Lodge. It was later given its present address of 9 Batts Hill. The property, privately owned, stands in the entrance to the drive leading up to Linkfield House (headquarters for the Redhill Territorial Army (TA) Centre). However, the TA have Lafcadio Hearn's old home recorded as Redhill Lodge. For main Lafcadio Hearn entry, see: [232].

ROCHESTER

(82) Guildhall Museum, High Street, Rochester, Kent (Tel: 0634–848717)

By the time of the death of Japan's first Englishman, William Adams [71] in 1620, his hosts were master gunsmiths and crack marksmen. When Lord Elgin arrived to sign the Anglo–Japanese treaty in 1857, his party were astonished to be welcomed by troops carrying bows and arrows! Between these two events, some two and a half centuries apart, is one of Japan's great technological enigmas.

When you see the superb example of a Japanese matchlock at the Guildhall Museum it only seems to deepen the mystery. The museum's gun was made 'using the double thickness wrapping method', as the inscription tells us, 'on a day in May in 1748'. This was almost midway between Adams and Elgin and showed the Japanese gunsmith as a master of his art. This musket would have made a formidable weapon. Yet to have even carried it onto the battlefield would have been almost unthinkable. It simply wasn't done.

A rather more bellicose attitude greeted the introduction of firearms by the first Europeans in Japan, the Portuguese, in 1543. These arquebuses, a type of musket, represented Western state-of-the-art technology and were demonstrated to Lord Tokita, the local *daimyo*, in whose territory the Portuguese landed. The delighted Lord Tokita saw the strange sticks pointed skywards. He heard a dragon's roar, saw the hot breath of smoke and Japan's first shot game dropped to his feet. Tokita made similar, immediate, and extravagant plans for opposing clans. He bought the two arquebuses for what is reported to have been several hundred times their worth. Then he appointed his swordsmith to be his gunsmith. Not having his master's financial means, the swordsmith resorted to the best available substitute to master the new technology: his very pretty 17 year old daughter. In exchange for her services, the delighted Portuguese skipper offered a crash course with the ship's armourers. Japan's first gun production line began to roll.

During the next century it was, ironically, the foreigner's gun that helped set up the Tokugawa shogunate, expel foreigners from Japan and root out the practice of Christianity there.

Then, a decade or so before the date inscribed on the Guildhall's musket, something happened that almost defies explanation. The Japanese warrior gave up the gun. In the pure, nationalistic, xenophobic, chivalric world of the samurai, the gun ceased to have a place. The weapon of the samurai was his sword. And no samurai would consider his sword being usurped by anything as vulgar as a gun.

It was perhaps for the same reason that the evolution of Japanese gun technology remained in a time warp. Guns continued to be made (and, as can be seen from the Guildhall example, very well indeed) but only for shooting ducks and the like. There is very little evidence, however, of technological change. The example here is almost identical to the Portuguese arquebuses introduced almost two centuries earlier.

The primitive matchlock was developed to near perfection. But the wheel-lock, the snaphaunce, and the flint-lock, all terms which marked the evolution of the gun elsewhere, were never made in Japan. When the gun bringers came again, from Europe and America, in the middle of the 19th century, it was virtually arquebuses to pin-fire in an afternoon.

There are other interesting examples of Japanese arms and armour at the Guildhall Museum (as well as a helpful, well-informed curator). Some are part of the permanent collections, like the splendid *magari-yari* polearm, and there are some very fine swords. Other items, including plenty of Japanese killing gear, come and go as part of changing exhibitions. Killing itself never went out of fashion – it was just the way a gentleman went about it. *Open daily 10am–5.30pm.*

RUDGWICK

(83) Rikkyo School in England, Rudgwick, Horsham, Sussex

The Rikkyo School in England, which opened in 1972, is a much sought-after boarding school for Japanese children. Set in ravishing Sussex countryside, it is an offshoot of the Rikkyo Anglican Christian Foundation in Japan, the roots of which go back to 1874.

SOUTHAMPTON

(84) Southampton City Art Gallery, Civic Centre, Southampton, Hampshire (Tel: 0703-223855)

The Southampton Art Gallery is another place to see works by master potters Shoji Hamada and Bernard Leach. If you're hereabouts, don't miss the opportunity. For main entry for Hamada and Leach, see: [100].

(85) Guardian Court, Westwood Road, Southampton, Hampshire

Richard Francis Trevithick (1845–1913), in Japan from 1887 to 1904 and responsible for Japan's first locomotive, spent his final years in Southampton. His last address in the local directory was at 7 Westwood Road. From later entries, this appears to have been renumbered to 49. Around 1974, Trevithick's house (49) and the two neighbouring houses (50, 51) were replaced with a block of flats – Guardian Court, Westwood Road. For main Richard Francis Trevithick entry, see: [96]. For main entry for Francis Henry Trevithick, Richard's brother, see: [107].

SOUTHSEA

(86) Royal Marines Museum, Marines Eastney, Southsea, Portsmouth, Hampshire (Tel: 0705-819385)

The Royal Marines Museum has connections with Japan going back to the 1860s. Exhibits include a remnant of the colours carried in action against the Choshu [43].

(87) 2 Sussex Road, Southsea, Hampshire

Basil Hall Chamberlain was born in Southsea in 1850 but was sent to France for his education. He joined the British merchant bank Barings but his health broke down and his doctor prescribed travel in order to restore it. He settled in Japan in 1873 and lived there until 1903 before retiring to Geneva where he died in 1935.

His first teacher of Japanese was an old samurai who always wore the traditional two-handed sword. Chamberlain's first post was that of English teacher at the Imperial Naval College in Tokyo but he ended his distinguished teaching career as Professor of Philology at the University of Tokyo and remained an Emeritus Professor after his retirement to Switzerland.

Chamberlain wrote many books about Japan and translated Japanese books into English, including *Kojiki*, the earliest known chronicle of Japan. His grammar, reader and handbook of colloquial Japanese helped many to learn the language and his *Things Japanese* remains a classic for those interested in Meiji Japan. He was born at 6 Queens Terrace which is now 2 Sussex Road.

TUNBRIDGE WELLS

(88) Ashburnhams, Bishops Down, Tunbridge Wells, Kent

Orientalist and translator of what some call the world's first real novel, *The Tale of Genji*, Arthur Waley (1889–1966) was born here on 19 August 1889, as Arthur David Schloss. He changed this German-sounding name at the outbreak of World War I, taking his mother's maiden name of Waley. The house in which he was born belonged to Major-General C.J. Godby at the time and is now a block of flats. For main Waley entry, the house in which he died and where he is buried, see: [35].

UCKFIELD

(89) High Street; National School; Parish Church, Uckfield, Sussex

John Batchelor (1853–1944) probably did more for the Ainu,

the blue-eyed, round-eyed, Caucasian people of northern Japan, than any other European. He also became an acknowledged authority on their culture and language.

Batchelor was born here, in what used to be 7 White Rails (now part of the High Street, just below the present post office). His father, William Batchelor, was tailor and parish clerk. John left school (almost certainly the National School, beside the parish church) at 12. He began work as a gardener

'As an old man with a long white beard, it pleased him greatly to be taken for an Ainu elder': John Batchelor [89]

John Batchelor's 'uniquely appropriate tombstone, in the shape of Hokkaido' [89]

in the churchyard of the Uckfield Parish Church, before his call to become a missionary. After his preparatory studies, the mission sent him first to Hong Kong. Then in 1877, for reasons of health, he obtained a transfer to the colder climate of Hokkaido, Japan's northern island.

The venerable John Batchelor, OBE DD, Archdeacon of Hokkaido, as he became, spent 63 years with the Ainu. As an old man with a long white beard, it pleased him greatly to be taken for an *ekashi* (an Ainu elder). This wasn't just for his physical appearance but especially because of the veneration in which he was held. Batchelor published a number of works, including his much respected *Ainu–English–Japanese Dictionary*. As an Ainu linguist, he was master of a tongue not known to relate to any other on earth. Disciple of God and man of letters, he was decorated by the emperor and became an honorary member of the Hokkaido government. John Batchelor returned to Britain in 1940. The distinguished missionary died four years later at the age of 90, at his wife's home town of Hertford.

John Batchelor is buried in Uckfield, in the Church of the Holy Cross where he once gardened. His uniquely appropriate tombstone, in the shape of Hokkaido, was commissioned by the Hokkaido Diocese and unveiled by the Bishop of Hokkaido, the Most Reverend John Masano Watanabe, on 6 July 1975. There is another, larger inscription to Batchelor inside the church, on the north aisle. The Hertford Museum [124], founded by Batchelor's in-laws, the Andrews family, has a collection of Batchelor's Japanese artefacts.

WINCHESTER

(90) Shoei Centre (at King Alfred's College), Winchester, Hampshire

In 1982, four years short of its centenary, Tokyo's Shoei Christian College for Girls opened a boarding college in Winchester. The new Japanese centre occupies a separate building in the grounds of the established King Alfred's College. It has a yearly intake of twenty female high-school graduates. They undertake a two-year course, during which the students are expected to become more proficient in the English language and to have learned something of British history and culture.

These young Japanese ladies play an active part in college life. As soon as their English is good enough, they are invited to join the other students of King Alfred's College in a subject of their choice.

At the inaugural ceremony in October 1982, attended by the Japanese ambassador and the Bishop of Winchester, the Mayor reminded his audience that Winchester under King Alfred, had been England's first capital in the ninth century, just as Nara had been Japan's first capital in the eighth.

WOKING

(91) Brookwood Cemetery, Woking, Surrey

Alexander William Williamson (1824–1904), who is buried in the Brookwood Cemetery, played a key role in helping

Japan catch up with the West after its period of self-imposed isolation had come to an end.

Williamson was Professor of Chemistry at University College, London when the first group of five Japanese students arrived in England in 1863. The professor acted as their guardian whilst they were in England, boarded three of them in his house and looked after the educational interests of all five. Hirobumi Ito went on to become Japan's first prime minister, Kaoru Inoue gave direction to the development of commerce, Masaru Inoue laid the foundation of the Japanese railway system, Kinsuke Endo introduced the European system of minting to Japan and Yozo Yamao developed methods of mining engineering and helped establish an engineering school in Tokyo. See Henry Dyer entry [216].

Williamson is best remembered in the academic world for carrying out original research which helped establish the molecular theory of chemical reactions, but he was also a brilliant teacher. After the first group of Japanese students had returned to play their pivotal role in developing the industrial infrastructure of Japan and its educational system, others followed and were taught by Williamson. The founder of scientific chemistry in Japan, Joji Sakurai, was a student and devoted admirer of Professor Williamson from 1876 to 1881; Professor Sakurai was made an Honorary Fellow of University College, London in 1937, the first foreigner to receive this distinction.

With the help of Hugh Matheson, the head of the eponymous trading company Jardine Matheson which had been instrumental in bringing the first Japanese students to London, a number of young English scientists recommended by Professor Williamson and other scholars were sent to Japan before the organization of Tokyo Imperial University. In 1874 R.W. Atkinson, Professor Williamson's prize student, was invited to become professor of chemistry at a college in Tokyo that was later amalgamated into Tokyo Imperial University. Professor Atkinson taught analytical chemistry, organic chemistry, theoretical and technological, as well as metallurgy, and conducted original research with his students, among whom was Joji Sakurai. Professor Atkinson was awarded the Order of the Rising Sun when he left Japan. See also: [34].

7 | South-west England

BATH

(92) The Bernard Leach Archive, Holburne of Menstrie Museum, University of Bath, Great Pultney Street, Bath, Avon (Tel: 0225-466669)

A Japanese once said of the potter Bernard Leach (1887–1979) that 'it is doubtful whether any other visitor from the West has ever shared our spiritual life so completely'. Strongly influenced by traditional Oriental pottery, Leach probably did more than anybody this century to revive the British craft movement. It was also partly through Leach's influence that his lifelong friend, Shoji Hamada (1894–1978) made a similar contribution in Japan.

The Holburne of Menstrie Museum has a Craft Study Centre with a collection of work by 20th century artist-craftsmen. Shortly before his death, Bernard Leach bequeathed his Study Collection and many of his personal papers. These have only recently been catalogued. The Leach Papers include his manuscripts, correspondence, diaries, original sketches and poems, broadcast scripts, book drafts, technical notes on kiln plans, clay bodies and glazes, and books and periodicals with material by and on Leach. The numerous photographs include many taken in Japan. Throughout his life, Leach collected a number of pots which acted as inspiration for what he was doing. Together, these make up the Leach Study Collection. The majority of the work is from China, Korea and Japan but there is also some traditional English slipware. Four Hamada pots made during his stay in St Ives are included as are about 100 of Leach's own work.

The Holburne's other collections include a group of *netsuke*, in ivory and wood; a finely carved reclining figure, c1800 or possibly earlier; and a figure of a hooded fisherman standing in water, of about the same date. For main Bernard Leach and Shoji Hamada entry, see: [100].

BEER

(93) The Bluff, New Road; St Michael's churchyard, Beer, Devon

The writer, diplomat with Britain's first legation in Japan, and translator of the *Nihon Shoki*, W.G. Aston (1841–1911), retired here in 1889. His large house, The Bluff, standing in an acre of woods and garden, overlooking the sea, is in New Road. Aston was buried in the local St Michael's churchyard. For main Aston entry, see: [226].

BRISTOL

(94) City of Bristol Museum and Art Gallery, Queen's Road, Bristol, Avon (Tel: 0272-223571)

That shrewd observer of things Japanese, Basil Chamberlain [87] once remarked that 'originality was so little understood

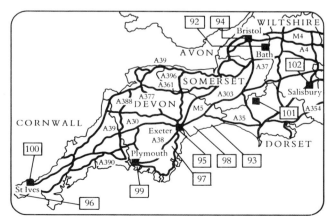

SOUTH-WEST ENGLAND

in Old Japan that an eminent man's descendants to the twentieth generation should be able to do the same standard of work as their ancestor'.

Given this premise, the *exceptions*, the innovators, can become milestones in Japanese art history. After a century of Tokugawa regimentation, the painter Okyo Maruyama (1733–1795) came as a gale of fresh air. He was the first farmer's son to become a significant artist. In a closed country that had learned to look in on itself, Okyo looked outward – to China and to the limited number of European canvases he managed to see. The results, although unmistakably Japanese, showed a distinct Western influence. Many of his works, extremely simple with bold darks and lights, have been compared to coarse-grained negatives. There is an outstanding Okyo at the City of Bristol Museum and Art Gallery painted at the height of his powers. It is an ink-painted flowering wisteria, dated 1774, on a fusuma sliding door re-mounted on a folding screen (*byobu*).

The Okyo is one of five paintings in Bristol's outstanding Japanese collection. The collection began in 1906, a year after the foundation of the museum and four years into the Anglo–Japanese Alliance. Much of it, however, has been acquired since 1949. There are around 600 wood-block colour prints, 300 *netsuke* and *okimono*, 150 sword-fittings and 50 ceramics, as well as lacquers, textiles, and Ainu artefacts. The Bristol Japanese collection is one of only a handful throughout the country with specialized curatorial expertise. This makes the 'Curator's choice' even more interesting. It includes the following: a rare example of a theatre print intended for mounting as an *uchiwa* screen-fan but instead kept as a memento of the performance; an early 17th century German-derived lacquered *escritoire* made for the export market; and an Arita late 17th century porcelain *kendi* flask. There are also some superb *netsuke* and *tsuba*. *Daily 10am–5pm, including Sunday.*

EXETER

(95) University of Exeter, Exeter, Devon

Cherry blossom bloom here every spring, thanks to a 1937 gift of cherry trees from Japan. The university is also trying to build up its collection of the famed Japanese carp.

GULVAL

(96) St Gulval Churchyard, Gulval, Cornwall

To everyone who *should* have known, the whereabouts of the tomb of Richard Francis Trevithick (1845–1913) was a mystery. The long search began in Cornwall. The Trevithick Society (set up in honour of the great railway pioneer, Richard Trevithick, 1771–1833, and Richard Francis's grandfather) were willing but unable to help. So logically, one had to start at his place of death. A number of things were already known about Crewe-born Richard Francis Trevithick. How he'd designed and built Japan's first locomotive, a design so efficient that many subsequent designs had been based on it. That, like his brother, Francis Henry [107], another railway engineer in Japan, he'd married a Japanese girl. Unfortunately, however, their only child, a daughter, had died.

It was also known that, having joined Japan's fledgling railway system as early as 1887, Richard Francis had been the last of all the foreign railway engineers to leave in 1904. He had settled in Southampton and died there on 13 February 1913. But where was the body? The local library, the clergy, the nearest cemeteries were all helpful. But sorry, no body – not in or near Southampton. Someone suggested the London Necropolis Cemetery at Brookwood, Woking [91]. The Victorians envisaged this vast area as a suburban Highgate. At the height of its popularity there were even special funeral trains from Waterloo. Eventually it was found that Richard Francis had been cremated in the Woking area at St John's Crematorium, just after he died in 1913. Then, some 40 years later, on 6 February 1953, the ashes were disinterred and reburied halfway across the country – at St Gulval Churchyard, Gulval in Cornwall.

At Gulval, there was a further hitch because at the time, the vicar had been too ill to record the re-interrment. But the grave is there all right. Enter the lower churchyard (sometimes referred to as the new churchyard) by the main gate, opposite the south lychgate. Walk down the central path, past the war memorial till you come to a whole cluster of Trevithick graves. Richard Francis Trevithick is the last of them. The granite cross has the clear inscription Richard Francis Trevithick. But why isn't it dated? There is also another inscription on the cross – to Ivy Trevithick and the words 'Remembrance (Kitten)'. Who was Ivy and who was Kitten? But these are small mysteries having finally tracked him down. For the retirement of Richard Francis Trevithick, see: [85]. For the birth and retirement of Francis Henry Trevithick, see: [107]. For the birthplace of both brothers, see: [165].

NEWTON ABBOT

(97) Newton Abbot, Devon

One of the British military advisers who schooled the Japanese in modern warfare during the Meiji era was born in Wolborough, an urban district of Newton Abbot, in October 1842. Albert George Sidney Hawes's father was a captain in the Royal Navy and his son followed him into naval service with the Royal Marine Light Infantry, which he joined in 1859 as a second lieutenant.

After 10 years service, Hawes was placed on the reserve list on half pay at his own request and went to Japan, where he 'worked strenuously, enthusiastically and earnestly to build up the personnel of the Japanese navy'. His early work laid the foundations of the Imperial Naval College for which the government built spacious quarters in 1872 and employed more naval instructors from Britain. Lieutenant Hawes was asked to organize the system of instruction and discipline to be observed in the Japanese men-of-war and in doing so he dared to break with many established Japanese traditions.

On the only training ship, the *Ryujo*, he began to teach the fundamentals of order, cleanliness and discipline to sword-bearing samurai arrayed in flowing robes and jealously mindful of their loyalty to their own feudal domain, or *han*. He introduced uniforms and abolished the wearing of swords; he stressed the political danger in the current practice of choosing all the officers and men on any ship from one *han* and gradually introduced men from different *han* into the complements of the various ships. He sent efficiency ratings of student officers to the Japanese government who paid his salary.

The *Ryujo* set the standards for other ships to which

Hawes's trained officers went as instructors. After two years at the Naval Training School Hawes left to undertake the organization of the Imperial Marine Light Infantry. The chargé d'affaires from the British legation sent a dispatch to the Foreign Office in London: 'The efficiency of the Japanese Navy is mainly due to this officer's exertions' and he was recommended for an honorary promotion to captain.

Hawes published a *Handbook for Travellers in Central and Northern Japan* in conjunction with the diplomat Sir Ernest Satow [98] in 1881 which was incorporated into Murray's well known guides some years later. He appears to have taken a Japanese wife and had children by her but what became of them is not known. In 1884 he was awarded the Order of the Rising Sun (Fourth Class) before leaving the service of the Japanese government. He then joined the British Foreign Office and served in Africa before being appointed HM Consul to the Society Islands in 1889. He was promoted to Commissioner and Consul General to the Sandwich Islands in 1894 and died in office in Hilo in 1897 a few days before he was due to marry a Miss Elsie Gay of Kauai. He is buried in Oahu Cemetery, section 2, lot 163.

OTTERY-ST-MARY

(98) Ottery-St-Mary Church; Beaumont House, The Ridgeway; Ottery-St-Mary, Devon

In the 1860s and 1870s, a new class of better educated, more outward looking young men were emerging in Japan, who would soon catapult their country from a medieval back-water to a world power. For a number of these future Japanese leaders, hungry for new ideas, the first Westerner to speak to them in their own tongue was a student interpreter at the British legation called Ernest Mason Satow (1843–1929).

London-born Satow had the kind of qualities which won him the genuine respect and lifelong friendship of such men as the young aristocrat, Hirobumi Ito – later to become Japan's first prime minister [34]. Satow was young, cultured, intelligent and a brilliant linguist. He had a wide knowledge of the world, of which the Japanese then knew virtually nothing. Satow's familiarity with the Japanese language and his close relationship with those engaged in changing their country's history, made him a unique intelligence gatherer. In the years leading up to the Meiji Restoration of 1868, Britain's old enemies, the French, were convinced that the established shogunate rule would prevail. From his vantage point centre stage, Satow was able to advise his superiors that it was in fact the Imperial Court that was about to reassert its power. This intelligence strengthened Britain's resolve not to provide support for the dying Tokugawa dictatorship. On the other hand, Satow's personal approval of the young emperor-to-be was thought by many to have the official blessing of the British government. The support, even the tacit support, of the world's greatest naval power was not something Satow's Japanese friends were ever likely to forget. The Meiji reign saw the formation of the Anglo–Japanese Alliance. In its wake came huge orders for British-built ships and Armstrong guns. It was also a time of many warm bonds between an old empire and the empire in the making.

When Satow first arrived in Japan in September, 1862, the English language had been as unnecessary as an ocean-going ship. During the closed centuries, the Japanese went no-where and welcomed nobody. A barely tolerated Dutch trading post existed on an artificial islet off Nagasaki. Dutch had thus become the only European language known to Japan's tiny linguistic elite. This bequeathed Satow a few flimsy Dutch/Japanese phrase books and grammars – virtually his only textbooks for learning Japanese. Yet within 12 months, he could speak and write Japanese better than any of his colleagues. In five years, he was all but master of the language.

Promotions and transfers took Satow to Bangkok in 1884; to Montevideo in 1888; to Morocco in 1893; back to Japan as British Minister in June 1895; to Peking in October 1900; then to a number of distinguished posts in Britain before finally retiring to Ottery-St-Mary in Devon. He was author or editor of over 30 books and articles about Japan, including a dictionary of colloquial Japanese, a guide book and *The Voyage of Captain Saris*.

When Sir Ernest Mason Satow died in August 1929, a commemorative brass plaque was erected in the chapel of his old embassy in Peking. In 1959, Britain's diplomatic mission there moved to new premises. Sir Harold Satow, Sir Ernest's nephew, suggested that his uncle's plaque be re-erected at his place of burial – the church in Ottery-St-Mary, Devon. Sir Ernst Satow's plaque is behind the pulpit in the Ottery-St-Mary Church. To see his grave, walk to the north-east corner of the churchyard, where it is located under a Celtic cross.

Satow's Ottery-St-Mary home, Beaumont House, not far from the church, seems more or less unchanged. It is in the road called The Ridgeway. In residence there with Satow during his last years was his final Japanese link. The local press coverage of the funeral cortege, which travelled between Beaumont House and St Mary's Church, makes special mention of Satow's 'faithful Japanese servant, Saburo Homma'. In the carefully prepared will, Satow remembered to provide his servant with his passage home – to the country Satow himself had known and loved so well for 67 years. For Satow's birthplace, see: [39]. Satow bequeathed his collection of Buddhist literature to the Bodleian Library, Oxford, see: [113].

PLYMOUTH

(99) Sutton Pool, vicinity of Mayflower Steps; Plymouth City Museum and Art Gallery, Drake Circus, Plymouth, Devon (Tel: 0752–264878)

On 4 November 1587, north of the Spanish Main and the route of the treasure galleons, the British circumnavigator and buccaneer, Thomas Cavendish, gave chase to 'a ship of the king of Spaine', the *Santa Anna*. Cavendish's *Globe* engaged the Spanish ship off the coast of southern California, overcame its crew, seized the '22,000 pezos of golde' and other treasure, set the ship alight, and put the Spaniards ashore.

There were however, some surprise passengers, whom Cavendish brought back with him to England. These included two Japanese Christian converts, boys aged about 17 and 20. The records show only their Christian names, Cosmos and Christopher. They arrived in Plymouth harbour on 10 September 1588, a couple of months after Drake had defeated the Spanish Armada.

It would seem from this account that Cosmos and Christ-

Plymouth Sound in the 17th century, much as it would have looked when the first Japanese arrived

opher would have been the first Japanese to reach Britain. As this was some 12 years before William Adams's arrival in Japan, it must also represent the first contact between the two peoples.

The next Japanese arrival, also in Plymouth, was on 27 September 1614. These were fifteen Japanese seamen. They had served under Captain John Saris (c1580–1646), on the voyage of the East India ship *Clove* from Japan. (The *Mayflower*, taking the Pilgrim Fathers to America, left from approximately the same spot some six years later, on 6 September 1620).

The Japanese seamen are believed to have returned to Japan about three years later. Saris, accused of private trading and attempting to import 'lascivious books and pictures', was dismissed from company service. For main Saris entry and tomb, see: [55].

About 15 minutes walk north from the harbour is Drake Circus, commemorating a rather more successful sea cap-

Du Buse, View of Plymouth Sound, from the collection of Plymouth City Museum and Art Gallery [99]

tain. The Plymouth City Museum and Art Gallery there has a small Japanese collection, the most interesting pieces being the ceramics and metalwork.

Like all museums, objects on view are constantly changing and the only way to be certain of seeing a specific item is by appointment. However, if you are lucky, you may be there when our 'Curator's choice' is on display. This is a *Ko*-Imari feeding vessel, about 6 inches high, warm to the touch with orange-peel texture, simply painted in blue and white with blue underglaze. It was made about 86 years after the arrival of the first Japanese here.

Ko-Imari (also known as Old Imari or Arita) was one of the two most important styles of Japanese porcelain (the other being *Kakiemon*) from the area of Arita on the Southern island of Kyushu, exported to Europe by the Nagasaki-based Dutch traders, from around the middle of the seventeenth century. *Open Tuesday–Saturday 10am–5.30pm; Sunday 2pm–5pm.*

ST IVES

(100) St Ives Pottery, St Ives, Cornwall

One of the most important Anglo–Japanese meetings this century – certainly in the arts and crafts movement – took place in Japan in 1919, between Shoji Hamada (1894–1978) and Bernard Leach (1887–1979). Their achievement in the coming years was nothing less than to change the way we look at art.

Men like William Morris had already started speaking out against mass produced commercialism that passed for Victorian good taste. Leach and Hamada, artist-craftsmen of genius, managed to persuade an entire generation of potters to examine the traditions of hand crafted ceramics in China, Korea, Okinawa and Japan. Far from being identical, these works reproduced the unevenness of colour, shape and texture found in nature.

Bernard Leach was born in Hong Kong and spent part of his childhood in Kyoto and Singapore. In 1897, he was sent home to school at the Beaumont Jesuit College near Windsor (now an ICL training centre). Then, after studying at the Slade and the London School of Art, he returned to Tokyo in 1909. He had intended to teach etching but instead became strongly drawn to Oriental pottery and had himself apprenticed to an old master of the Kenzan, graduating as the VIIth in the Kenzan tradition. As well as his life-long friendship with Shoji Hamada, Leach established close contacts with Japan's most prominent potters and won acclaim for exhibitions of his own work there.

Shoji Hamada, born in Kawasaki and a graduate of the Tokyo Industrial College, found Leach's enthusiasm irresistible and agreed to accompany him to England in 1920. By this time, Leach had married his cousin, Murial Hoyle and had two children. David was born in 1911 and Michael in 1913. Shortly after their return to Britain, their twin daughters, Betty and Jessamine, were born in Cardiff, where Leach's father-in-law, Dr William Evans Hoyle, was director of the National Museum of Wales.

The family settled down in St Ives, then a small fishing village where the smoke from the kipper houses turned harbour views to smog. Here Leach and Hamada built Europe's pioneer Oriental Climbing Kiln. At first, home demand was slow, but there was a ready export sale in Japan. As the fame of the kiln grew, so did the number of British buyers. Over the years, more than 100 potters, many from Japan, came to visit, study and work in the St Ives pottery.

Hamada went back to Japan in 1923 but throughout their lifetime friendship, both potters made a number of further visits to each other's country. Hamada became a major figure in the Japanese Folk Crafts (*mingei*) movement and through his connection with Leach, found an international market. As Japan's most renowned potter, Hamada was designated a Living National Treasure in 1955, followed in 1968 with the award of the Order of Culture.

On the other side of the world, Bernard Leach became a rallying point for the whole craft movement. He exhibited widely, gave lecture tours, and published a number of pamphlets and books, including in 1976, *Hamada* – a homage to his old friend. Among his many honours were the CBE, the Binns medal of the American Ceramic Society, the Japanese Foundation cultural award and the Order of the Sacred Treasure, second class.

Leach married three times. In 1936, he obtained a divorce from his first wife and married his secretary, Laurie Cookes. They separated a few years later and in 1955, Leach married a young Texan potter he met in Japan, Janet Darnell, who took over the management of the St Ives Pottery.

Samples of the work of both Leach and Hamada can be found in museums and galleries all over the world. Some places to look out for in the British Isles are the Aberystwyth Arts Centre [191]; Holburne of Menstrie Museum [92]; Southampton Art Gallery [84]; and York City Art Gallery [158].

SHERBORNE

(101) Sherborne Castle, Sherborne, Dorset

It is often chastening to be reminded that so many of the things we think of as part of Europe's common heritage derived not from the West but from the East. In the 17th century, fine Oriental porcelain was seized upon by rich Europeans not just because it was elegant and well made, but, put quite simply, no European craftsman had yet cracked the secret. It wasn't until 1710 that the alchemist, Bottger, after countless experiments, finally succeeded in making the first European porcelain.

True porcelain is a hard-paste, fired to about 1,400 degrees centigrade. The Chinese have been making porcelain for about a thousand years. Skills passed from China to Korea. Then, at the end of the 16th century, a Japanese invasion of Korea under Hideyoshi Toyotomi (1536–1598) returned with a number of Korean potters, who settled in Arita, Kyushu. Around the middle of the 17th century, two events catapulted Japan into the porcelain export market. In China, the collapse of the Ming dynasty in 1644 put a temporary halt to that traditional source. The principal trader, the Dutch East India Company, realized that if it was to stay in business, an alternative supplier had to be found quickly. Meanwhile in Japan, the Arita potters discovered a new technique for overglazing enamel pigments, resulting in a vastly superior product. By the middle of the century, the Dutch base near Nagasaki was supplying Europe and South East Asia with vast quantities of what came to be known as *Ko*-Imari, Old Imari or Arita.

Then, as the Arita potters continued to experiment with shapes, colours and enamels, a new style of even higher quality emerged. Its beauty, elegance, translucence and whiteness of glaze was to ravish the palaces of Europe. This new style, which continues to command the world's highest prices, came to be known as *Kakiemon*. And it is the *Kakiemon* particularly that you should seek out when you visit the Porcelain Room at Sherborne Castle. *In park by Sherborne Lake, about five miles east of Yeovil off the A30 to the south. Open Easter Saturday–end September Thursday, Saturday, Sunday and bank holidays 2pm–6pm.*

WOODFORD

(102) Heale House Gardens, Woodford, Salisbury, Wiltshire (Tel: 072273-504)

When a disciple of the great 16th century teamaster, Rikyu (c1520–1591), was asked why his master had not precisely defined the trappings of the tea ceremony, he replied that to have done so would have been to define nature itself. Some

Stone lantern at Heale House Gardens [102]

say that all the things which go to make up the aesthetic nature of the Japanese people are combined in the tea ceremony. This includes more than just finding a quiet place to meditate. It is also the simplicity, architecture, ceremonial, ceramics, calligraphy, group activity, garden design, flower arranging and spirit. It is the rustic simplicity of nature that is so admired. And nowhere is this better seen or are Rikyu's ideals so well applied as in the *chaya* or tea-house.

The room must be small, just adequate for perhaps five guests and the teamaster to sit in. It is likely that a peasant's house provided the original model. This was seen by the aristocratic originators of the tea ceremony as a direct contrast to their own lordly grandeur. The room should be sparse, without furniture but carefully organized. The building materials must be light unfinished wood, the windows small and made from paper, the doorway low to encourage humility. On the floor should be the soft natural colour of *tatami* matting. It must be open to nature – and to the soft sounds of nature.

Rikyu the grand teamaster, would have been much pleased with the *chaya* at Heale House Gardens. This small fragile tea-house was brought to Wiltshire by the present owner's great uncle, the Hon Louis Greville. Greville was Britain's diplomatic Second Secretary in Tokyo, 1882–87. Along with the tea-house, he also brought a stone temple lantern and a snow lantern, a red lacquer bridge and four Japanese gardeners.

The tea-house and red lacquer bridge were reassembled and laid over two irrigation canals. The soft gurgle of water underneath is the only sound. From it can be seen acers, magnolias and flowering shrubs. The vivid red arched bridge is sometimes referred to as a Nikko bridge (there is a similar bridge in Nikko although the style and vivid colour are more Chinese-derived than Japanese). The bridge provides a lovely and dramatic contrast to the pale tones of nature of which the *chaya* is composed.

Those concerned about the fragility of such a structure may be comforted to learn that there are thought to be about eight original tea-houses from the 16th and early 17th centuries extant in Japan.

The tea-house at Heale House Gardens, although over a century old, has withstood all that British weather could throw at it. On advice from experts involved in Salisbury Cathedral's maintenance, work has recently been done in propping up the foundations imbedded in the irrigation canal. The hand-made paper windows are regularly renewed. A gift from an appreciative Japanese lady, Mrs Kimiko Monsen, has meant a complete renewal of the *tatami*.

To be fair, however, it wasn't just the Japanese corner, exquisite as it is, that won Christie's first Garden of the Year award. The rest of Heale House Gardens, devoted to other cultures, covers a total of some five acres. The house, although partly restored after an 1835 fire, is still much as it was when it provided a brief sanctuary for Charles II after the Battle of Worcester in 1651. *Located four miles north of Salisbury on the Woodford Valley road between the A345 and the A360. Open throughout the year 10am–5pm.*

8 | *Central England*

BATSFORD PARK

(103) Batsford Park Arboretum, Moreton-in-Marsh, Gloucestershire

In a lecture given to the Authors' Club on 6 November 1911, Algernon Bertram Freeman-Mitford, the First Lord Redesdale (1837–1916) claimed to have achieved in fact what H.G. Wells's fictional inventor of the time-machine did in fantasy. Mitford's journey of 1866 was not, however, into the future but to the past. From the bustling, changing England of the industrial revolution, he travelled back centuries, to the last days of the shogunate – to a still feudal Japan entrenched in the Middle Ages. As somebody later observed, it was rather like stumbling across Camelot and taking tea with King Arthur. Mitford was a snob, an aristocrat and medievalist, and no period could have pleased him better. Here were real knights in armour, acting out codes of chivalry, fealty and honour that hadn't existed in Europe for centuries.

Mitford was born in South Audley Street, London [22] and had a house in Cheyne Walk, Chelsea [8] after his marriage in 1874. In 1886, he inherited Batsford Park, an estate to which he developed a great attachment – but could not always afford to keep up. In 1910 he was forced to lease out Batsford Park and moved to 1 Kensington Court [13].

The young Mitford's Japan adventure began in 1866, when he was transferred from Peking to the newly opened British legation. It was an exciting and a dangerous time. Much of the country was in turmoil. The old system of rule by shogun was breaking down, to be replaced in 1868 by the restoration of the emperor. Mitford, along with his col-

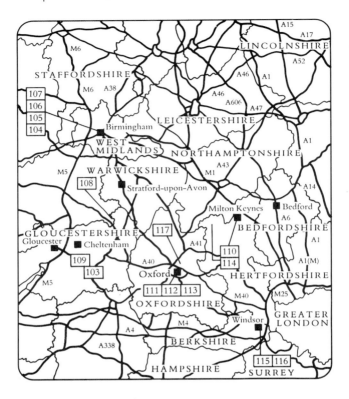

CENTRAL ENGLAND

leagues, had to be on constant guard against a particularly violent faction, whose war cry was 'expel the foreigners!' Mitford writes that a loaded pistol was always beside him on his desk. Much of this is set down in Mitford's own biographical works, written long after he had left Japan. The minor classic for which he is probably best remembered is his *Tales of Old Japan*, which is really a collection of stories. This was first published in 1871 and has never been out of print since. Mitford's Japanese memoirs were published in 1985 (*Mitford's Japan: The Memoirs and Recollections 1866–1906*, edited by Hugh Cortazzi, Athlone Press).

Mitford left Japan in 1870, made a brief visit in 1873 and accompanied Prince Arthur of Connaught there in 1906, an account of which was published in Mitford's *Garter Mission to Japan.* Between Mitford's first visit and his last, Japan had undergone a metamorphosis. Where had the medieval knights gone? With Britain's help, Japan had built up one of the world's most up-to-date navies, sufficient to beat the Russian fleet in the previous year. The country was rapidly catching up on its missed centuries of isolation. When Mitford attempted to refer to his own early experiences in Japan, in almost forgotten Japanese, he learned that those times were now referred to as belonging to the *mukashi* – the ancient times of long ago.

Mitford's memory lives on in Batsford Park, a beautiful arboretum with one of the largest collections of rare trees in the country. Mitford became fascinated by Japanese plants, particularly bamboos. He later published a book called *The Bamboo Garden* and after he had inherited Batsford Park in 1886, created a bamboo garden with some 50 different types. Sadly, there is little left of Mitford's bamboo garden but there are many flowering cherries and other Japanese species as well as a number of objects Mitford brought back with him from the Far East. His Buddha still looks rather splendid amongst the trees, but the derelict tea-house is sorely in need of repair and the antlers of the Japanese bronze deer are a constant prey to present day souvenir hunters. Mitford is buried in St Mary's churchyard, on the north western edge of Batsford, together with all the rest of the famous (and notorious) Mitfords. The commemorative marble plaque is inside the church. *The arboretum is situated near the intersection of the A44 and the A429.*

BIRMINGHAM

(104) Hockney Brook; Schools of King Edward VI, Edgbaston Park, Birmingham, West Midlands

Britain's second minister in Japan – after Alcock [77] – from 1865 to 1883, Harry Smith Parkes (1828–85), played a significant role in strengthening Anglo–Japanese relations, during the difficult years just before and after the 1868 Meiji Restoration.

Harry Parkes was born on 24 February 1828, at Birchill's Hall, Bloxwich, a district of Walsall. (In 1850, home on leave from the Far East, Parkes learned that iron ore had been

The conferring of the Order of the Garter by Prince Connaught on Emperor Meiji, 20 February 1906: from a contemporary Japanese print

found on the site and saw that two-thirds of the house had been knocked down.) Parkes lost both his parents when he was still very young, in 1832–33. After their deaths, Harry and his two older sisters went to live with their father's brother, Lt John Parkes, RN, vet and gentleman. Parkes's uncle, who seems to have been in the habit of frequently moving house, apparently lived in two addresses in the Birmingham area while Harry was with him. These were in Hockney Brook, an area of Birmingham and Exeter Row which, due to redevelopment, no longer exists. In 1838, Harry became one of the first pupils of the new King Edward's Grammar School, now the Schools of King Edward VI in Birmingham. The old school building that Harry knew was demolished in 1937. In 1841, Sir Harry Parkes, as he was to become, was invited to join his two sisters in China. His future in the Far East had already begun. For main Parkes entry, including his tomb and that of his wife, Fanny Parkes, see: [33]. For Parkes's bust, see: [11].

(105) Birmingham Museum and Art Gallery, Chamberlain Square, Birmingham, West Midlands (Tel: 021-235 2834)

During the long, peaceful Tokugawa centuries (1600–1867), life could be rather dull for the samurai. There were no battles, little rape and pillage to speak of, and all the fun seemed to be happening elsewhere. The upstart merchants, who were *supposed* to have nothing, gave every impression of doing very nicely – with lots of yen, beautiful geisha and more hedonistic pleasures than the average samurai on a stipend could hope for in a lifetime.

There was really only one way for the samurai to show off what a marvellous fellow of taste he was. This was by the superb workmanship of his weapons. Probably the most prized and decorated of these were his sword-guards – the marvellous Japanese *tsuba*. The early *tsuba*, plain and functional, were less marvellous and came from the same smith who made the rest of the sword. But by the 16th century, *tsuba*-making had become the art of the specialist *tsuba*-smith. The finest and most intricate designs were produced with coloured metal inlays and incrustations. As the smiths' skills increased still further, the basic *tsuba* metal, iron, was transferred from a modest black to a harvest of patinas. There were blues, browns, reds, and russets. Designs were intricate and imaginative. Dragons coiled, demons snarled, and there were also gentler scenes of birds and flowers.

Two examples from the 'magnificent tsuba collection' at the Birmingham Museum and Art Galley [105]

The Awabi Fishers, c1798 – an Utamaro ukiyo-e woodblock print:
Birmingham Museum and Art Gallery [105]

Precious metals were used but more particularly decorative
metals like copper.

The Birmingham Museum and Art Gallery has a magnifi-
cant *tsuba* collection. Many of the over 200 pieces were the
gift of Richard Hancock. Hancock was a successful Birmingham estate agent and valuer and a collector of great expertise
and knowledge. In 1932, aware that his *tsuba* collection was
one of the last in the country not to have been broken up and

dispersed by auction, Hancock prepared a detailed and scholarly *Catalogue of Tsuba*. It is still a respected work of reference.

There is a lot more Japanese weaponry in the Birmingham collections, well worth showing off. Some outstanding examples are the gold and silver hilt ornaments; the *yoroi-toshi* or armour-piercing blade, c1500; and a rare *fuchi* (collar) and *kashira* (cap) from one of the five great masters of the 1750s. Too numerous to cite individually are the swords, daggers, mounts, blades, handles, collars, washers and out-standing examples of fine inlays.

There are also collections of *netsuke*, *okimono* and *inro* and a little-known but fine collection of *ukiyo-e* prints. *Open Monday–Saturday 9.30am–5pm, Sunday 2pm–5pm.*

(106) St Thomas's Church, Bath Row, Edgbaston, Birmingham, West Midlands

Isabella Bird (1831–1904), inveterate traveller, and the author of the best selling *Unbeaten Tracks in Japan*, lived in Edgbaston, Birmingham, in her early teens, from 1842 to 1848. It was here in 1847, that she produced her first written work, an essay, printed for private circulation.

Her father, the Rev Edward Bird, had lost his previous Tattenhall parish because of his failure to stop Sunday working. He now suffered a similar failure in the tough working class parish of St Thomas's. The area where the rectory was located, in Frederick Street, has been rede-veloped. St Thomas's church, in Bath Row, was bombed in the last war but part of it remains.

Isabella was deeply sympathetic to her father's cause, but as a girl of 16, a lover of riding and country pursuits, she must have been particularly pleased when he accepted the offer of a living in the quiet rural parish of Wyton in Cambridgeshire. For main Bird entry, see: [133].

(107) 64 Portland Road, Edgbaston; 5 Vernon Road, Edgbaston; St Augustine's Church, Edgbaston; Lodge Hill Cemetery, Wooley Park Road, Birmingham, West Midlands

It was grandfather Richard Trevithick (1771–1833) who really made the family name – by inventing the world's first steam locomotive. Two generations on, grandsons Francis Henry Trevithick (1850–1931) and his brother, Richard Francis (1845–1913) joined the hundred or more other foreign engineers who were helping to put Japan's railways on the right tracks.

Both brothers married Japanese girls. Richard Francis had only one child, a daughter, who died young. Francis Henry, however, had four children. His eldest son, Yoshitaro Richard, studied navigation and seamanship in London then joined the NYK Japanese steamship company. A bright lad, he did well and in 1916 was offered the rank of captain, to command the 10,000 ton *Hakusan Maru*, on the Yokohama to London run. There was one snag. Who ever heard of someone with a name like Trevithick captaining a Japanese ship?

There was nothing for it. Out went Trevithick and in came Okuno (his mother's maiden name). His father, after 20 years on the Japanese railways, ran into health problems and retired to Birmingham. Here his old age was comforted by his son, Captain Okuno, bringing regular deliveries of *sake*, rice crackers and other delicacies not generally sold at your usual Birmingham corner shop.

From around 1911 to 1919, Francis Henry was at 64 Portland Road, Edgbaston. He then moved a short distance away, to 5 Vernon Road, where he remained until his death in 1931, aged 81. The funeral service was at St Augustine's Church, Edgbaston. He was buried in the Lodge Hill Cemetery. The Japanese Trevithick descendants, now all Okunos, live in Yokohama. For main entry and tomb of the brother, Richard Francis Trevithick, see: [96]. For the birth-place of both brothers, see: [165].

BROADWAY

(108) Snowshill Manor, near Broadway, Hereford and Worcestershire (Tel: 0386-852410)

Japanese weaponry reached one of its highest stages of perfection at a time when it was militarily least needed. From the beginning of the 17th to about the middle of the 19th century, Japan was unified, at peace, and strongly ruled under the Tokugawa shogunate at Edo (modern day Tokyo). There was to be no serious foreign incursion until the Americans arrived in 1853.

This is approximately the period represented in the extraordinary Green Room at Snowshill Manor. During this time, Japan produced some of the finest arms and armour the world has ever seen. Japanese armourers had previously been asked to produce effective methods of killing enemy clans. Now it was necessary to outshine the erstwhile enemy in sartorial elegance. Knights all over the medieval world had similarly paraded the wealth and good taste of their lords. However, the Japanese didn't have the inconvenience of wars to get in the way of fashion. The shogunate's own system of government provided another opportunity for displaying armour and dress. In order to check possible rebellion by the previously warring *daimyo* (medieval lords), the system of 'alternative attendance' was established. All were compelled to spend part of the year as 'guests' of the shogun at Edo. When they returned to their fiefs, the *daimyo's* families remained as hostages. The resulting toing and froing resulted in travelling fashion shows of lords and retinue as each procession vied with the others to demonstrate their finery. Japan's master armourers, with a long tradition of skill and craftsmanship, were encouraged to make full use of fine metalwork, coloured lacquer and rich textiles. The result was technical brilliance. It was also about as battle-ready as the bearskins and scarlet jackets paraded today at Buckingham Palace.

The Green Room collection is mostly bellicose, though there are a number of other Japanese artefacts. These include lacquerware, bronzes and pottery. The man responsible for these and the other collections at Snowshill Manor was Charles Paget Wade – architect, artist, craftsman, eccentric, and a man of private means. Wade's means were not too sorely strained by his purchases for the Green Room, however. He picked up many items in junk shops during the last war. Japanese artefacts were then unfashionable. Buying them was probably unpatriotic but certainly cheap.

A visitor to Snowshill Manor will find a lot more to wonder at than just the Japanese Green Room. The house and its contents have been described as a 'clutter of curiosities collected by a magpie'. Here is everything from Venetian cabinets and Flemish tapestries to one section entirely crammed with bicycles! The house was presented in its entirety to the National Trust in 1951, five years before the Magpie's death.

Curiously, like the Japanese scholar and translator, Arthur Waley, Wade is thought never to have set foot in the land of the samurai. If he had, perhaps he would have been disappointed. Modern Japan is nothing like his Green Room. *Three miles south-west of Broadway, four miles west of junction of the A44 and the A424. Open Easter Saturday, Sunday and Monday 11am–1pm and 2pm–6pm. April and October Saturday and Sunday 11am–1pm and 2pm–5pm. May–September: Wednesday–Sunday, bank holiday Monday 11am–1pm and 2pm–6pm.*

CHARLTON KINGS

(109) St Mary's Church, Charlton Kings, Gloucestershire

'From the Imperial Japanese Navy, in memory of their dear friend, Bob, aged 14'. The Anglo–Japanese Alliances (1902–23) and the huge British shipbuilding programme for Japan produced many warm personal friendships. But the story behind the memorials to a 14 year old Edwardian schoolboy in St Mary's Church must be among the most curious.

For Robert Buckley Podmore (known for miles around simply as Bob) riding to hounds was everything. At the age of only eight, he won the distinction of being England's youngest-ever Master of Hounds.

Bob's father, Edward Boyce Podmore, was a director of the shipbuilders, Vickers Son and Maxim. Shortly after the start of the Russo–Japanese War (1904–05), the firm received a Japanese order to build the battleship, *Katori*. It was launched on 4 July 1905, by Princess Arisugawa. While the ship was being equipped, Mr Podmore invited a number of her officers to sample the delights of rural Gloucestershire. Charlton House, where the officers stayed, is little changed and is used as offices. Bob was 14, master of horse and hound. He so impressed his father's distinguished guests with his equestrian prowess that he was invited on board the *Katori* for her gun trials in April 1906. One can imagine the boy's excitement to be so close to the action of one of the world's most modern battleships.

But four months later, Bob was dead. The cause was attributed to a riding accident. He was widely mourned but nowhere more so than by his new found friends from the *Katori*. A brass tablet on the west of the nave of St Mary's Church refers the visitor to a stained glass window at the south-west of the chancel. The inscription reads, 'erected by Engineer-Captain T. Fuji and brother officers of the Imperial Japanese Navy, in memory of their dear friend Bob, their companion of the gun trials of HIJMS Katori'.

Outside in the churchyard, Bob is also remembered by a large marble Cornish cross. Below the cross, on the stone edging of the plot itself is the single inscription, 'Bob'. The *Katori* was broken up in 1924/25.

MILTON KEYNES

(110) Anglo–Japanese Liaison Officer; Peace Pagoda, Willen Park; Nipponzan Myohoji, Willen; Gyosei International School, Milton Keynes, Buckinghamshire

There is more to Milton Keynes than concrete cows and a gridiron road network. Its central location, accessibility and go-ahead Development Corporation have meant that more than two dozen Japanese companies have set up in the garden city just off the M1. Because of the Japanese presence, the city has its own Anglo–Japanese Liaison Officer, the first to be appointed in the UK.

Another first, this time in Europe, is the Peace Pagoda completed in September 1981 and built on a reclaimed tip beside a lake in Willen Park. The leader of the Buddhist sect Japan Buddha Sangha, 96 year old Most Venerable Nichidatsu Fujii, was present for the opening ceremony and gave a discourse on peace. Sixteen nuns and monks of the sect spent less than two years building the reinforced concrete structure which has a sacred white dome with a roof to protect it from the weather and a decorative spire. Below the dome are superbly carved stone panels depicting the life of Buddha and there is a large niche facing east containing the gilded statue of the young Buddha pointing to the earth and the heavens. The original design of the pagoda was by Professor Minoru Ohka, a Japanese architect and an authority on stupas. His preliminary designs were interpreted by British architect Tom Hancock, whose meeting with a lone Buddhist monk

'The first in Europe': the Milton Keynes Peace Pagoda [110]

in 1977 in London led to the project being undertaken. The structural engineers Anthony Hunt Associates worked with Hancock to produce plans for the local authority and working drawings for the nuns and monks who did the building.

The idea of erecting peace pagodas was conceived by the Most Venerable Nichidatsu Fujii, the Preceptor of the Japan Buddha Sangha, soon after atomic bombs were dropped on Hiroshima and Nagasaki in 1945. The Milton Keynes pagoda is one of more than 50 erected so far, mostly in the Far East. The site is significantly located at the epicentre of England, visible from the M1 and was chosen to give a sense of belonging to the whole nation. The ridge above the pagoda is planted with cedar trees forming a backcloth to a thousand cherry trees donated by the residents of Yoshino in Japan as a tribute to people who suffered in World War II.

Adjacent to the pagoda is a Japanese temple, presided over by the Venerable Teresawa. The design of the buildings and the lay-out of the gardens are authentic and construction was carried out by members of the sect. *Willen Park is located just north of route H6 (A509), two miles from Junction 14 of the M1.*

Adding to the Japanese presence is nearby Gyosei International School, a Japanese boarding school for the increasing numbers of children of expatriate Japanese families who want their children to continue a Japanese education while living abroad. The overall architectural style of the buildings suggests a cross between a fast food establishment and an airport hotel, but there are some traditional touches including a tea ceremony building with shoji screens surrounded by a gravel and rock Japanese garden.

OXFORD

(111) Ashmolean Museum of Art and Archaeology, Beaumont Street, Oxford, Oxfordshire (Tel: 0865-278000)

During the long 'closed centuries' in Japan's history there was always a small opening in the not-quite-shut door. In the far south-west, where Kyushu stretches out towards China and the world beyond, two foreign communities agreed to being corralled, in exchange for a licence to trade.

The Dutch were isolated in the artificial island of Deshima in Nagasaki; the Chinese in a separate compound in the city. For some two and a half centuries, these two communities formed the narrow waist of an hour glass – the only conduit through which goods and ideas could squeeze in or out.

In some instances, however, the squeeze could become a flow. The exquisite ceramics in the Ashmolean Museum of Art and Archaeology, for example, were part of an export drive. Those involved showed a talent for business not exactly lacking in Japan today. By the middle of the 17th century, well after all exits and entrances are generally thought to have been locked and barred, pioneer merchant traders were already well established.

In fact, so impressive were the orders from Dutch and Chinese merchants that the local *daimyo*, Lord Nabeshima, found that no single kiln or enamelling workshop could hope to cope alone. His agents organized and coordinated a number of sources whose output could be chanelled through the port of Imari. The port gave its name to the exported ceramics, as did the general area where they were made, Arita.

The Ashmolean's outstanding collection includes an ex-

19th century inro – the Courtesan Morokoshi of Echizen-ya Writing a Letter by Shunsho: Ashmolean Museum [111]

ceptional, 17th century large enamelled jar. It is decorated in overglaze blue, red, green, yellow, aubergine and black enamels and depicts a continuous landscape of pavilions and temples among trees, rocks and mountains. Don't miss it.

The export of Japanese lacquerware, also strongly represented at the Ashmolean, was kept up almost uninterrupted from its first appearance in Europe at the beginning of the 17th century. One of the museum's more unusual Japanese items was bought in Holland in 1982. It is a lacquered leather shield, believed to be one of only a handful still in existence.

The leather itself comes from Bengal, but such was the fame of the Japanese craftsmen that it was shipped to Japan for lacquering in 1675.

Japanese lacquerware was traditionally made of wood. An earlier example in the Ashmolean shows the long-held Japanese talent for caricature. It is a rare flask, used for keeping musket powder. Only three are known to exist. One is in the Ashmolean and one of the other two (probably from the same hand) is in the Tokyo National Museum. The figure is of a hairy Portuguese barbarian, dressed in a red hat and baggy trousers, the height of fashion when the image was made around 1600. On the obverse are two other figures. The subject matter indicates that it was made for a Japanese patron. Images for the overseas market depicted native subjects – clearly designed for a foreign market.

'The Ashmolean's outstanding collection includes an exceptional 17th century large enamelled jar': Ashmolean Museum [111]

China long exerted the strongest foreign influence on Japanese art. The two countries shared many cultural similarities and the threat of colonization, Japan felt, came not from Asia but from the proselytizing Europeans. Chinese artists continued to work in Japan and the mainland remained to some extent a source of artistic example.

One of the last Chinese painting styles to make a distinct impact is known as *Nanga* – meaning from the south. Of the Japanese artists to have painted in this genre, the visitor to the Ashmolean has a reasonable chance of seeing two outstanding examples. These are Buncho Tani (1764–1840) and Bai-itsu (1783–1856).

Most of the Ashmolean's major Japanese exhibits date from the 17th century or later. In addition to the types described above – ceramics, painting and lacquerware – there is also some excellent metalwork. The museum's Japanese collections from earlier periods are of less importance. The senior curatorial staff at the Ashmolean also teach at the university. They participate in the various disciplines where Japan is involved – language, history and literature – as well as working closely with other bodies and institutions concerned with Japanese studies. *Open Tuesday–Saturday 10am–4pm. Sunday 2pm–4pm.*

(112) Pitt Rivers Museum, South Parks Road, Oxford, Oxfordshire (Tel: 0865-270927)

In Japan today, where the polls tell us most think of themselves as middle class, the mask of the *Noh* theatre has become just another popular symbol for Japan – like the rising sun or a snow-capped Mt Fuji. This is a spectacular fall from the aristocratic heights of its origins.

The *Noh* mask, sculpted with such cunning that a tilt of the actor's head would change the expression and the mood of the performance, was both a work of art and a symbol of aristocracy. In Tokugawa Japan, the chasm that separated the nobility of the *Noh* theatre from the *Kabuki* of the common people was the width of feudalism. So lowly was *Kabuki* that, in a census, the numerals denoting the *Kabuki* actor's existence were those used for counting animals.

The original notes accompanying the priceless collection of *Noh* masks at the Pitt Rivers Museum are thus entirely appropriate. They state that (in 1884) there were only two other collections of equal quality in existence – and these belonged to lords. There are more than 50 masks, most dating from around the end of the 17th century and are the first of this museum's 'Curator's choice'.

The *Noh* masks are together as a Japanese collection on their own. This is an exception to the way most Pitt Rivers material is arranged. It is one of the few museums where most items are set out not by nationality but by type or article. You are thus able to compare say, a sword or a cooking pot of one culture with a sword or a cooking pot of an entirely different culture – side by side. What's more, the range and diversity are staggering.

In 1864, less than a decade after Perry's Black Ships and the same year that the French joined the Royal Navy's bombardment of Shimonoseki, a Japanese delegation visited Paris. The French photographer, L. Rousseau, persuaded these 'kimonoed men from the middle ages' to sit before his camera. The detail – showing the clothing patterns, even the sword decorations – is quite remarkable. There are altogether more than 80 photographs in this Pitt Rivers collection. (Please contact museum in advance for access to Photographic Archive.)

Less than 40 years later, in 1900, things had so changed that an actress and former geisha, Sada Yakko, was appearing on the London stage, acclaimed by contemporary critics as 'the Ellen Terry of Japan'. You can still visit the London Coronet Theatre at Notting Hill Gate (now a cinema) where she and her troupe played [1]. The Pitt Rivers has her original hand crafted *koto*. *Entrance through University Museum. Open Monday–Saturday 1pm–4.30pm.*

(113) The University (University College, Merton College, St John's College); The Bodleian Library, Broad Street (Tel: 0865-277000); Nissan Institute of Japanese Studies, 1 Church Walk (Tel: 0865-59651); The Botanical Gardens, near Magdalen Bridge, Oxford

The University has close associations with the Japanese Imperial family. In 1921, Crown Prince Hirohito was awarded an honorary degree when on his tour of Britain, and later his son, Crown Prince Akihito, planted a tree in University College when he visited in 1953. Both the current emperor's sons carried out graduate studies at Oxford –

Crown Prince Naruhito was at Merton College (1983–85) studying medieval transport systems and Prince Fumihito studied zoology at St John's College (1987–89).

The Bodleian Library possesses about 30,000 volumes in Japanese. The collection is particularly strong in the fields of religion, literature, history and Sinology. Of some note are the 2,000 books relating to Japanese local history. The Department of Oriental Books undertakes to provide materials in support of the research into modern history undertaken at the Nissan Institute of Japanese Studies. One of the library's great treasures as far as Japanologists are concerned is the log book of Captain William Adams in which he records four voyages made from Japan between 1614 and 1619 to Siam, Cochin and China. The library also possesses a number of examples from the Jesuit Mission Press, which was operating in Japan at the beginning of the 17th century prior to the banning of Christianity and the expulsion or death of all those who practised it.

In 1881, the Japanese Buddhist scholar Bunyu Nanjo visited Oxford and published a catalogue of Japanese books purchased from Alexander Wylie and donated by Max Muller. Following this, 328 volumes of Buddhist literature were presented to the Bodleian by Sir Ernest Satow (1843–1929), the British diplomat who served as ambassador in Peking and Tokyo [98].

The Botanical Gardens near Magdalen Bridge have a large number of species of Japanese origin but no formal Japanese garden. See also, Cambridge University: [121].

WADDESDON VILLAGE

(114) Waddesdon Manor, Waddesdon village, near Aylesbury, Buckinghamshire (Tel: 0296–651211)

Japan's best is not always in Japan. Japanese visitors would do well to seize the opportunity to come to Waddesdon Manor to see the beautiful and rare examples of Arita porcelain here, for they are unlikely to find such pieces in Japan. Like early Japanese cars with 'long leg room for foreigners', much of the famed early Arita porcelain, as well as Imari porcelain, went exclusively to the export market.

The origins of Waddesdon's Arita collection go back to

the middle of the 17th century, one of the greatest periods in the development of the Japanese porcelain industry. The well established supply of Oriental porcelain to Europe via the Dutch East India Company ceased with the collapse of the Ming dynasty. In Japan, new techniques from Korea, including the use of overglaze enamel pigments, greatly improved the quality of the local porcelain. This applied especially to the kilns of Arita, an area close to the Dutch trading post off Nagasaki.

The Dutch traders found they shared a common interest with the local *daiymo*. These Kyushu lords, not entirely in sympathy with the shogun's seclusion policies, were sufficiently distant from Edo (present day Tokyo) to enjoy a degree of autonomy. As the nearest neighbours of the Dutch, they were eager to profit from the only Japanese export point to the outside world. In time, this cooperation meant that huge quantities of porcelain passed through the nearby port of Imari to South-east Asia and Europe. So both the name of the port as well as the area became identified with the porcelain.

Look particularly for Waddesdon's splendid pair of early 18th century Arita eagles. No similar pieces are thought to exist in Japan. The same could be said of the *Fontaine à Parfum*, shaped in a form of fish and probably unique in Arita porcelain (its general style, however, is described as Louis XV). The Dutch did in fact ship various styles to Japan for the local potters to copy. Characteristically – and not for the last time – the Japanese craftsmen so improved the original that the finished product often surpassed anything yet in existence.

There is more Japanese wildlife outside in the grounds of Waddesdon Manor, including a small herd of Japanese Sika deer. The first of these hardy, easily-tamed species were exhibited at London Zoo in 1860 and later in the same decade introduced to Powerscourt, County Wicklow, Ireland [234]. From here they were supplied to stock other parks in the British Isles and Waddesdon Manor was an early recipient.

The immensely wealthy Rothschild family, who built the sumptuous Waddesdon Manor in 1874–89, have banking links going back to Japan's first contact with Britain. Edmund de Rothschild tells of a meeting his great grandfather, Baron Lionel de Rothschild, had with one of the early Japanese delegations to England in the 1860s. The family bank later participated in a number of loans, including support in the Russo–Japanese War and disaster relief following the great 1923 earthquake. *At western end of Waddesdon village six miles north-west of Aylesbury on Bicester Road (A41). Closed for refurbishment until 1993.*

WINDSOR

(115) Eton College, Windsor, Berkshire

Eton College has been visited on several occasions by members of the Japanese Imperial family, including the present emperor when he was crown prince in 1953.

When his father, the late Emperor Hirohito (now referred to as Emperor Showa), visited the college in 1921, the librarian informed the prince that it was a matter of regret that the library had no Japanese books. The Imperial visitor promised to remedy this defect.

Four years later, in 1925, the college received a case containing 400 volumes and an explanatory note in English giving the title of the collection as *Nijuichi-Dai-Shu* or 'The Tanka collections of the One-and-Twenty Reigns'.

Apparently the college has had no adequate appraisal as to their merit or value. The archivist has been advised that the books probably date from the 15th to 16th centuries. *Genuine researchers should write to The Archivist, Eton College, Windsor, Berkshire SL4 6DL.*

(116) Dean's Cloister, St George's Chapel, Windsor, Berkshire

'The shame be his who thinks badly of it!' This extraordinary outburst (which became the motto of the Knights of the Garter) is attributed to King Edward III when, during a dance in 1348, he picked up a lady's garter from the floor. The king then tied the garter onto his own leg. Members of the order have followed suit ever since, even having the motto inscribed on their pretty blue garters.

The order of the garter is awarded to a finite number of those leading 'a blameless life' and has been held by the three Japanese emperors following the Meiji Restoration.

The Emperor Meiji was nominated on 4 November 1905.

The Queen and Emperor Hirohito (now referred to as Emperor Showa)

In 1906, Prince Arthur of Connaught travelled to Tokyo to carry out the investiture on 20 February, on behalf of King Edward VII. The prince was accompanied by that old Japan hand, Lord Redesdale [103], who wrote his own account of the visit in *The Garter Mission to Japan*, published in the same year. There was no ceremony for either the Emperor Taisho (installed 19 September 1912) or the Emperor Hirohito (invested 3 May 1929).

As is normal practice, each of these knights was allocated a stall in St George's Chapel. A metal stall plate is affixed to the back of the stall, showing the heraldic achievement of the knight, his name and year of appointment. The plates remain in position after death but the banner which hangs above the stall is removed. The banner is prepared under the supervision of the Garter King of Arms. The late Emperor Hirohito's was in the form of a chrysanthemum, the *mon* (insignia) of the Imperial family. Emperor Hirohito's banner was removed on 20 December 1941 and replaced on 22 May 1971, the year of his visit to Britain.

WOODEATON

(117) Parish Church, Woodeaton, near Oxford, Oxfordshire

The historian George Richard Storry (1913–81) made his home in this village six miles north east of Oxford and he is buried in the churchyard. His interest in Japan began in 1932 when as an undergraduate at Merton College he met, in his own words, 'the gentle poet Edmund Blunden' who had returned from his teaching position in Tokyo and was a fellow of the college [127]. In his talks with Blunden, Storry's imagination was aroused and in 1937, with Blunden's encouragement, he accepted an appointment as lecturer in English at Otaru Higher Commercial School in Hokkaido where he stayed until 1940.

It was his intense experience of life as a young man in this remote northern part of Japan and in the uneasy atmosphere of the eve of the Pacific War that fostered Storry's lifelong commitment to the study of the Japanese and their history. Upon returning to England he joined the Intelligence Corps, served in the Middle East, Singapore, India and Burma, and was responsible for interrogating Japanese prisoners-of-war.

After the war, he launched himself into the full-time academic study of Japan's history, first as a Research Scholar at the Australian National University (1947–55) then as a Fellow of St Anthony's, Oxford. There over the years his dedication to Japanese studies prepared the ground for a major benefaction from the Nissan Motor Company. The Nissan Institute at Oxford is a memorial to the scholar who is best remembered for his book *History of Modern Japan*. In 1981, he was awarded the Japan Foundation Prize – in appreciation of his Japanese friendships and understanding of his 'second country'. In his acceptance speech in Tokyo, Storry said: 'It is thanks to many Japanese friends and colleagues that I have come to appreciate, however clumsily, certain lessons that Japan has to teach – among them the cardinal virtues of loyalty, patience, artistic restraint and good manners'. For Storry's birth and baptism, see: [135].

9 | *Eastern England*

BEDFORD

(118) Bedford Modern School, Manton Lane, Bedford, Bedfordshire

'Father of Western architecture in Japan', Josiah Conder (1852–1920), was born in the vicinity of Bedford, and went to the Bedford Modern School, on the site of what is now the Harpur Centre shopping precinct. In 1974, the school moved to its present position in Manton Lane. For main Conder entry, see: [32].

CAMBRIDGE

(119) The Fitzwilliam Museum, Trumpington Street, Cambridge, Cambridgeshire (Tel: 0223–332900)

The Fitzwilliam Museum holds a number of coloured wood block prints by Kitagawa Utamaro (1753–1806) and some Japanese ceramics. *Open Tuesday–Saturday lower galleries 10am–2pm, upper galleries 2pm–5pm, Sunday 2.15pm–5pm. Also open Easter Monday and spring and summer bank holidays. Closed 24 December–1 January.*

(120) Shaftesbury House, 4 Shaftesbury Road, Cambridge, Cambridgeshire

Shaftesbury House, where in 1871, Togo (later Admiral Togo, 1847–1934) came to study English and mathematics, is now the home of the German Lutheran Church in Cambridge. Togo came not to the university but to the home of the curate, Mr A.D. Capel, a private tutor.

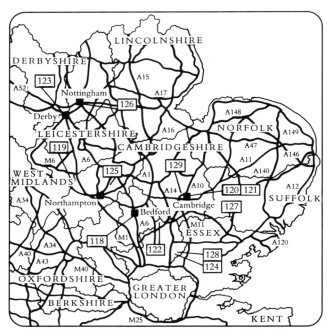

EASTERN ENGLAND

Years later, when Togo's name was on everyone's lips, Mr Capel wrote about his now famous student in the *Strand Magazine* of April 1905, almost on the eve of his astounding victory at Tsushima. Mr Capel described Togo's 'rapid strides in elementary mathematics'. His progress in English, on the other hand, was 'by no means great'. Capel also refers to Togo's near blindness. His sight was saved by the skill of a Harley Street surgeon. For the main Togo entry, see: [65].

(121) The University (Newnham College, Trinity College, Girton College, Corpus Christi College); The University Library, West Road, Cambridge (Tel: 0223-337733/333045); The University Museum of Archaeology and Anthropology, Downing Street (Tel: 0223-337733); Leys School

Although the Imperial family connections are not as close to Cambridge University as they are to Oxford [113], there are some links. Crown Prince Hirohito spent a day in the university town in 1921 and was awarded an honorary Doctorate of Law. The future emperor also visited the Leys School where a number of the Japanese aristocracy had been educated in the last years of the 19th century; there is a photo of the prince reviewing the school's Combined Cadet Force. Also in the school chapel is a plaque given by the Japanese who fought in World War I. The Crown Prince also visited Newnham College, which was celebrating its Golden Jubilee and stopped near the Pike and Eel in Water Street to watch the college eights rowing on the Cam after a side trip to Ely Cathedral. The Crown Prince dined at Trinity College before leaving on his private train for the overnight journey to Edinburgh.

A cousin by marriage of the current emperor went to Girton College – Miss Hisako Tottori studied at Cambridge when her father was stationed in the UK with Mitsui and Company. She is now Princess Hisako and married to Prince Norihito.

Rugby football was first introduced to the Japanese by a Cambridge man. Edward Bramwell Clarke was born in Yokohama to a Japanese mother and he studied at Corpus Christi College. He returned to Japan at the turn of the 20th century and taught English at Keio University. In a letter addressed to the secretary of the Keio rugby football club (the oldest in Japan) in 1931, Clarke explains how it came about.

'I introduced rugby to the men of my then classes at Keiogijiku because they seemed to have nothing to occupy them out of doors after class on summer and winter days. Winter baseball had not yet come in and the young fellows loitered around wasting the hours and the lovely autumn weather. I thought if I could get them interested in rugger their hours during their free afternoons would not be so long and wearisome. My Japanese was too rough and ready, my vocabulary far too scant to explain the fine points of the game, so I asked my friend Tanaka Ginnosuke (a graduate of Trinity Hall) to come to my help, which he did with great readiness and enthusiasm and so the game started'.

The first proper game involving Japanese players took place on 5 January 1901, between Keio and a team known as the Yokohama Foreigners. The Keio side lost 39–5 and according to Clarke: 'the team came to the conclusion that they had been beaten chiefly because their legs were too short, and they expressed their intention of making their children (when they got them!) sit on chairs in preference to squatting on *tatami!*'

The University Library contains what is usually acknowledged to be one of the finest collections of Japanese books in Britain. It is particularly strong in literature, religion and art. The collection was inaugurated by Eric Ceadel, who later became librarian and it contains among other treasures the Aston Collection, about 9,500 books in Japanese including rare block printed books donated by W.G. Aston (1841–1911). Also in the library are the Parkes Papers belonging to Sir Harry Parkes, the British minister plenipoteniary in Japan during the 1860s and 1870s [33]. The Jardine Matheson Papers is a huge uncatalogued collection from the company that was one of the first to set up in Japan after the period of isolation came to an end in 1853. The library also has one *Hyakumanto-darani*, one of the earliest examples of printing in the world to survive. A further five are in the British Library [7], plus a unique set of eight (four sutras in various editions). *Non-university users must apply for prior permission from the Librarian.*

The University Museum of Archaeology and Anthropology has a teaching collection of Japanese archaeological material including Ainu artefacts, musical instruments, clothing, *netsuke*, metalwork and lacquer. *Open Monday–Friday 2pm–4pm, Saturday 10am–12.30pm and bank holidays in full term. Closed 24 December–1 January and Easter week.*

COTTERED

(122) Garden House, Cottered, Hertfordshire

The Japanese Gardens at Cottered (or the Garden House) is one of only a limited number in Britain with some genuine claim to authenticity. Their creator, Herbert Goode, had the enthusiasm, integrity and financial means to reproduce the gardens he had seen with such delight on his 1905 visit to Japan.

He sought and received expert advice from skilled Japanese garden designers. The essential elements of the garden, from the simple stone lanterns to the more intricately planned and sited tea-house, were either tailormade for Mr Goode in Japan or constructed by Japanese craftsmen in the UK. He went even further. Many features are in fact reproductions of famous landmarks in their home country. The sacred bridge at Nikko was one model, Kyoto's Golden Temple another.

Work began almost immediately upon the Goodes' return. On a flat, virtually treeless Hertfordshire pasture, tons upon tons of earth were moved and out of this metamorphosed a Japanese garden with all the traditional elements: a miniature Mount Fuji, the lovely Waterfall, a Turtle Pond and a lilliputian gorge.

It is not only superficially pleasing to look at. For those able to see, there is significance in every mark and symbol. Even magic. The garden's Japanese name is *Koraku En*, meaning good luck and long life. There is the Fox Shrine, sacred to the god of prosperity and stepping-stones. Below the waterfall is the huge six foot tall *Fudo-seki* (guardian stone), blueish-green and dedicated to the guardian god of the garden.

In the Japanese way, nature must be constantly curtailed. In more affluent days, 12 gardeners were kept on the go – to clip and prune and to pinch the buds of the fairy-tale forest so that it would never grow up. Creation, preservation and improvement were maintained by the founder until his death in 1937. Then after Mrs Goode died in 1964, the property passed to Mr Ironside Tetley-Jones. Faithful to the garden's traditions, he continued the work, repairing and re-building bridges, and re-siting ornaments. In 1966, the picturesque Garden House was built – to become the residence of the new owners, Mr and Mrs Engelmann.

The Engelmanns opened the gardens to the public on a number of days each year, under the Gardens Scheme Charitable Trust – with enormous response. However, the property was sold in the mid-1980s and since then, there has been some uncertainty as to when the gardens will be open again. Hertfordshire has two of the country's most interesting historic Japanese gardens – at Cottered and Fanhams Hall near Ware [128]. At the time of going to press, neither Cottered nor Fanhams Hall was exactly welcoming visitors. *No access at present.*

The mountaineer the Reverend Walter Weston who 'opened the eyes of the Japanese to the beauty of their mountains', with his wife and Japanese hunters as guides and porters [123]

DERBY

(123) Mile Ash House, Derby, Derbyshire

Walter Weston was born at Mile Ash House in Derby on Christmas Day 1861. He went to Derby School before Clare College, Cambridge and took Holy Orders in 1885. In 1888, he went to Japan as a missionary under the Church Missionary Society.

Weston spent three extended periods in Japan and wrote four books about the country. He is best remembered, not for saving souls, but for introducing the sport of recreational mountaineering and opening the eyes of the Japanese to the beauty of their mountains – a noteworthy achievement for a foreigner, particularly as he looked at the beauties of the mountains with only one. For all of his long life (he died at the age of 79 in 1940) Weston was blind in one eye.

This handicap did not prevent him from recording at least 15 mountain first ascents, nor from climbing Fuji four times, on one occasion accompanied by his wife. His first book *Mountaineering and Exploration in the Japanese Alps* was published by John Murray to whom he had been introduced by his friend Isabella Bird [133]. The book came out in 1896 and was critically well received; it stood out from the countless numbers of 'impressions' that were being published at that time. Weston satirized these books when he wrote that he fully expected to see published in the near future *Five Minutes in Japan in Two Volumes.*

It was through Weston that the Japanese Alpine Club came to be founded and he was made an Honorary Member. In 1937, Japanese mountaineers erected a bronze tablet in his honour at Kamikochi in the Japan Alps and the emperor bestowed on him the Order of the Sacred Treasure in

The Weston memorial tablet at Kamicochi in the Japan Alps – 'it was through Weston that the Japanese Alpine Club came to be founded' [123]

recognition of his pioneering work in mountaineering. According to an obituary written soon after his death: 'His worst failing was an inability to keep his pipe alight for more than two minutes'.

HERTFORD

(124) 25 Castle Street; Hertford Museum, 18 Bull Plain, Hertford, Hertfordshire (Tel: 0992-582686)

John Batchelor, the man they called the 'father of the Ainu' died here in 1944, at 25 Castle Street, the home of his wife's family, the Andrews. The Andrews were a prominent local family during the late 19th and early 20th century.

The Hertford Museum, founded by the Andrews family, has a small Japan-related collection. A number of items were donated by John Batchelor, including his Ainu–English–Japanese dictionaries. For main Batchelor entry, including his place of birth and tomb, see: [89].

KETTERING

(125) Alfred East Gallery, Sheep Street, Kettering, Northants (Tel: 0536-410333)

At the height of his fame, Sir Alfred East RA was described as 'England's greatest living landscape painter'. He was born in Lower Street, Kettering on 15 December 1844, the youngest of a family of eleven. From an early age he painted and drew, at first the horses and carts passing the window, then later, the trees along the nearby Ise Brook. At Kettering Grammar School, his artistic ability was recognized but not encouraged. He was a compulsive painter. 'Painting was a passion with me; I neglected everything else to follow it', said East.

His parents were not in favour of an artistic career, so on leaving school he was sent to work in a shoe factory owned by his brother, Charles. Shortly after his marriage to Ann Heath in 1874 he was sent to Glasgow as the shoe firm's representative; he attended evening art classes and after a while decided to make it his career. After attending the Glasgow School of Art, East went to study in France, before returning to England about 1883.

In recognition of the growing interest among late Victorians for all aspects of Japanese art and culture, in 1889 The Fine Art Society in London commissioned East to spend six months in Japan producing a series of paintings and etchings which were exhibited on his return. East produced a staggering total of 98 works from his trip, as well as writing a journal, published for the first time in 1991: Alfred East, *A British Artist in Meiji Japan* (edited by Hugh Cortazzi), In Print Publishing, Brighton, UK, 1991.

Alfred East was knighted in 1910 and the Alfred East Art Gallery was opened on 31 July 1913, just two months before the painter died and was buried in Kettering Cemetery. As part of the collection there are a number of etchings and watercolours that East painted during his time in Japan including one of Fuji, a street scene in Kyoto, his cottage in Hakone and other scenes of Hakone in the rain. Sir Alfred East was a founding member of the Japan Society. *Open Monday–Saturday 9.30am–5pm, closed public holidays.*

LINBY

(126) Newstead Abbey, Linby, near Nottingham, Nottinghamshire (Tel: 0623-792822)

'You can't be a Gulliver here any more', the head gardener tells visitors to Newstead Abbey's Japanese garden. 'Once you could have stood at the bottom and had a crane's-eye-view of a toy Japan'.

He was referring to the little make-believe land described in the early guidebooks, published when the garden was young. The Japanese landscape-architect designed Newstead's Japanese garden as a compressed vista, with everything small and to scale. He had supervised the specially imported Japanese gardeners and told them where to plant each dwarf tree and dwarf shrub. Precise instructions were laid down concerning clipping and pruning. In the first decades of the century following the completion of the garden in about 1910, everything was kept to no more than two or three feet tall. Alas, time, neglect and high labour costs have meant that these first plantings have been allowed to shoot up naturally to 25 or 30 feet high. So, in the sense of the garden representing a swathe of miniaturized countryside, Newstead Abbey's garden is no longer purely Japanese. You have to meander as the paths do, to see the features of its famous 'Willow-plate pattern' bit by bit. Much beauty, however, lingers in this lovely old garden and many of the original Japanese features can still be seen.

To find your way to the Japanese garden, go to the south side of the Abbey's very ample grounds and enter through a green, mossy tunnel. Then, as you go through the ancient carved stones from the original 12th century priory that once stood on the site, you will pass the weir. Here water cascades from the main lake and divides into two streams, crossed by traditional Japanese humped bridges and stepping stones.

There are old well weathered stone lanterns, made in Meiji Japan. But, sadly, the specially imported tea-house has had to be re-roofed 'in more vandal-proof materials'.

Inside the Abbey, the original Henry VII Room has been re-named the Japanese Room. Here the Japanese landscape retains a permanent perspective. Around the walls, native pine trees, cranes, waves and plum blossom flutter and bloom from the magnificent Japanese screens, dating from the 17th century.

Newstead Abbey has a long and romantic history. It was founded as a priory around 1170 and became a secular estate during the Reformation. The poet Lord Byron was probably the most famous of the later owners. In 1860, the Abbey was bought by William Frederick Webb, the African explorer and friend of Dr Livingstone. His daughter, Ethel, visited Japan and loved what she saw. It was she who introduced the Japanese garden and Japanese interior decorations on her return. *Twelve miles north of Nottingham on the Mansfield road, the A60. House: Good Friday–30 September 11.30am–6pm. At other times: by prior arrangement. Gardens: all year 10am–dusk except the last Friday in November.*

LONG MELFORD

(127) Holy Trinity Church, Long Melford, Suffolk

In the burial ground adjoining Holy Trinity Church, the poet Edmund Blunden is buried. Part of the epitaph on his grave reads: 'I live still to love still things quiet and unconcerned'.

'I live still to love still things quiet and unconcerned': Edmund Blunden [127]

Blunden was born in Tottenham Court Road, London in 1896 but grew up in Yalding, Kent where his father was a schoolmaster, organist and choirmaster. His education at Oxford was interrupted by volunteering for war service in the Royal Sussex Regiment. In 1916 he was commissioned and in 1917 he was awarded the Military Cross.

In 1924, he was appointed Professor of English Literature at Tokyo Imperial University and stayed there for three years. Blunden's lectures were so popular that one contemporary described him as 'like some Victorian revivalist preacher, filling a huge hall to bursting with a rapt congregation'. *Undertones of War* was written while he was in Japan and on publication in 1928 was immediately recognized as a masterpiece.

Blunden's wife Mary and their two surviving children (Joy, their first born daughter had died of a fever when only a few months old) stayed behind in England while he carried out his teaching duties in Japan. In 1925, he met Aki Hayashi, a 36 year old teacher of English at a junior high school. He was lonely and the dumpy Miss Hayashi was well passed the usual marrying age in Japan; they began an affair and Blunden signed more than one undertaking to make her his wife, should he ever become free to do so.

According to Sumie Okada, the author of *Edmund Blunden and Japan*, the professor, on his return to England, committed the folly – reminiscent of Shelley, whom he so much admired, in its impetuousness and unintentional cruelty – of taking Miss Hayashi back with him as his 'secretary'. Once there, a secretary (without the inverted commas) is what she soon became, beavering away for him, year after barren year, in the British Museum Reading Room, while he married first a second wife and then a third (by whom he had four daughters). By all accounts he became more and more perfunctory in his attentions and more and more dilatory in the payment of her meagre wages.

When she predeceased him, Miss Hayashi left the carefully hoarded sum of £2,000 – all that she possessed after years of living in drab bedsitters – to her adored employer in her will.

In 1947, Blunden returned to Japan for another three-year period, serving with the British Mission as Cultural Liaison Officer. He was regarded with the greatest esteem and affection in Japan – sentiments which he fully reciprocated – and in 1950 he was elected to the Japan Academy, the highest honour that could be paid.

In July 1948 Blunden was present at the unveiling of a monument to William Adams, the first Englishman in Japan [71]. The poem he wrote specially for the occasion is respectfully addressed to the citizens of Ito:

> 'Here then, while Shakespeare yet was living, came
> An Englishman to win another fame,
> And, with his different skill, to find a place
> In the long chronicle of Nippon's race;

How gladly I, after three hundred years,
Come where Will Adams led the pioneers
Of ship-design in Ito; still you praise,
You men of Ito, his laborious days,
And still, though time so far has borne him hence,
Call him the Pilot in pre-eminence.
I know his home in England and I know
At last his home by the Pacific's flow,
And am most happy thinking of that man
Who first united England with Japan;
Happy, to find that spirit flowering still
Which set your garland on the brow of Kentish Will'.

In 1963, Blunden was awarded the Order of the Rising Sun (Third Class) as a further mark of the respect and admiration with which he is held in Japan. He died in 1974 and continues to be remembered for his sincerity, modesty and gentleness, his wisdom, his humour and generosity – and his rare poetic temperament. *The grave is located at the bottom of the burial area by the path that crosses in front of the copse.*

WARE

(128) Fanhams Hall Japanese Garden, Ware, Hertfordshire

You had to be rich. And not just rich but *very* rich. Those who had Japanese gardens made in Britain around the turn of the century didn't go in for half measures. Japanese gardens went with grand country estates, world cruises and large private incomes. These green fingered millionaires set out to make their gardens as authentic as possible. This meant importing huge heavy artefacts such as stone lanterns and tea-houses from Japan. It wasn't just objects – Japanese gardeners who knew what to do with them were also needed. When the wealthy brewing family, Page (later Page-Crofts), commissioned the Fanhams Hall Japanese Gardens in 1901, imported gardeners and artefacts were only part of the deal. There was also a Mr Inaka to carry out the original designs and a Professor Suzuki for general supervision and day-to-day planning. Nor did the activity stop with the completion of the garden. For summer after summer afterwards, a maintenance team of Japanese gardeners would cross the world to tend them.

Of the three principal styles of Japanese garden – the hill and water garden, the tea garden and the dry garden – it was generally the first that captured the hearts of the Edwardian rich. The Fanhams Hall Japanese Garden has lakes, a miniature Mount Fuji and plantings of cherry, pine and Japanese cedar. But the designers also introduced some features of the dry garden, such as a waterfall made of rock.

Fanhams Hall remained in the Page family until 1950, when it was bought by the National Westminster Bank. In 1959, a visit by the Japanese ambassador was highlighted by the gift of a rare dawn redwood. Known as a living fossil, this was thought extinct until 'rediscovered' in China in 1945.

In 1971, Fanhams Hall became the institute and training college of the Building Societies Association. In 1986, it was purchased by Sainsbury's, the supermarket chain, to serve a similar purpose as a training centre.

In 1990, there was considerable local protest against the felling of an avenue of Scots pines there. Defending this action, Sainsbury's said that the avenue of trees had been looking very sorry for itself, after the ravages of gales in recent years. The 19th century trees were being replaced with mature, native chestnuts, 12–15 feet high. This was all part of a much wider £200,000 Fanhams Hall restoration programme. Sadly, the gardens are not normally open to the public. However, aware of the gardens' historic interest, the owners have, in the past, considered group visits by prior appointment.

WYTON

(129) Old Rectory, Wyton, Cambridgeshire

Isabella Bird (1831–1904), author of *Unbeaten Tracks in Japan* and many other books, first came to the lovely Old Rectory here, overlooking the River Ouse, in 1848, when she was 16. It was the third benefice for her father, Isabella's fourth home and always her favourite. In 1850, Isabella underwent an operation on her spine and in 1854, when she was 24, took her first trip abroad on the recommendation of her doctor. It was the beginning of a lifetime of world travel.

The Old Rectory at Wyton remained in the family until

the rector's death in 1858, when Isabella, her mother and her only sister, Henrietta, made their home in Edinburgh [207]. Today, the Old Rectory, protected as a Grade II Listed Building is privately owned. For main Bird entry and her place of birth, see: [133]. *Wyton is a village three miles east of Huntingdon.*

10 | North-east England

BAMBURGH

(130) Bamburgh Castle, Bamburgh, Northumberland (Tel: 06684-208)

This 6th century seat of Northumbrian kings seems a fitting place for the Japanese lords and princes, who at one time or another have been guests here of the Armstrong family. Bamburgh Castle is one of two mansions – the other being Cragside, Rothbury [150] – bought by the first Lord Armstrong in the latter part of the 19th century. The first lord died without a direct heir and his estate passed to his great-nephew William Watson-Armstrong (1863–1941) who in 1903 became the first Lord Armstrong of the second creation.

In 1953, when Crown Prince Akihito (now Emperor Akihito) stayed with the Armstrongs at Cragside, he visited Bamburgh. He was presented with two paintings of the castle by another recent Japanese guest, the artist Takanori Ogisu. (Two other Takanori paintings of Bamburgh and Cragside are in the Japanese ambassador's residence in London.)

Although the present Armstrong family have made Bamburgh their home, some of the rooms are open to the public. The displays include the star and order insignia of the Order of the Rising Sun, awarded to the first Lord Armstrong; a pair of fine 19th century *tanto* (a short dirk, worn thrust through the girdle); and a number of the formidable *naginata* (pole-handled weapons with slim curved blades, like glaives) c1800. *The castle is 16 miles north of Alnwick, six miles from Belford, three miles from Seahouses. Open Easter to last Sunday of October daily at 1pm.*

BARNARD CASTLE

(131) Bowes Museum, Barnard Castle, County Durham (Tel: 0833–690606)

The Bowes Museum has a rather domestic collection of Imari porcelain of the late 17th and 18th centuries of the sort used in British country houses at that time – bowls, teapots, dishes and a few large vases. These seem to have been inherited by John Bowes, co-founder of the museum with his wife, from various relatives. There is also a Japanese

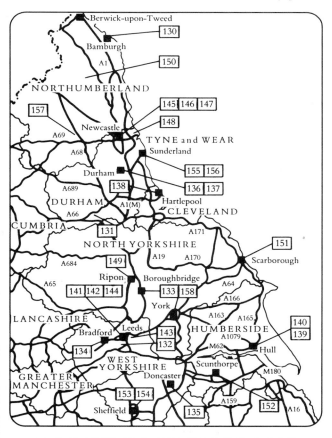

NORTH-EAST ENGLAND

black lacquer armour trunk raised on four square sectioned legs, each set in the centre of one side, probably of the 19th century. Other lacquerware include four small cabinets possibly bought in connection with the 1867 Paris Exhibition. *Open Monday–Saturday 10am–5.30pm, Sunday 2pm–5pm. March, April, October 5pm closing, November–February 4pm. Closed 20–26 December, 1 January.*

BATLEY

(132) Bagshaw Museum, Wilton Park, Batley, West Yorkshire (Tel: 0924–472514)

When the Bagshaw Museum's most publicized Japanese art donor, John Hilditch, died in 1930, his obituary in the Manchester Evening News merited twice the space given to D.H. Lawrence, the day's other prominent death. Hilditch's collections had been proudly exhibited all over the north of England and his personal files were crammed with letters of praise and veneration – from public and museum curators alike. His entry in *Who's Who in Art* spilled over one and a half full columns. It attributed to him authorship of a shelf of scholarly works and all but described his travels as those of another Marco Polo.

Not everyone, however, shared these feelings of adulation. To many well known Oriental art experts at the British Museum, the Victoria & Albert and the local Manchester Art Gallery, Hilditch was thought of as an eccentric, fraud, hoaxer and pest. Hilditch had personally valued his entire art collections (including his Japanese collection which really did contain some nice pieces) at some £2.5 million. When in fact it was sold after his death, the most valuable item fetched a trifle over £20. Speculating on Hilditch's much vaunted Oriental expeditions seeking after antiquities, newspaper accounts pondered whether he had actually ever been further afield than Southend!

For Hilditch, Oriental collecting seems to have become an obsession that left him supersensitive to criticism and blind to reason. From his home, *Minglands*, Hilditch would speed through his morning's work as the agent for a sewing machine company – sometimes reportedly keeping three secretaries in equally frenzied activity. Then, come high noon, John Hilditch the rep would become Mandarin John the Orientalist. Next door to *Minglands* there was his Peking Villa, crammed with all his treasures of the Orient. He would be seen darting about, costumed for all the world, they said, like a Chu Chin Chow. Each weekday at 7 o'clock and twice on Sundays, dressed as a Buddhist priest, Hilditch acted out the rites of an Oriental ceremony in the Hilditch-McGill Palace Temple he had created out of a garage.

The Bagshaw Museum has a wide and varied Japanese collection. A modern valuation would certainly result in a considerably higher valuation than that made at the time of Hilditch's death, more than 60 years ago. Some of the 19th century lacquer combs, for example, are beautiful by any standard. Exquisite Japanese embroideries are among the items selected for the 'Curator's choice'. Cranes, tortoises and prunus blossom, symbols of longevity, are stitched in threads of fine silk and gold.

Another local donor was John Speak, the son of a Keighley mill-owner. His collection includes some superb Japanese Satsuma ware. Among these, 'Curator's choice' was a small, extremely fine bowl. The inside of this treasure is decorated with chrysanthemums and around the outside march 47 ronin. *The Bagshaw Museum is situated in the 40 acre Wilton Park, between Birstall and Batley. Batley is about seven miles south-west of Leeds. Open Monday–Saturday 10am–5pm, Sunday 1pm–5pm.*

BOROUGHBRIDGE

(133) Boroughbridge Hall, Boroughbridge, North Yorkshire

The publication of *Unbeaten Tracks in Japan* by Isabella Bird (1831–1904) in 1880 punctured the myth of Japan as a land of ever-bowing natives with quaint habits and nice manners, tea-houses and strange gardens. For the first time since Japan had emerged from its seclusion some quarter of a century earlier, an astute, observant, experienced travel writer had penetrated *beyond* the artificiality of the so-called 'civilized' port areas. What Isabella Bird found along her unbeaten tracks was a very long way from the accepted stereotype.

Isabella's friend and publisher, John Murray, had pleaded

Dean Cemetery in Edinburgh, where Isabella Bird is buried [207]

with his recalcitrant author to tone down her descriptions of the poverty, ignorance, disease, and stupefying medieval backwardness she had found in Japan's northern hinterland. But Isabella was a faithful reporter of the truth before her eyes. Travelling with a Japanese guide as her sole companion, she found herself back in the dark ages, exchanging curious stares with the bottom layers of the Japanese feudal heap. At night, after finding what lodgings she could, prying eyes would trespass into every crack of the flimsy walls. She had begun to learn Japanese and understood something of what was said about her. 'Was this a man, a woman, or a monkey?', came the curious whispers. Isabella realised she was probably the first European woman they'd ever seen. Her audience might be a gaggle of undernourished children. Or at other times, the entire village!

After these experiences, Isabella told her publisher she was determined to 'de-cherry blossom' Japan. When *Unbeaten Tracks in Japan* appeared, it seemed that this was precisely what her readers wanted. Murray wrote later that never in all his years as a publisher had he known a book to win such acclaim.

Isabella Bird's *Unbeaten Tracks* was re-published in 1984.

Princess Chichibu, the late emperor's sister-in-law, suggested that somebody might like to try re-tracing Isabella's 'tracks'. Japan Society member James Blewitt rose to the challenge. Mr Blewitt found that news of the pilgrimage had preceded him. At Tokyo station, and then at every stage of the journey, television crews were there in force. Isabella's *Tracks* had begun in Nikko – in 'Mr Kanyo's house'. The room where Isabella had stayed, Mr Blewitt discovered, had been preserved by Mr Kanyo's descendant as something of a showpiece. 'Mr Kanyo's house' was now Nikko's best hotel.

The daughter of a clergyman, Isabella Lucy Bird was born on 15 October 1831 in Boroughbridge Hall, Boroughbridge. The house, which belonged to her maternal grandmother, appears to be little changed today. In early 1832, Isabella's father was appointed curate at Maidenhead. Throughout Isabella's childhood, rectory followed rectory. Others were in Birmingham (St Thomas's Church [106] still exists but not its rectory where the Birds lived); Wyton Rectory, Wyton, Cambridgeshire [129], and Tattenhall Rectory, Tattenhall, Cheshire [189]. Isabella's last residence – she was by now Mrs Bishop – was in 18 Melville Street, Edinburgh [207]; she was buried in Edinburgh's Dean Cemetery. There is also a clock erected in memory of her sister Henrietta, near Henrietta's cottage in Tobermory, Mull [219].

Isabella was only 24 when, after a spinal operation, her doctor advised her to recuperate abroad. This began a lifetime of often very unconventional travel. Most of her journeys appeared in print. In book after book after book, this Victorian Marco Polo described the wild fringes of the 19th century world with insight, distinction, and obvious enjoyment.

Isabella Bird had a number of interests and at various times was a nurse, photographer, missionary advocate, and social worker. She even busied herself as a stay-at-home housewife but the husband she took in later life, Dr Bishop, died after only about five years of marriage. Isabella pursued her unbeaten tracks until the last. Only one thing could still her travels. Mrs Isabella Bishop, née Bird, died in Edinburgh at the age of 73. Under her bed, her bags were packed and ready for the one journey she'd never make. *Boroughbridge is a small town on the bank of the River Ure six miles south-east of Ripon.* See also: [106, 129, 189, 207, 219].

BRADFORD

(134) Cartwright Hall, Lister Park, Bradford, West Yorkshire (Tel: 0274-493313); Cliffe Castle, Spring Gardens Lane, Keighley, West Yorkshire (Tel: 0535-618230/1)

Bradford Art Galleries and Museums owns a moderately sized, but good collection of Japanese material, most donated by several collectors early in the 20th century. The collection of 18th and 19th century prints is stored at Cartwright Hall. *Open 10am–6pm daily, closed Monday except bank holidays, October–March 10am–5pm.*

Netsuke, inro, ivory carvings, metalwork and armour are held at Cliffe Castle. *Open daily 10am–6pm, closed Monday except bank holidays. Appointments to view the material not on display can be made Monday–Friday 10am–5pm.*

DONCASTER

(135) St George's Church; 47 Thorne Street; Midland Bank, 1 High Street, Doncaster, South Yorkshire

The historian Richard Storry was born in Doncaster on 20 October 1913 and baptised a month later at St George's Church. The family home was 47 Thorne Street and his father Frank Spencer Storry was bank manager at the London Joint Stock Bank (later the Midland Bank) at 1 High Street, Doncaster. For main entry on Storry, see: [117].

DURHAM

(136) Oriental Museum, Elvet Hill, Durham, County Durham (Tel: 091-374 2911)

All areas of Japanese artistic and craft output are represented in the University of Durham's Oriental Museum. The items date from 1600 and are spread across religious, military, aristocratic and everyday leisure fields. There is quality metalwork including a wide range of weaponry, as well as good examples of ivory carving and lacquer with small but interesting holdings of *netsuke* and *inro*. An excellent range of modern calligraphy supplements the print collection which is strong on warrior prints, and there are individual works of historical calligraphy and *sumi-e*. Over 500 slides and prints provide a comprehensive and often unique record of 19th century Japan. Japanese ceramics in the museum are mainly export ware but there are representative examples of work for all levels of the home market. Outside is a fine and rare Japanese temple lantern, and there are Japanese flora in the museum grounds and in the University Botanic Gardens. *The museum is open April–October Monday–Saturday 9.30am–1pm and 2pm–5pm, Sunday 2pm–5pm. November–March closed weekends.*

(137) Ushaw College, Durham, County Durham

Some ten miles west of Durham is the Roman Catholic Ushaw College, where the author, Lafcadio Hearn (1850–1904) went as a boarder, when he was 13. According to the school register, which can still be seen, he was at Ushaw between 9 September 1863 and 27 October 1867. The young Hearn was quite popular with the other boys but was considered something of a rebel and non-conformist by the teachers. In 1863, an accident, variously reported as a punch or a direct hit from the knotted end of a rope, blinded Lafcadio in the left eye. In November of the same year, his father (who had previously more or less abandoned the boy) died abroad of malaria. It was about this time that Lafcadio's great-aunt and guardian, Mrs Brenane, came under the influence of a Henry Molyneux. Molyneux had little time for Lafcadio and Hearn's later writings accuse Molyneux of swindling him out of his inheritance. Molyneux also per-suaded Mrs Brenane to leave her Dublin house and move to his house in Redhill, Surrey [81]. This is the address given in the Ushaw registers. Molyneux seems to have been a poor businessman, losing not only his own capital but Mrs Brenane's as well. With no more funds available, Lafcadio was forced to leave school and lived for a time at the Molyneux house at Redhill. For main Hearn entry, see: [232].

HARTLEPOOL

(138) Gray Art Gallery and Museum, Clarence Road, Hartlepool, Cleveland (Tel: 0429-266522)

Sir William Gray II was the owner of the town's shipyard at the turn of the 19th century and he was the main benefactor of the Gray Art Gallery and Museum. Sir William persuaded a number of local people to donate items to the museum, one of whom was Colonel Thomlinson who owned the Seaton Carew Ironworks from about 1890 onwards. The colonel travelled all over the world and the bulk of the museum's Oriental collection came from him, including a fine 19th century carved wooden figure of an abbot from Japan. The piece is in three sections: the monk, his black lacquered throne and his footstool with slippers. His legs are tucked up under his habit, as if in the lotus position and the empty slippers indicate that this is a commemorative portrait made after the Abbot's death. Also donated by the colonel, who achieved his rank in the Volunteers (later the Territorials), was a large Imari vase decorated with panels of chrysanthemums and a female figure at the top. A Major Jobson donated most of the museum's extensive *netsuke* collection; some of these are of mythological groups while others illustrate genre scenes, poets, samurai, literary and folkloric subjects. About half of the 86 items have legible signatures, including Shogyoku, Hoichi and Gyokusan. There are also good examples of Japanese armour in the museum collection. *Open Monday–Saturday 10am–5.30pm, Sunday 3pm–5pm.*

HULL

(139) St Barnabus Church, corner of South Boulevard and Hessle Road; Town Docks Museum, Queen Victoria Square, Hull, Humberside (Tel: 0482-593902)

Before dawn on 22 October 1904, in the vicinity of the Dogger Bank, ships and men of the Hull trawler fleet became innocent casualties of the Russo–Japanese war. Out of the peaceful blackness of the North Sea, suddenly and without warning, the blinding glare of searchlights was followed by the splintering crash of heavy shells. Within less

Prime Minister Toshiki Kaifu welcomes Prime Minister Margaret Thatcher at Akasaka Palace in October 1989

than 30 minutes, some 300 shells had sunk the *Crane*, instantly killing her skipper and third mate and badly wounding the third engineer. Two other ships, the *Gull* and the *Moulmein* were badly damaged. The *Moulmein* had had a shell burst clean through her galley.

This senseless, unprovoked attack had been carried out by a trigger-happy Russian Baltic Fleet. The Russians were openly scornful of the Japanese, referring to them as harmless butterflies. 'We'll pin one on a postcard and send it home as a souvenir', ran a popular joke. But for the Russians to have opened fire on the first vessels they saw may suggest they were less sanguine than they would have had everyone believe. Although still some 15,000 sea miles from Japanese waters, they had taken the Hull trawlers for Japanese torpedo-boats.

First reports reaching the British mainland were treated with disbelief. That a supposedly friendly country would make an unprovoked attack on unarmed fishermen belonging to the world's greatest maritime power was almost inconceivable. Then, as news of the casualties was confirmed, disbelief turned to fury. The Russian embassy was stoned. At Victoria Station, the ambassador was confronted by hoots and raised clenched fists. Compensation was demanded of the Tsar. The Royal Navy was ordered to sea to detain all Russian vessels. On the brink of war, an apology was received from St Petersburg. Russia agreed to meet all parliament's demands. A promise was made to recall the Baltic Fleet. Britain accepted the apology. But in the end, the Tsar reneged on most of his promises. His Baltic Fleet was not recalled. It would have been better for Russia if it had been.

At the end of an eight-month voyage, the Russians met the Japanese in the Straits of Tsushima and were almost totally destroyed. The Japanese fleet, mostly British built and under British-trained officers, had won the most dramatic and decisive sea victory since Trafalgar. The British, most especially the men of Hull, were delighted.

The Russian Outrage (also known as the Dogger Bank Incident) is remembered at two places in Hull. In the centre of what used to be Hull's fishing community, outside the church of St Barnabas, at the corner of South Boulevard and Hessle Road, is the statue of a fisherman. He is a grey figure wearing a sou'wester, a jersey and fearnought trousers tucked into his seaboots. The names of the dead are inscribed.

The local Russo–Japanese War casualties are further commemorated in Hull's Town Docks Museum. Here the Fishing Gallery has a three-dimensional display of the actual shell-torn companionway cover of the trawler *Mino*.

The Town Docks Museum also has a fine carved ivory example of the traditional *takara-bune*. This is the treasure ship, carrying the seven gods of good fortune. How easily the Japanese have adapted and absorbed the superstitions and faiths of their neighbours – and so often with such wit and nonchalance. No wonder the Christian evangelists have never managed to convert more than about one per cent of the population.

Ebisu is the only one of the mostly jolly septet who is indigenous to Japan. He is the god of small businesses. Daikokuten, from Indian Buddhism, is the deity of the kitchen. Bishamonten, also from India, represents power and authority. The laughing Chinese Buddhist Hotei dispenses gifts from his bottomless sack. Jurojin, from Chinese Taoism, should be solicited for sagacity and longevity.

Fukurokuju, also Taoist, brings popularity. Benzaiten is the token woman on board the treasure ship and was once a Hindu Goddess. Her areas of responsibility are maternal love and artistic grace. What more could you want? *Town Docks Museum is open Monday–Saturday 10am–5pm; Sunday 1.30pm–4.30pm.*

(140) Wilberforce House, 25 High Street, Hull, Humberside (Tel: 0482-593921)

In Wilberforce House there is a fine collection of *hina matsuri* or dolls from the doll festival. The festival dates back a thousand years but its greatest period of development was the Tokugawa era (1603–1867). The dolls used in the traditional display are not everyday children's toys but meant to be looked at and admired as a display. The set in Wilberforce House consists of 15 dolls dressed in formal classical court costumes including the emperor and empress, three ladies-in-waiting, five musicians, two retainers and three guards. On the lower shelves are miniature weapons, armour, musical instruments, lacquered tableware, chests, folding screens, lanterns, a palanquin, a carriage and two flower arrangements. The set on display was given by the then Princess Royal in 1951. *The museum is open Monday–Saturday 10am–5pm, Sunday 1.30pm–4.30pm.*

LEEDS

(141) Hall Park Japanese Garden, Horsforth, Leeds, West Yorkshire

Hall Park Japanese garden at Horsforth was created in 1987 as a community project by 15 participants on a joint Leeds Leisure Services/Manpower Services Commission programme. Like many Japanese gardens the design is a direct expression of a deep and religious appreciation of nature. The group of rocks adjacent to the stone bridge represents Mount Fuji. The carp stone in the garden represents man as a fish swimming in the river of life; as it overcomes the current and ascends the last obstacle, it changes into a dragon and is allowed to enter heaven.

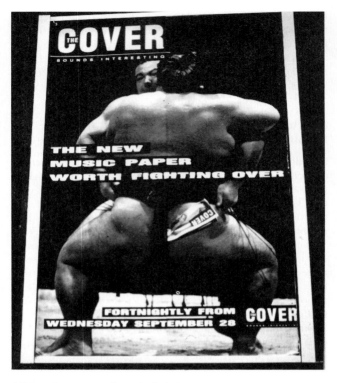

Things Japanese catch on in Britain

A feature of the one-acre garden is a pair of wrought iron gates, the design of which incorporates plum and cherry blossom and three oak leaves gleaned from a rare book on ancient Japanese family crests. In the surrounding wall is a window with another samurai crest – *kikusui*, or chrysanthemum on water, made famous by Masasige Kusunoki, a 14th century warrior. The Kusunoki family crest is supposed to have originated in China where in the depths of the Nanyanghsien mountains was a valley overgrown with chrysanthemums. Anybody who drank at the stream running with the floating blossoms enjoyed longevity. Professor Kanzawa of Asia University in Tokyo did the calligraphy for the garden signs.

(142) Leeds City Museum, Municipal Buildings, Leeds, West Yorkshire (Tel: 0532–462632)

One of the most unusual Japanese items in Leeds City Museum is an example of contemporary Japanese advertising: plastic food which is displayed outside many restaurants in Japan to indicate what is available inside. In the museum's Ethnography Department is a *bento* – a lunchbox complete with plastic rice balls, shrimp, giant radish, seaweed and noodles. It is one of about 200 Japanese items including armour, swords, costumes, toys, domestic items and a wedding kimono. Very little of the material is displayed as a rule, but visitors are welcome to examine the stored collections after making an appointment a week in advance.

(143) Lotherton Hall, Aberford, near Leeds, West Yorkshire (Tel: 0532–813259)

Lotherton Hall was the former home of Sir Alvary and Lady Gascoigne. Sir Alvary was a British diplomat in Japan immediately after World War II. In his collection, on show in the house, are some Japanese items: a fine pair of screens, a pair of picnic boxes and other lacquer and a few pieces of porcelain. The garden shows Japanese influence but it was created before Sir Alvary spent time in Japan: in 1912 his mother, Mrs Laura Gwendolen Gascoigne CBE (née Galton 1859–1949) created the Japanese rock garden and incorporated some lanterns and maples. *Located three and a half miles north-east of Garforth on the B1217. Open throughout the year daily 10.30am–dusk.*

(144) Temple Newsam House, near Leeds, West Yorkshire (Tel: 0532–647321/641358)

Temple Newsam House, an Elizabethan mansion with gardens designed by Capability Brown, has a few pieces of Japanese work, mostly 17th century porcelains, among its ceramics collection. There are also some handsome Japanese lacquer panels incorporated in the so-called Chinese drawing room, which was decorated with hand-painted Chinese wallpaper by Lady Hertford in the 1820s and is considered a fine example of the Regency taste for the Orient. *Located two and a half miles east of Leeds on the A64. Turn south-east onto the*

A63, turn south after one mile at Halton. Open throughout the year Tuesday–Sunday (and bank holiday Mondays) 10.30am–6.15pm (8.30pm May–September).

NEWCASTLE UPON TYNE

(145) Central Library, Newcastle upon Tyne (Tel: 091-261 0691); Archives Department and Museum of Science and Engineering, Blandford House, Blandford Square (091-232 6789); Elswick Cemetery, Elswick, Newcastle upon Tyne, Tyne and Wear

Admiral Togo and a party of Japanese naval officers visited Newcastle in 1905 soon after the Battle of Tsushima in which he defeated the Russian fleet in Japanese ships built in Britain, many from Tyneside. His visit is recorded in the Central Library in contemporary photographs. Togo and his staff were visiting Sir Andrew Noble, a partner in Armstrong Whitworth, the ship builders, a firm that no longer exists. The library also has photos of a number of ships built for the Japanese Navy – *Takasago* (1898), *Asama* (1898), *Tokiwa* (1898), *Kashima* (1905). One ship built on Tyneside at the Swan Hunter Shipyards at Wallsend was the *America Maru*, launched in 1898 as a twin screw steamer which carried 91 First, 28 Second and 300 Third Class passengers on the Japan/Hong Kong/San Francisco service under a subsidy from the Japanese government. The ship was commandeered during the Russo–Japanese War of 1904–05 and again during World War II when she was torpedoed and sunk by the American submarine USS *Nautilus* in March 1944 en route between Iwojima and Ladrone Island while in service as a troop transport. Other records of companies doing business with Japan at the turn of the century (electric power generating, paper making, leather working using 'japanner' – a hard black varnish from Japan) as well as photos and launch cards of ships destined for the Imperial Navy are held in the Archives Department. In the same building is the Science Museum, which has a couple of builder's models of warships built by Armstrong, Mitchell and Co for the Japanese Imperial Navy. The *Naniwa Kan* (1885) and *Yoshino* (1893) were cruisers combining speed with quick-firing guns. Both ships took part in the Sino–

Japanese War of 1894–95 and the Russo–Japanese War of 1904–05. The latter was lost while taking part in the bombardment of Port Arthur in 1904 and the former was wrecked in 1912 after striking a rock off Urupa Island in the Pacific Ocean.

Elswick Cemetery contains a number of graves of Japanese naval seamen who died, presumably from illness, on Tyneside while learning how to build and operate naval vessels. Iwamoto Kato (grave space B consecrated 36) died 21 June 1877 aged 20 years and Katsujiro Yamazaki, a paymaster in the Imperial Japanese Navy, died in Gresham House Hospital, Newcastle on 12 November 1899 aged 33 years and is buried in grave space B consecrated 40.

(146) Hancock Museum, University of Newcastle upon Tyne, Barras Bridge, Newcastle upon Tyne, Tyne and Wear (Tel: 091-222 7418)

There are some 90 items of Japanese origin in the Hancock Museum. The Ainu material is of interest as it includes a collection of 11 photographs of men and women showing their face tatoos. Other notable items include swords and armour, models of insects and a 'mermaid', and a moustache-lifter for keeping facial hair out of a cup. *Open daily 10am–5pm.*

(147) Laing Art Gallery, Higham Place, Newcastle upon Tyne, Tyne and Wear (Tel: 091-232 7734/232 6989)

The most revered craft in Japan was sword making and the process of manufacture amounted almost to a religious rite. A local man, William Parker Brevis (1867–1939), made a life-long study of cutting and thrusting weapons and was especially knowledgeable about Japanese swords and *tsuba*. His collection is now in the Laing Art Gallery and has some examples of great interest including a *katana* with a 16th century blade mounted in an attractive inlaid 19th century scabbard with contemporary accessories. The symbolism of the fine inlaid spider's web on the scabbard is carried through to the *menuki*, a large fly, and the *tsuba* which has an inlaid spider. Other curiosities in the collection are an articulated iron carp, a large black lacquer *norimono* or palanquin, a gold lacquer saddle frame and stirrups and two picnic boxes.

Another local benefactor was Albert Howard Higginbottom, a successful restaurant and pub owner who pioneered the idea of taking 'snack' lunches. In 1919 he donated his 1,000-item Japanese collection (which included prints by famous 18th and 19th century artists) to the Laing Art Gallery. The range of subject matter is comprehensive, from leaves from the finest 18th century books, through portraits of actors, musicians and courtesans, theatrical productions and riverside picnics, to examples of the best landscape pictures.

NORTH SHIELDS

(148) Local Studies Centre, Old Library, Howard Street, North Shields, Tyne and Wear (Tel: 091-258 2811)

The Local Study Centre has some limited material related to ships built on Tyneside for the Japanese Imperial Navy. These include the *Kashima* and its sister ship the *Katori*, battleships built at the Vickers Yard at Elswick.

RIPON

(149) Grantley Hall College, Ripon, North Yorkshire (Tel: 0765-620259)

Concealed behind banks of laurel opposite the car park of Grantley Hall, an adult education centre belonging to North Yorkshire county council, is a Japanese rock garden constructed in the latter part of Victoria's reign. It incorporates the usual maples, azaleas and bamboos. The college is not open to the public but anybody particularly interested in Japanese gardens is welcome if arrangements are made in advance with the Warden.

ROTHBURY

(150) Cragside House and Country Park, Rothbury, Morpeth, Northumberland (Tel: 0669-202333)

Like most successful, productive partnerships, Japan and the first Lord Armstrong (1810–1900) met at just the right time.

This page *A Kingfisher, Irises and Pinks by Hokusai – colour print from woodblocks, c1830: V&A [26]. Katsushika Hokusai (1760–1849) was one of the greatest of all ukiyo-e artists. He is most famous for his Thirty-six Views of Mount Fuji (actually a series of forty-six landscape prints). The V&A has all forty-six Fuji prints.*

Overleaf *Screen – Flowers of the Four Seasons, attributed to Shiko Watanabe 1683–1755: Ashmolean Museum [111]*

When the Iwakura Mission arrived in Newcastle upon Tyne on the evening of 21 October 1872, Japan was just beginning to realize how vulnerable its long seclusion had left it. Armstrong, to whom they were introduced the following morning, was the inventor of the world's most advanced gun. He was soon to become a major builder of ships. Japan had urgent need of both.

The son of a local merchant, politician and reformer, the man who would become the first Lord Armstrong, Sir William George, Baron Armstrong of Cragside, was born at 9 (formerly 6) Pleasant Row, Shieldfield, Newcastle upon Tyne. By the time of his fateful meeting with the Iwakura Mission, he had already established himself as an inventor and industrialist of genius and had been knighted by Queen Victoria.

In 1875, Japan began an official naval shipbuilding programme, extended in 1882 with the first navy expansion bill. Early orders were mostly dealt with by southern British yards but with Armstrong's new shipyard at Elswick open for business in 1884, substantial Japanese orders began to be placed with the new partnership of Armstrong–Mitchell.

In the same year, the architect Norman Shaw completed the task of turning Armstrong's original modest shooting lodge into the 100 bedroom Cragside mansion (and the first house in the world to be lit by hydro-electric power). The Elswick works, which grew to rival Krupps as the largest in the world, were to build a good portion of Japan's Imperial Navy and the buyers were lavishly entertained at Cragside.

Cragside's visitors' book reads like a *Who's Who* of Japanese society, past and present. Prime ministers, admirals, princes and princesses, even the direct descendants of the Tokugawa shoguns – all were entertained at Cragside. In 1953, the present emperor, then Crown Prince Akihito, said that Cragside's pines and lakes and flowering shrubs reminded him of home. With the same spade that his father had used at Blair Athol in Scotland in 1921, the young prince planted a cyprus tree overlooking the tennis court where he had played during his stay.

In 1977, the mansion of the armaments king was acquired by the National Trust, to become Cragside House and Country Park. The so-called Japanese Room is named after personal family friends, the Marquess and Marchioness Yorisada Tokugawa, aunt and uncle of the present emperor's mother. Family friends, the Tokugawas stayed at Cragside in 1916, 1921, and 1951. There are a number of traditional Japanese prints and various personal photographs and mementoes, including a 1953 gift from Crown Prince Akihito – a set of gold lacquer boxes. For Armstrong's other residence, Bamburgh Castle, see: [130]. *Entrance by Debdon Gate one mile north of Rothbury on Alnwick road (B6341). House open 1 April–31 October Tuesday–Sunday and bank holidays, 1pm–5.30pm.*

SCARBOROUGH

(151) Peasholm Park, Dean Road, Scarborough, North Yorkshire

Peasholm Park has a number of Japanese touches to it but is not laid out as a Japanese garden. The park runs along a glen with a small stream and there are a number of ponds laid out like a Japanese water garden. The bridges and other ornamental buildings are in the Japanese style and plants, such as the Chusan Palm with its enormous fan shaped leaves, give a subtropical feel similar to parks in Kyushu.

SCUNTHORPE

(152) Scunthorpe Museum and Art Gallery, Oswald Road, Scunthorpe, South Humberside (Tel: 0724–843533)

The J.A. Jackson bequest made to Scunthorpe Museum and Art Gallery in 1965 includes a few Japanese ivory carvings which would be of interest to collectors. *Open Monday–Saturday 10am–5pm, Sunday 2pm–5pm.*

SHEFFIELD

(153) Archives Division, Sheffield Central Library, Surrey Street, Sheffield, South Yorkshire (Tel: 0742–734711)

The Archives Division has records of several local companies that had dealings with Japan in the Meiji era. Of particular interest are photographs and plans of railway locomotives supplied by the Yorkshire Engine Company to the Imperial Japanese Railways about 1871. Accounts taken from the local newspapers can also be seen recording a visit by Japanese Embassy staff accompanied by Sir Harry Parkes [33], the British minister in Japan, to the city in 1872.

(154) Sheffield City Museum, Weston Park, Sheffield, South Yorkshire (Tel: 0742-768588)

One of the most popular exhibits in Sheffield City Museum is a life-size painted wood carving of two sumo wrestlers by the artist Hannanuma. The carving was donated in 1891 by Mr Harry Deakin, born and bred in Sheffield, who worked in the Yokohama art dealers firm of Messrs Deakin Brothers. Other Japanese items in the museum include bronze vases, braziers, paperweights and brooches as well as a fine collection of swords. The Japanese longsword is renowned for its strength, sharpness and quality of design. It was used almost entirely as a cutting weapon and was generally used with two hands. Until 1877 when Imperial edict abolishing the wearing of swords was issued, samurai wore swords openly. They always carried their swords in pairs. When in armour, a long sword called *tachi* hung suspended at the left side, and a short dirk called *tanto* was thrust through the belt. When in civilian dress a long sword, *katana*, and 'companion sword', *wakizashi*, were both carried uppermost in the belt. The majority of the blades are mounted for civilian wear and skilled metalworkers made beautiful 'sword furniture' to adorn the hilt and sheath. When not in use the blades were stored in plain white wood sheaths, *shira saya*, for protection. The swordsmith and maker of sword furniture stood socially amongst the highest in the artisan class, the swordsmith's occupation in particular earned him much respect. *Open Monday–Saturday 10am–5pm, Sunday 11am–5pm. June–August 8pm closing.*

SUNDERLAND

(155) Bishopwearmouth Cemetery, Sunderland, Tyne and Wear

Among the first Japanese monuments to be erected in the British Isles was a memorial to the child of a Japanese couple

'One of the most popular exhibits is a life-size painted wood carving of two sumo wrestlers by the artist Hannanuma': Sheffield City Museum [154]

who were members of a troupe of artistes who appeared in Sunderland for two weeks in February 1873. The acrobatic troupe was called Tannaker's Japanese. Tannaker Buhicrosan was a Dutchman married to a Japanese who brought his touring troupe around Britain in the 1870s and the local paper says the show 'was well worth seeing for its new tricks'. However, the entertainers must have had sad memories of Sunderland because of the death of Godie, a 15-month old toddler whose grave is in Bishopwearmouth Cemetery Ward 4 Section C Grave Number 527. The full inscription reads: 'Here lies Little Godie, who died February 21 1873. Aged 15 months, the only son of Omoterson and Godie, natives of Japan, members of Tannakers Japanese. This is claimed to be the first Japanese monument erected in this country'. For Tannaker's Japanese village, see: [17].

(156) Sunderland Museum and Art Gallery, Borough Road, Sunderland, Tyne and Wear (Tel: 091–514 1235); Grindon Museum, Grindon Lane, Sunderland, Tyne and Wear

Chinese pirates, the Ming dynasty, the Tokugawa trade descriptions act and the fickleness of samurai haute couture. A profound knowledge of these disparate elements went into the identification of the most remarkable Japanese exhibit in the Sunderland Museum and Art Gallery.

The museum's Exhibit A is a magnificent long sword with red lacquered scabbard. The first clue to its history was the signature of the swordsmith – Kunetsuga of Fujiwara. However, there were three succeeding generations of that name in the area around Kyoto, between 1526 and 1629. For further evidence, we have to look to contemporary developments across the China Sea. Here the Ming Dynasty was fighting for its survival against the invading Manchus. Normal arrangements between China and Japan had broken down and control of the maritime trade had been seized by the most successful pirate of his time, Ching-kung Cheng.

Faced with the inflationary effects of virtually unrestricted imports, the Japanese Tokugawa regime made it mandatory for all swordsmiths to indicate, when appropriate, the use of 'foreign' (which really meant Chinese) raw materials. This is precisely what the experts found on the Sunderland Museum's masterwork.

The inscription clearly says *namban tetsu*, which means 'made with foreign iron'. Documented evidence indicates that Cheng's piratical reign lasted from 1620 to 1644. So this is the most likely period when the sword was made.

There are further clues, matching the *style* of the sword with the requirements of contemporary Japanese society. During the peaceful Tokugawa centuries (1600–1867), the samurai turned his sword, if not to plough shares, at least to something fashionably acceptable to his peers. Look closely at the Sunderland Museum sword and you can find the rivet holes that suggest the sword was shortened to the more fashionable length of two *shaku* (about two feet). This length made it much easier for the young samurai to tuck the sword into his waist sash. The gorgeous red scabbard would then protrude flamboyantly.

The history behind Sunderland's Japan exhibits is what makes them exciting. Not just this sword but all the others. And the sword fittings. The art of the *tsuba* alone has filled libraries. There are ceramics, armour, lacquer, even the saddle made for the *daimyo* of Nagaota in 1787. It is a moveable feast. *Open Tuesday–Friday 10am–5.30pm, Saturday 10am–4pm, Sunday 2pm–5pm.*

The Grindon Museum in Sunderland has a few Japanese costumes, shoes, weapons and dolls in store.

WALLINGTON

(157) Wallington Hall, Wallington, near Cambo, Northumberland

Owned by the National Trust, Wallington Hall has a good collection of Japanese ceramics. The pieces date mainly from the late 17th and 18th centuries and are mostly Imari and Arita porcelain dishes, jars, vases and teapots.

YORK

(158) York City Art Gallery, Exhibition Square, York, North Yorkshire (Tel: 0904–623839)

The opening of Japan created a two-way traffic. Western technology flowed in. Japanese art – and what passed for Japanese art – became *de rigeur* almost everywhere else.

Japanese art was also copied and adapted. Perhaps the most significant genre to emerge from this adaptation was *Japonisme*, the Japanese form of the much older *Chinoiserie*.

The York City Art Gallery has an interesting *Japonisme* painting by the English artist, Philip Wilson Steer. It is of a (European) girl dressed in a kimono, the costume that gives the work its title, 'Kimono'. Like Whistler's similarly clad girl of 1864 and the later 'Red Kimono' of 1893 by Henrich Breitner, the Japanese garment was simply used as a prop. No attempt was made by the artist to actually copy the Japanese painting style.

The gallery's other Japan-related items are the result of a much more two-sided interchange of craft and inspiration. York is fortunate to have some of the most brilliant pottery to come out of the partnership of Bernard Leach and Shoji Hamada [100].

The originator of this outstanding ceramics collection was the Very Reverend Milner-White, Dean of York. He was one of the first to discover the importance of the partly Japan-inspired English stoneware and collected the works of Leach and others long before they became national institutions. Steer's 'Kimono' was another example of the Dean's generosity and his recognition of significant works of art.

An exceptional Hamada piece is a dark green olive pot, rust glaze over a cream lip and with wax resist. Mr Milner-White had it brought over specially from Japan. It later proved the inspiration for Leach's famous pot *à la Hamada*. The best known of the Leach pieces is his 'Leaping salmon' – a matt white glazed vase decorated with the salmon in full flight. There is also his magnificent 'Tree of life' in beaten copper, c1927.

The fusing of the two masters' skills is perhaps best seen in our 'Curator's choice' – Shoji Hamada's four-sided, moulded dish with paddle decorated rims. The inspiration clearly comes from the potter's admiration for English slipware. The finished bowl, however, is pure Japanese.

Other relevant holdings include a mixed collection of Japanese prints, usually available only by appointment. *Open Monday–Saturday 10am–5pm, Sunday 2.30pm–5pm.*

11 | *North-west England*

BLACKBURN

(159) Blackburn Museum and Art Gallery, Museum Street, Blackburn, Lancashire (Tel: 0254-667130)

In the term *ukiyo-e*, *e* means 'picture' and *ukiyo* 'the floating world'. Thus: 'picture of the floating world'. This was the underbelly of Tokugawa Japan, contemptuously tolerated by the ruling classes. It was peopled by courtesans, geisha, sumo wrestlers, playwrights and novelists – the purveyors of transitory pleasures. These characters became the first subjects of the *ukiyo-e* artists and print makers. The riches that maintained the sparkle of this underworld came from the despised *shonin* (merchants). Feudal Japan placed the merchants at the bottom of the broad class structure. The social scale rose up through artisans, farmers and then to the samurai. In practice, however, many samurai lived in impoverished gentility while those 'in trade' lived very comfortable lives.

The pleasures of the flower and willow world, as it was called, were extremely inviting, and even the samurai became models for the *ukiyo-e*. Samurai often had little money – what a rich merchant might lavish in a night on his favourite geisha, a samurai could hardly earn in a year. So with his swords in hock, wooden replicas in their scabbards and often in disguise, the aristocratic samurai would often sneak silently to join the lower orders in their delicious pleasures.

As time went by, other subjects were also included by *ukiyo-e* artists – such as flowers, birds, landscapes and mythological scenes. The first *ukiyo-e* date from the middle

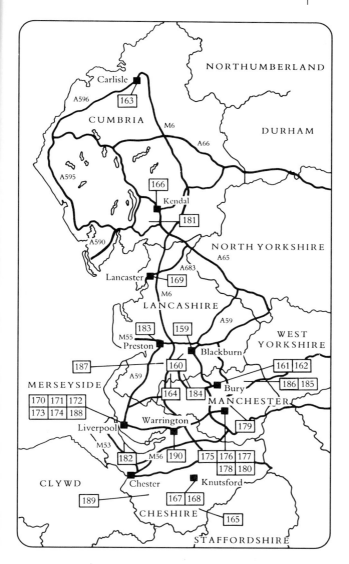

NORTH WEST ENGLAND

of the 17th century and *ukiyo-e* evolved as a continuing art form until it began to be replaced by Western-introduced newspapers and photography in the late 19th century.

Nevertheless, even as these Western techniques began to replace the *ukiyo-e* in their native country, the impact of *ukiyo-e* in Europe was considerable. The wonderful colours, styles and printing techniques that the Japanese had developed through their centuries of near isolation came as a startling revelation to the rest of the world. There was another important reason for the popularity and rapid spread of *ukiyo-e*. They were quick and easy to produce and therefore cheap. Western dealers and collectors could provide generously for themselves with very little outlay. The *ukiyo-e* became so ubiquitous in Europe and America that even today, the *ukiyo-e* has become synonymous with *all* Japanese art.

Of contemporary European artists, perhaps the closest in subject matter to that of the *ukiyo-e* artist was Toulouse-Lautrec. His prostitutes from the Paris brothels found their counterparts in Utamaro's flower and willow maidens from the red light districts of Osaka and Edo (modern Tokyo). Lautrec and his contemporaries saw not only a kinship in the subjects. The very style of the *ukiyo-e* was soon to have an influence on the whole European art and craft scene. A new word entered Western vocabulary, appropriately through the French. It was *Japonisme*.

The outstanding collection of over a thousand *ukiyo-e* at the Blackburn Museum and Art Gallery gives a very good representation of the genre. Included are the well known names of Harunobu, Utamaro, Hokusai and Hiroshige. Space, however, is insufficient for the museum to exhibit even a small proportion all the time. However, the keeper is happy to give visitors a private view if prior arrangement is made.

The man responsible for bringing this large collection together was Mr T.B. Lewis, and his widow presented the collection to the museum in 1944. Mr Lewis was from the local Blackburn merchant class and in addition to being a prosperous cotton manufacturer, he was also a poet, collector, antiquary and playwright. Just the sort of qualities that he would have found in the characters of his collection. *Open Tuesday–Saturday 10am–5pm.*

(160) Bolton Museum and Art Gallery, Le Mans Crescent, Bolton, Lancashire (Tel: 0204-22311)

Bolton's stunning example of the aristocratic *oyoroi* armour was obsolete for fighting some five centuries before it was made in the 18th century. However, by the peaceful Tokugawa Period (1600–1867), armour was made principally for show. It was a kind of status symbol that flaunted the wealth and position of both the wearer and his lord. Japanese armourers chose freely from previous styles, sometimes adding impressive horns from one period, and another interesting bauble from another. The *oyoroi*, or 'the great harness', in the Bolton Museum and Art Gallery is reasonably true to the original.

Early Japanese armour initially evolved from styles worn on mainland China. Then it was perfected and adapted during the civil strife waged from the 10th to the 12th centuries. The *oyoroi* provided far better protection than the simpler *haramaki* (wrapping the belly) armour worn by the lower ranks – but also proved far more unwieldly. It was particularly burdensome on horseback, and the *oyoroi* was gradually replaced by lighter more practicable fighting garb.

However, as the Bolton example shows (notice the fine lacquering, colourful lacing and gilt embellishments), the *oyoroi* armour is a grandiloquent expression of knightly elegance. It was donated by the local firm of H. Murray & Co in 1892.

Most of the museum's other Japanese pieces, a varied collection, are the result of local generosity. Donors include the wealthy businessman, antiquarian and supporter of good causes, Sir Samuel Scott, the second baronet of Yews. His nice inlaid and lacquered panel, for example, was given in 1942. The museum's collection of over a hundred *netsuke* and *inro*, including many excellent specimens, was also a gift. Although of no great material worth, the curator is proud of the museum's Bernard Leach [100] link – a late 19th century Japanese book on bird studies, initially given by Leach to local artist, Edith Norris. Like many of the smaller collections, the museum has no Japanese specialists amongst its curatorial staff. So it is quite likely that the worth of some of Bolton Museum's pieces is yet to be discovered. *Open Monday, Tuesday, Thursday, Friday 9.30am–5.30pm, Saturday 10am–5pm.*

BURY

(161) Bury Art Gallery and Museum, Moss Street, Bury, Lancashire (Tel: 061-705 5878)

The museum contains a scale model of a Shikishima class battleship, the *Hatsue*, built for the Japanese Imperial Navy by Armstrong Whitworth at their Elswick shipyard on the Tyne in 1901. The original was 15,000 tons normal displacement, measured 439 feet 9 inches in length and had a crew of 741. On completion and before sailing to join the Japanese fleet, the battleship represented Japan at the funeral of Queen Victoria. Her active service life was not long. During the bombardment and subsequent blockade of Port Arthur during the Russo–Japanese War she struck two Russian mines in quick succession and sunk on 15 May 1904. The model was presented to Bury during the early part of the century by the head of a local firm of calico printers, John Whitehead Ltd, whose premises were at Elton, on the outskirts of the town. Mr Whitehead was a director of Armstrong Whitworth and he also presented a huge ornamental bronze urn, 15 feet high which is Japanese in origin. The museum also possesses three Japanese photographic albums from about 1890 with front and back covers lacquered and depicting Japanese scenes and inlaid with ivory and mother of pearl. Two of the albums contain hand tinted black and white photos of a number of Japanese cities as well as the interiors of houses and people at work and leisure. *Open Monday–Friday 10am–6pm, Saturday 10am–5pm. Closed Sunday.*

(162) Lancashire Fusiliers Museum, Wellington Barracks, Bury, Lancashire (Tel: 061-764 2208)

On 24 May 1921, five years before he became emperor, Crown Prince Hirohito visited the Twentieth Lancashire Fusiliers in Manchester, to thank them for their part in bringing about the end of the samurai. After inspecting the guard of honour, he gave each man a silver-headed ebony walking cane, embossed with the rising sun and the Twentieth's regimental crest.

There was a healthy whiff of diplomatic nostalgia about this visit of the 21 year old prince. It had been at the specific request of the War Office that the Twentieth was appointed to mount guard over the future emperor's Manchester residence.

Fifty seven years earlier, on 23 January 1864, the second Battalion of the Twentieth Lancashire Fusiliers disembarked at Yokohama. They were the first British troops in Japan. The battalion had only recently reported for duty in Calcutta. Their sudden transfer had been at the urgent request of Britain's pioneer minister in Japan, Rutherford Alcock [77]. Alcock had become increasingly concerned by the activities of the extreme anti-foreigner faction, who were demanding the expulsion of all foreigners and death to those who remained. There had been a number of frightening attacks on the legation and on the new foreign community, resulting in deaths and serious woundings. In a time of country-wide unrest, the weakened Bakufu government had proved incapable of providing adequate security.

Many Japanese as well as foreigners welcomed the reassuring presence of British troops. By October, according to the Twentieth's official regimental history, a request was made that Japanese troops be permitted to join the Twentieth on the parade ground. However, as the samurai were still resplendent in full chain armour and carried their whole panoply of swords, spears, bows and arrows, it was felt appropriate that they perform their exercises separately!

This was, in a sense, the samurai's last parade. The smartly turned out British troops, with their organization and discipline, armed with the world's most advanced weapons, could not fail to impress the invited Japanese officials (although eventually Japan would look to Germany as the model for its army). In 1864, it was the Twentieth who began the transformation of medieval knights into what was to become the most efficient army in Asia. The silver-headed Japanese cane on display in the Lancashire Fusiliers Museum is a way of saying thank you. *Open daily (except Monday and Thursday) 9.30am–4.30pm.*

CARLISLE

(163) Tullie House Museum and Art Gallery, Tullie House, Castle Street, Carlisle, Cumbria (Tel: 0228-34781)

Although not on view on a regular basis, the museum and art gallery has a small representative collection of Japanese prints which may be viewed by prior arrangement. There are prints by Gakutei, Harunobu, Hiroshige, Hokusai, Kiyonaga, Koryusai, Shuncho, Sumiyoshi, Torin, and Utamaro as well as various unknown artists. *Open April–September Monday–Friday 9am–6.45pm, Saturday 9am–5pm, Sunday (June–August) 2.30pm–5pm. October–March Monday–Saturday 9am–5pm.*

CHORLEY

(164) Astley Hall Museum and Art Gallery, Astley Park, Chorley, Lancashire (Tel: 02572-62166)

Among the collections of pottery and paintings in Astley Hall are two from Japan. A Mrs Swarbrick donated a 19th century 33-piece Japanese tea service of porcelain, painted with groups of figures in a landscape dominated by Mt Fuji. A Manchester businessman donated a collection of paintings and photographs. Richard Alexander Doxy was a partner in the firm Brooks and Doxy of West Gorton and Miles Platting, Manchester; the company made cotton spinning machinery and Mr Doxy travelled widely in the Far East on business. In 1893 he visited Japan and it is believed that the collection was acquired then. Although not exceptionally fine or rare examples of Japanese art, they throw an interesting light on the type of 'quality souvenir' that attracted English visitors to Japan in the 19th century. There are approximately 50 paintings on silk, hand-made paper and pith paper featuring people from various social classes, birds, landscapes and boats. There are also 18 double-sided photographs of scenes of Japanese life. *Open April–September daily 12am–6pm. October–March Monday–Friday 12am–4pm, Saturday 10am–4pm, Sunday 11am–4pm.*

CREWE

(165) Chester Street, Crewe, Cheshire

The Japan railway engineers, Richard Francis Trevithick (1845–1913) and his brother, Francis Henry Trevithick (1850–1931) were both born here at what was once 22 Chester Street. Chester Street itself still exists but the north side, where the Trevithick house was, has been redeveloped into shops, offices and car park. For main Trevithick entries, see: [85, 96 and 107].

KENDAL

(166) Abbot Hall Art Gallery, Kendal, Cumbria (Tel: 0539-722464)

Abbot Hall is a fine mid-18th century house which has a highly selective collection of Japanese prints and porcelain. Toyokuni, Kuniyoshi and Yeisen are represented among over 100 examples of the woodblock cutters' art. The porcelain includes Imari tea caddies, plates and a pair of pilgrim flasks painted in underglaze blue. Not all items are on permanent display but may be seen by prior arrangement. *Open Monday–Friday 10.30am–5.30pm, Saturday and Sunday 2pm–5pm.*

KNUTSFORD

(167) Tatton Park Japanese garden, Knutsford, Cheshire (Tel: 0565-654822)

English gardens bloom in the warm weather. Tatton Park's Japanese garden blooms all year round. This is because – like the gardens in the home country – Tatton has skillfully used different natural materials to look good in each of the four seasons.

Take moss, for example. The Tatton Park Japanese Garden can hardly boast the 100 species traditionally claimed by Kyoto's world famous, 14th century Kokedera Moss Garden. However, there is sufficient variety of this beautiful, ever-changing plant to make a visit to Tatton a unique experience. The Japanese say the texture and luminosity of moss look best after rain. It is also fascinating to see how the colours of the moss gradually change – from a spring green slowly darkening to an autumn russet.

In spring, Tatton Park gives you a taste of Japan in cherry blossom time – with a gorgeous blaze of *sakura* (cherry blossom), one of Japan's most enduring symbols. For the samurai, *sakura* represented the brief glory that foreshadowed death on the battlefield. The *kami-kaze* pilots in the Pacific war were told they shared this same ephemeral nobility.

On a merrier note, Japanese still gather under the blossoms in springtime. There are songs and poetry and warm strong *sake* rice wine (after which the songs and poetry get even better). Second only to cherry blossom time are the colours of autumn. Tatton Park's Koyo lake takes its name from the blooded hues of the maples reflected in its waters. On the right day, it is a sight to remember.

Northern Japan can be white for months on end and few people know better than the Japanese how best to exploit the extraordinary beauty of nature's changing moods. The specially imported stone snow lanterns at Tatton are designed to collect and display what is picturesquely called 'winter blossom'.

Plant selection is taken very seriously. Those foreign to Japan are excluded. So there are cherry, plum, magnolia, bamboo, pine, azalea and iris. But no English roses. No lawns.

Different species are not just appropriate or inappropriate. They are lucky and unlucky. A wedding is likely to have pine, bamboo and apricot – constancy, prosperity and purity. Basil Chamberlain, writing towards the end of the last century observed that camellia was avoided because its red blossoms reminded the Japanese of decapitated heads.

At the heart of Tatton's Japanese garden is the tea-house, its doorway traditionally low to compel the obeisance of humility. The stand-in for Mount Fuji is snow-capped with white stones. Then beyond, over the arched bridge, is the Shinto shrine, surrounded by water. This shrine, like all the main elements in the garden, was imported from Japan and erected and put into place by Japanese gardeners, around 1910. The shrine was paid for by the third Lord Egerton.

After the garden, go up to the library of the great house. Here there are four volumes of Japanese prints – by Kuniyoshi, Kunisada and others – in mint condition. There are also two framed woodcuts by Tokokumi and Utamaro. Tatton Park's title and estate passed to the fourth and last Baron Egerton in 1920. In 1960, the house and garden were taken over by the National Trust. Today the estate is administered and financed by the Cheshire County Council on behalf of the Trust. *Two miles north of Knutsford, three and a*

Top *'The bridge provides a dramatic contrast to the pale tones of nature': cherry tree and red laquer bridge, Heale House Gardens* [102]

Bottom *The Beckford Cabinet, 'the greatest single item' in Chiddingstone Castle* [67]

Top 'An early example of Japanese talent for caricature' – 17th century wood and laquer powder-flask decorated with Portuguese figures: Ashmolean Museum [111]
Bottom 'One of the most fascinating men of his generation': the grave of Laurence Oliphant, Twickenham Cemetery [60]

half miles off the M6 (exit 19), four miles south of M56 (exit 7), A556 Chester road or A50 from Stoke on Trent. Station Knutsford (2 miles). 21 March–30 September open daily (closed Mondays except bank holidays). Park open 11am, last admission 6pm, closed 7pm. Mansion, gardens, old hall, farm open 12am, last admission 4pm, closed 5pm. 1 October–31 March open daily (closed Mondays, Christmas eve and Christmas day). Park open 11am, last admission 4pm, closed 5pm. Mansion, old hall closed. Gardens open 12am, last admission 3pm, closed 4pm.

(168) Knutsford, Cheshire

After his first school in Rochdale [185] John 'Earthquake Milne' was sent here as a private pupil to the Rector of Knutsford from 1859 to 1864. From here he went on to Liverpool College [173]. For main Milne entry, see: [78].

LANCASTER

(169) Lancaster City Museum, Market Square, Lancaster, Lancashire (Tel: 0524–64637)

Britain did not just supply the locomotives and rolling stock for the Japanese National Railways (founded in 1872), it also supplied the ticket printing machinery. The inventor of the machinery Thomas Edomonson was born in Lancaster and the Museum was presented with the very first ticket issued by the Museum of Transportation in Tokyo to their permanent Edomonson Memorial Exhibition which records his meritorious services to the railway world. *Open Monday–Friday 10am–5pm, Saturday 10am–3pm.*

LIVERPOOL

(170) Botanic Garden, Calderstones Park, Liverpool, Merseyside (Tel: 051–724 2371)

The city and port of Liverpool have had trading links with Japan for many years and there are a number of strong Japanese connections (including the marriage of one of its most famous sons, John Lennon of the Beatles, to Yoko Ono).

In the Harthill and Calderstones Botanic Garden there is a Japanese garden created by trainee gardeners employed by the City Council but modelled on the temple gardens of Kyoto. The hope is that the arrangement of the water, rocks and plants creates 'a fitting abode in which the soul can rest and find spiritual refreshment'. Visitors are encouraged to proceed slowly through the garden in order to relax and appreciate each vista as it comes into view. Bridges in Japanese gardens usually do not have handrails; this is not a safety oversight but follows the belief that nothing must come between man and nature as he lingers to watch the falling water of the cascade or the water rushing into the small lake. There is a *tsukubai*, or water basin, fed by water from a bamboo pipe which is the place where guests wash their hands on entering the garden and symbolically wash away all unclean thoughts to enable them to enjoy the garden more. The deer scarer is another simple device which uses a bamboo stem suspended on pins so that it can swing freely; when the stem is full it tips up and empties the water in a pool and makes a clacking sound as it falls back to rest on the rock. *Open daily 8am–5.45pm.*

(171) The Liverpool Record Office, William Brown Street, Liverpool, Merseyside (Tel: 051–225 5147)

The Record Office has a number of papers and books relating to the city's connections with Japan. The *Annals of Liverpool* is a chronological list of events and contains references to visits by Japanese ambassadors in 1862 and 1872, members of the Imperial family in 1886, the founding of the Bowes Museum of Japanese Art Work in 1890, the Japanese Fancy Fair of 1891 organized by the Japanese consul James L. Bowes, visit of the Japanese ambassador in 1905 and of the Japanese battleship *Katori* in 1906. In a copy of *News from the Missions* of August 1898 there is an article describing Christmas in Japan.

(172) Merseyside County Museum, William Brown Street, Liverpool, Merseyside (Tel: 051–207 3759)

The museum has a substantial Oriental collection created through maritime trade from the Port of Liverpool. The

Japanese portion of this collection covers a broad spread of the decorative art from Japan such as *netsuke* and lacquer-work as well as such everyday items as toys, games and snuff bottles. The finest items in this field are nearly 600 swords and sword fittings of outstanding quality. *Open Monday–Friday 10am–5pm, Sunday 2pm–5pm. Closed 24–26 December, 1 January and Good Friday.*

(173) 3 Mount Vernon Place, Edgehill; Liverpool College, Liverpool, Merseyside

3 Mount Vernon Place seems to have been the birthplace of John Milne (1850–1913) 'the father of Japanese seismology'. The house was actually John's father's family home. The father, also called John and a successful wool broker, had business in the district and had taken his wife (in advanced pregnancy) with him. When the baby was three weeks old, the family moved back to their home in Rochdale. The area has now been redeveloped. Following primary school, John Milne was a pupil at Knutsford, Cheshire [168] until at 13, in 1864, he went to the famous old Liverpool College. For main Milne entry, see: [78].

(174) 5 Princes Street; Toxteth Cemetery, Smithdown Road, Liverpool, Merseyside (Tel: 051-733 5591)

Although born in Leeds and a member of the Bowes family whose ancestral home is Streatlam, near Barnard Castle in County Durham, James Lord Bowes was educated in Liverpool and founded a wool-broking business in the city. Bowes became Japan's first Honorary Consul despite admitting in an interview with the *Pall Mall Gazette* of 1888 that he had never done any business with the country: 'My connection with Japan has been one of purely a sentimental and friendly nature and as a matter of fact Japan is one of the few countries in the world in which there were no sheep until twenty years ago, when a few were imported, but they have not thriven, and do not appear likely to do so'. Even though Bowes did not trade with Japan, the Port of Liverpool certainly did. Bowes estimated there was £3,700,000 worth of exports to Japan in 1887: cotton yarns and cloth £1,557,000; woollen goods £720,000; iron £400,000; machinery £152,000; alkalies and chemicals £92,000 and the balance consisted of 'almost everything from tin-tacks to steam hammers, ladies' gowns to armour-clads, soda crystals to diamonds'. What made Bowes's honorary position so important was that 90% of the exports to Japan were produced north of Liverpool.

In 1871 Bowes married and built a home in the Scotch Gothic style at 5 Princes Street which he called Streatlam Towers after the ancestral home in County Durham that had been in the family since the 13th century. In a building attached to his home he kept his magnificent collection of Japanese art and curios which he opened to the public from time to time. In 1891 the Japanese Fancy Fair was held in his museum and in the same year he was awarded the Imperial Japanese Order of the Sacred Treasure for his work as Honorary Japanese Consul.

Bowes had great respect for the culture and history of Japan and took pleasure in telling people that its painters and potters had matched anything in the West over the centuries. His Consul's Commission was dated 'the two thousand five hundred and forty-eight year from the coronation of the Emperor Jimmu'. (The mythical Jimmu Tenno – from whom the Imperial line claims direct descent – is said to have mounted the throne on 11 February 660 BC. This is still year zero in the Japanese calendar.)

During his life, Bowes published a number of books on Japanese art and craft: *Japanese Marks and Seals*, *Japanese Enamels*, and *Japanese Pottery*. He is buried in Toxteth Park Cemetery (Section I, grave number 729) with his wife, mother–in–law, daughter and two other children who died in infancy.

MANCHESTER

(175) Central Library, St Peter's Square, Manchester (Tel: 061-234 1900)

The *Annals of Manchester* to be seen in the Central Library record two visits by Japanese ambassadors during the Meiji era when Japan was keen to catch up with the West and industrialize as quickly as possible. Manchester was one of the great industrial powerhouses of the world at that time and on 4 October 1872 a group of Japanese came to the city and 'visited various manufactories, also the Royal and Prince's Theatres, the Assize Courts and the City Gaol'. In 1884 Ambassador Mori and his wife made a private visit on 15 January and on the following day they were shown over the mills of Sir Elkanah Armitage and Sons and the print-works of Messrs T. Hoyle and Sons and were also entertained to luncheon by the Mayor at the Town Hall.

(176) Museum of Science and Industry, Liverpool Road Station, Castleford, Manchester (Tel: 061-832 2244)

In the summer of 1944, Japanese military commanders were faced with the overwhelming material strength of the Allied Forces who were island-hopping inexorably towards Japan. They had little hope of forestalling defeat by conventional tactics and many of the military began to advocate the use of drastic new combat methods. One officer, Ensign Mitsuo Ohta, a transport pilot serving with the 405th Kokutai, conceived the idea of a rocket propelled suicide plane. The ensign's plans were accepted by the navy and engineers went to work on the aircraft which was primarily designed as an anti-invasion or coastal defence weapon to be launched from a parent aircraft. The tiny aircraft was built of wood and non-critical metal alloys and great care was taken in its planning to enable it to be mass produced by unskilled labour. As the aircraft was to be flown on its one-way mission by pilots with only limited flying experience, instruments were kept to a minimum and good manoeuvrability was demanded to achieve reasonable accuracy. Named Navy Suicide Attacker Ohka (Cherry Blossom) Model II, it carried a 1,200 kg warhead in the nose and was launched from the bomb bay of a specially modified Mitsubishi G4 attack bomber. Between September 1944 and March 1945, 755 were built. They went into action on 21 March 1945 but the parent planes were intercepted and forced to release their weapons short of the target. Their first success came on 1 April when they damaged the battleship *West Virginia* and three transport vessels and eleven days later the Ohka aircraft sunk the destroyer *Mannert L. Abele* off Okinawa. The slow and cumbersome parent aircraft proved to be extremely vulnerable when approaching within a few miles of well-defended targets and production of the model ceased in March 1945. Other more advanced models were planned but never went into production. One of the original Ohkas can be seen at the Manchester Air and Space Museum. It is listed as Yokosuka (the place of manufacture) MXY-7 Ohka II 'Baka' Piloted Bomb. *Baka* means 'fool' in Japanese. *Open Tuesday–Saturday 10am–5pm, Sunday 11am–5pm. Closed Monday unless bank holiday.*

(177) Manchester City Art Gallery, Mosley Street, Manchester (Tel: 061–236 5244)

Manchester City Art Gallery has an extremely rare and beautiful *norimono* (the palanquin restricted by law for the exclusive use of the shogun and his *daimyo*) that is believed to have belonged to the last of the shoguns. This was Hitotsu-bashi Keiko Tokugawa, whose fall in 1867 brought an end to two and a half centuries of Tokugawa rule.

The palanquin became a fashionable mode of transport early in the Tokugawa era (1600–1867). Not only was it well able to cope with a landscape of mountains and appalling roads, it represented a literal demonstration of the rich riding on the backs of the poor. While the shoguns ruled, the emperor was kept in his place at Kyoto. His mode of transport was a bullock cart.

Keikō's *norimono* has as its personal numberplate the heraldic Tokugawa insignia in gold leaf and gilt copper. Its black lacquered wood gleams. Luxury features come as standard: front observation window, slatted doors and exquisitely painted decorations of birds and flowers. (At the time of going to press, the *norimono* was undergoing interior restoration, but it will be out again in good time for the 1992 opening of the refurbished ground floor galleries.)

The Manchester City Art Gallery's next important link is with the beginning of Tokugawa rule, 253 years earlier. It is a beautifully preserved suit of armour, supposedly from Osaka Castle. Osaka was the final major fortress to fall to the first of the ruling shoguns, Ieyasu, in 1615. This style of armour would certainly have been familiar to Britain's Gillingham-born William Adams [71] – then one of Ieyasu's closest advisers.

Both Adams and the Portugese introduced European ideas into the art of war. Japanese armour became lighter and simpler; solid plating replaced the old intricate lacing. The Gallery's suit is a particularly interesting example, as it is believed to have emanated from the Myochin armoury. In both output and excellence, the Myochins dominated the armourer's art, through successive generations, for some four centuries.

The armour was one of a number of items given to the museum by Earl Egerton of Tatton. For Tatton Park's superb Japanese garden at Knutsford, see: [167]. The Earl presumably acquired the armour personally in Japan.

The gallery also has a collection of over 100 Japanese woodblock prints. All the most popular *ukiyo-e* artists are represented including Masanobu Okumura (1686–1764), who can take credit for a number of innovations. Examples are the *hashira-e* (pillar print), the *uki-e* (perspective picture), the first use of lacquer in the *urushi-e* (hand-coloured print) and the *bijin-ga* – the glamour pin-ups of the time. Masanobu may have even been one of the first to exploit colour printing.

NB While the ground floor galleries here are being refurbished, much has had to be put in store. The curator apologizes for this but bids visitors a warm welcome for the 1992 opening. For researchers and others who need to view material sooner, please telephone the curator for a private view. *Open Monday–Saturday 10am–5.45pm, Sunday 2pm–5.45pm.*

(178) Manchester Museum, Oxford Road, University of Manchester (Tel: 061-275 2634)

So revered is the Japanese swordsmith, there is a roll of honour going back to the beginning of the 8th century which contains over 12,000 names. The Japanese sword is invested with religious significance, drawn from the beliefs of Shinto, Zen and Confucianism. It is a work of faith and dedication that compelled the swordsmith to begin each day with ritual purifying ablutions.

The heating, forming, hammering and finishing could take many weeks for a single blade, but the result was a work of art and a symbol of veneration. To its user, it was his status and honour. His sword, as has been often quoted, was the 'soul of the samurai'. As a bone splintering weapon of death, no edged weapon in the world has been able to match it – not even the legendary blades of Toledo and Damascus.

The Japanese collection in the Manchester Museum is

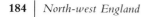

18th or 19th century inro – laquer inlaid with tortoise-shell and mother-of-pearl: Manchester Museum [178]

wide, varied and interesting. But the museum had little hesitation in making its 'Curator's choice'. This is undoubtedly the 14th century *tachi*. The *tachi* is the ancient, heavy, sling sword. The name *tachi* probably derives from the character *tachikiru*, meaning 'to cut in two'. But it could also have meant 'great sword' or 'horizontal sword'. It pre-dates the samurai custom of wearing two swords (both lighter and shorter).

Manchester's blade is signed *Sadanaga* and was probably smithed around 1360 in what is now Okayama. As the old province of Bizen, the area gained such a reputation that records show whole villages almost exclusively populated by swordsmiths and their families. The mounts on the museum's *tachi* came later. The type of decoration that was used indicates techniques developed during the Tokugawa years (1600–1867). To be more precise, experts have dated the decoration to the 18th century.

The rest of Manchester's fine Japanese collection includes various types of arms and armour, ceramics, metalwork, lacquer, woodcarving, archery, ivories and also *inro*. Most are from the 18th and 19th centuries. The bulk of the Japanese material came to the museum through the generosity of Mr R.W. Lloyd, a director of Christie's. In 1958, he bequeathed part of his collection to the British Museum and part to the Manchester Museum. Manchester also has a quantity of modern 1980s Japanese tea ceremony utensils. *Open Monday–Saturday 10am–5pm except Christmas, Easter and bank holidays.*

(179) Oldham Art Gallery and Museum, Union Street, Oldham, Greater Manchester (Tel: 061-678 4653)

The second Mongol Invasion of 1281 is probably as significant in Japanese history as the defeat of the Spanish Armada is to Britain. A superb *katana* sword blade, thought to be a survivor of Japan's great battle against the Mongols, is held at the Oldham Art Gallery and Museum.

The *katana*, dating from about the 12th century was the samurai's long sword, worn with the edge upwards. It is one of the most formidable swords ever invented. Oldham's example is a fragment from an event that nearly changed the course of Japanese history. It was witness to an invading force of some 150,000 troops from the contemporary world's most powerful conqueror – the great Kublai Khan.

It wasn't, however, the *katana* that defeated Kublai Khan's legions. A typhoon more terrifying than anyone could

19th century ivory carving, showing Mashahige Kusoniki, an outstanding samurai commander born in 1294 AD. He fought on the side of Emperor Go-Daigo until he was defeated in 1336 AD, when he had to commit suicide: Manchester Museum [178]

remember devastated the invading fleet and sent its men to the bottom of the sea. Like the British in 1588, the Japanese attributed their deliverance to the gods. They called that typhoon *kami-kaze* – the divine wind. It is a term the Japanese have evoked in times of crisis ever since.

The museum does have a number of other Japanese items well worth the visit. For the 'Curator's choice', we move forward several centuries – to the well-run bureaucracy of the Tokugawas. This is a brass and bronze figure of one of a pair of samurai messengers. As was the custom, one is holding a lantern aloft to light the way for his compatriot, carrying the official dispatches. It can perhaps be seen as a small cameo of the time.

In common with many museums, Oldham acquired most of its Japanese collections around the turn of the century. Two prominent local donors were Charles E. Lee, an Oldham industrialist, and Francis Buckley, writer and historian. Try to see the two small bronze mirrors from the 14th to 15th centuries. There is also some 19th century Satsuma ware, a Hamada bowl, other swords, sword furniture, *inro*, and *netsuke*.

This then is the flavour of what's on offer. The Oldham collection is varied and exciting, but as with any museum, space is limited and displays change. If you genuinely want to see something special, please telephone the curator direct for a personal viewing – or even just information. *Open Monday, Wednesday, Thursday, Friday 10am–5pm, Tuesday 10am–1pm, Saturday 10am–4pm.*

(180) Whitworth Art Gallery, University of Manchester, Whitworth Park, Manchester (Tel: 061-273 4865)

Among the 11,000 items held by the Whitworth Art Gallery is a large collection of Japanese prints, ranging in date from the early 17th century to the present, and including examples by almost every artist of importance working during that time. Formed over a number of decades during the course of the 20th century, the collection is substantially the result of gifts and bequests made during the late 1930s and early 1940s by Dr Percy Withers, and during the early 1950s by Joseph Knight, followed in 1960 by the transference of a number of fine examples which had been collected by the History of Art Department of the University of Manchester. Dr Withers was a master at Manchester Grammar School from 1888 to 1892, as was Joseph Knight some time later. Knight was a Governor of the Whitworth and from 1900 to 1930 headmaster of the Bury School of Art; an artist in his own right he was much influenced by the use of colour in Japanese prints.

One work which has always been especially popular at the Whitworth Art Gallery is the stunning triptych *Ryuko Ai Shitate* ('Fashionable Blue: Concert on a Balcony') by Keisai

Eisen (1790–1848). The three sheets, each printed in a range
of tones of the richest blue, show two elaborately dressed
oiran, or senior courtesans, attended by young girls, or
kamuro, who are making origami paper models. They are
listening to the playing and singing of four other women,
ranged against the background of a busy river, the blue flush
of the sky beyond the distant shore suggesting the fading
light of evening. Some Japanese prints are usually on display
although an appointment to see more should be made by
writing in advance. *Open Monday–Saturday 10am–5pm,
Thursday 10am–9pm.*

MILNTHORPE

(181) Dallam Tower, Milnthorpe, Cumbria
(Tel: 05395 63368)

Dallam Tower is owned by Brigadier C.E. Tryon-Wilson
whose family has been connected with the area since the 13th
century. The house and magnificent gardens are just 200
yards from Milnethorpe which was Westmorland's only
port until 1853. Part of the garden was laid out in Japanese
style in 1930. There are Japanese bridges, pools and cascades
and shrubs and trees including a *Cryptomeria japonica* nearly
100 feet high. The gardens are open to the public several
times a year in aid of the National Gardens Scheme. *Milnthorpe is 7 miles south of Kendal and 7 miles north of Carnforth,
near junction of the A6 and B5282. Four miles from Arnside
station.*

(182) The Lady Lever Art Gallery, Port Sunlight
Village, Wirral (Tel: 051-645 3623/645 7888)

The Lady Lever Art Gallery has a small collection of
porcelain with examples of 17th century Arita, 18th century
Imari and 19th century Hirado pieces. There is also a horse
tackle and trappings of wood, lacquer, brass, leather and
cloth believed to have been acquired by Lord Lever during
his only visit to Japan for two weeks in 1913. See also: [194].
Open Monday–Saturday 10am–5pm, Sunday 2pm–5pm.

PRESTON

(183) Harris Museum and Art Gallery, Market Square, Preston, Lancashire (Tel: 0772-58248)

The Harris Museum and Art Gallery has a small Japanese collection including enamel vases, lacquer ware, *tsuba*, *netsuke*, some export porcelain and a *Noh* theatre mask of a young girl. *Open Monday–Saturday 10am–5pm.*

RIVINGTON

(184) Rivington Terraced Gardens, Lever Park, Rivington, Lancashire

William Hesketh Lever was born in Bolton in 1851, the son of a prosperous local wholesale grocer. Lord Leverhulme, as he was to become, founded the Lever Brothers Empire (now the Unilever Organisation) and in 1900 purchased the Manor of Rivington and began the development of the estate. By 1920, Lord Leverhulme had spent some £250,000 on the work, including replacing his original timber residence which was burnt down by a suffragette in 1913 while he was away dining with the King. The most famous and dramatic feature of Rivington Terraced Gardens was not begun until 1922, when the landscape architect T.H. Mawson created a Japanese garden, consisting of tea-houses, lanterns, pagodas,

The waterfall in the Japanese garden – 'the most famous and dramatic feature' of Rivington Terraced Gardens [184]

'A Japanese area on a Lancashire estate': Rivington Terraced Gardens [184]

bridges, miniature waterfalls complemented with plant species from Japan and a one acre lake. Lord Leverhulme had visited Japan in 1913 to inspect his company's soap factory at Tori Shinden in the Inland Sea, and although only there for a fortnight at the end of October on business he did have a little free time to appreciate the beautiful autumn colours. One day he took the staff of the soap factory on a picnic to Morimo, a beauty spot famous for its maples half an hour by tram outside Osaka, and this experience could well have influenced his decision to incorporate a Japanese area on his Lancashire estate. After his death in 1925, Rivington gradually fell into disrepair and the lanterns, tea rooms and pagodas were all vandalized. Now owned by the North West Water Authority, the Terraced Gardens have been restored and a self-guided nature trail includes the Japanese garden. *Rivington Terraced Gardens is in Lever Park just north of Junction 6 of the M61.*

ROCHDALE

(185) 147 Drake Street, Rochdale, Lancashire

This was the family home of John Milne, the world famous seismologist. He was actually born in his grandmother's house at Mount Vernon Place, Liverpool [173] but the family moved back here when he was three weeks old. The house, near the corner of Milkstone Road, appears unchanged today. The young John had little distance to travel to his first school. Run by a Miss Fisher, it was then a Dame School in Milkstone Road. For main Milne entry, see: [78].

(186) Rochdale Library Local Studies Department, Area Central Library, Esplanade, Rochdale, Lancashire (Tel: 0706 47474)

The Local Studies Department here has a fascinating photographic record of Meiji Japan. Richard Heape, a wealthy local businessman, set off on a Grand Tour in the 1870s visiting Egypt, India, Australia and the Far East. Whether he took photographs himself or purchased prints as he visited places of interest is not known, but the department has eight photographic albums of his tour, including one of Japan and China. Altogether there are 48 photographs of Japan and Japanese lifestyles taken between 1874 and 1876, including a pedlar selling pots and pans, a barber dressing the hair of a top-knotted samurai and a *daimyo* getting into a palanquin.

ROSSENDALE

(187) Rossendale Museum, Whitaker Park, Rawtenstall, Rossendale, Lancashire (Tel: 0706-217777/226509)

Rossendale Museum has a few Japanese items in its collection, including a drawing on silk done around 1800, examples of footwear (*geta* and *tabi*), some porcelain and a cake stand. *Open Monday–Friday 1pm–5pm, Saturday 10am–12 noon, 1pm–5pm, Sunday (April–October) 2pm–4pm. Groups at other times by arrangement. Sunday April–October 1pm–5pm, November–March 1pm–4pm.*

ST HELENS

(188) The Museum and Art Gallery, College Street, St Helens, Merseyside (Tel: 0744-24061)

St Helens Museum has a small collection of Japanese items – bronzes, ceramics and textiles, mainly from the 19th century. The textiles are silks acquired from the Horniman Museum and others donated in the 1960s by a Mrs Gamble, a St Helen's resident whose family had lived in Japan. The bronzes include a pair of vases showing *Shoriken* (the Japanese pronounciation of the Taoist immortal *Chung-li Ch'uan*) walking on water.

TATTENHALL

(189) The Rectory, Tattenhall, Cheshire

In 1834, when the future author and traveller, Isabella Bird (1831–1904) was three years old, her father was forced to give up his position as curate in the busy Reading parish to become the Rector of Tattenhall. The major part of the Tattenhall Rectory is much the same as it was, except that about a third of the Regency style building has been demolished.

It was a quiet comfortable parish, with a good living of £300 a year and with the Birds' cousin, the bishop, on hand whenever his influence was needed. Everything might have stayed that way if it hadn't been for the Reverend Bird's attitude to Sunday Observance.

Many of Rector Bird's Cheshire parishioners had long practised Sunday cheese-making and its abolition became the rector's personal crusade. Instead of changing local traditions, however, he managed to drive his flock away. So in 1842, with little left to do in Tattenhall, he looked around for a place where sin and vice could be confronted. There were lots of both in crowded, noisy St Thomas's in Birmingham [106], to where he next moved his family. The salary was a miserable £60 a year. For the main Isabella Bird entry, see: [133]. *Tattenhall is a village seven miles south-east of Chester.*

WARRINGTON

(190) Warrington Library, Museum Street (Tel: 0925-751232); Warrington Museum and Art Gallery, Bold Street, Warrington, Cheshire (Tel: 0925-30550/44400)

The Library has a collection of 57 Japanese wood engravings by Kunisada, Kunichika, Kuniyashi, Yashitori and Kamiaki purchased around 1910 from a dealer. The Museum has three collections with Japanese associations. One consists of swords, fine arts and household items; the second is of Oriental silks, including Japanese; and the third is an ethnographic collection including some items from Japan. *Museum open Monday–Friday 10am–5.30pm, Saturday 10am–5pm. Closed bank holidays.*

12 | *Wales*

ABERYSTWYTH

(191) Aberystwyth Arts Centre, University College of Wales, Penglais Road, Aberystwyth, Dyfed (Tel: 0970–623232)

There can have been few more propitious times than 1919 for starting a ceramics collection. It was the same year that the meeting took place in Japan between Shoji Hamada and Bernard Leach [100]. It was also the beginning of a decade that changed the way East and West looked at the art of the potter.

The Aberystwyth collection began with a £5,000 bequest from two wealthy spinster sisters, Margaret and Gwendoline Davies. The man appointed as consulting curator was Sydney Greenslade, architect of the Welsh National Library but better known as a passionate collector of ceramics and glass. Greenslade had the knack of being able to spot the master-potter-to-come and acquired for the gallery representative examples of all of Leach's early work. He roamed the galleries, countrywide, and brought back two rare pieces from Hamada's first exhibition in Britain, at the Paterson Gallery in 1923.

This unique collection of the University College of Wales Aberystwyth, is housed in the Aberystwyth Arts Centre. It eventually included examples from the entire movement. The first Straite Murray joined the collection in 1921, a Bernard Leach in 1922, a Michael Cardew in 1928 and a K.P. Bouverie in 1929. Invariably, it was the first flowering of each potter's production. The result you see today is a collection of over 400 pieces, representative of the best of

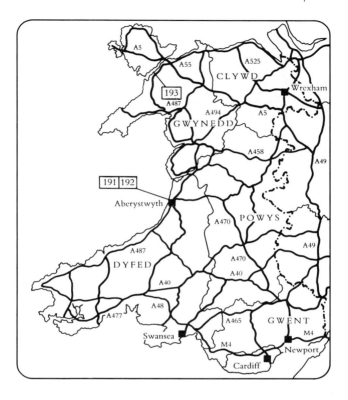

WALES

both Japanese and European potters of the period. *Open Monday–Saturday 10am–5pm and evenings.*

(192) The National Library of Wales, Penglais Road, Aberystwyth, Dyfed (Tel: 0970-623816)

Perhaps the most significant Japan-related item in The National Library of Wales is a collection of Japanese albums and addresses presented to the Prince of Wales (later Edward VIII) during his tour of Japan, in April and May 1922.

The papers of Lord Rendel include correspondence from various liberal politicians relating to Japanese foreign policy during the late 19th century. There is also a collection of

'Japan's most renowned potter', Shoji Hamada [100] made this 'Chrysanthemum bowl' in 1923: University College of Wales [191]

some 400 books and periodicals (most in English, some in Japanese) relating to the history and literature of Japan. These were purchased from the library of Professor Whitfield (1899–1974), who succeeded Edmund Blunden [127] as Professor of English Literature in the University of Tokyo from 1931–1934. A recent addition, the papers of the scientist Sir Benjamin Davies, include a scrap book of press cuttings on Japanese international relations 1931–1939.

CAENARFON

(193) Caenarfon, Gwynedd

As a small boy, the author Lafcadio Hearn (1850–1904) was brought here on holiday by his great-aunt, Mrs Brenane. In the cottage of a seaman from the China run, the young Hearn would sit for hours among the sailor's collection of grotesque objects and statues of Oriental gods and hear strange stories of the mysterious Orient. At night, Hearn would dream about them and vowed one day he would go East. For main Hearn entry, see: [232].

13 | *Scotland*

ABERDEEN

(194) Aberdeen Art Gallery, School Hill, Aberdeen, Grampian (Tel: 0224-646333)

The art gallery has a small collection of Japanese items including soapstone, ivory and wood carvings, *netsuke*, lacquered boxes (including a brush box), a lacquered quiver, sword guards, some parts of Japanese armour, a miniature ivory cabinet, a ball-shaped incense burner and a figure of the Buddha painted in the 18th century.

Among the print collection is a small group of Japanese 19th century prints, including examples by Toyokuni, Gakutai, Kuniyoshi and Kunichika. For ornithologists there is a bound volume of bird studies. *Open Monday–Wednesday, Friday and Saturday 10am–5pm, Thursday 10am–8pm, Sunday 2pm–5pm.*

(195) Alexander Hall Shipyard, Aberdeen, Grampian

When the American Commodore Matthew Perry and his Black Ships steamed into Edo Bay in 1853 he effectively pulled Japan out of its feudal isolation and into the modern world. Over the next decades Japan scrambled to catch up with the West and looked to America and Europe for role models and technical expertise – a Prussian constitution was adopted, a French legal code, an American/German education system and a British navy. The Imperial Naval College in Japan was founded in 1872.

Over 100 years ago shipbuilding was thriving in Aberdeen. After the Meiji Restoration in 1868, three warships

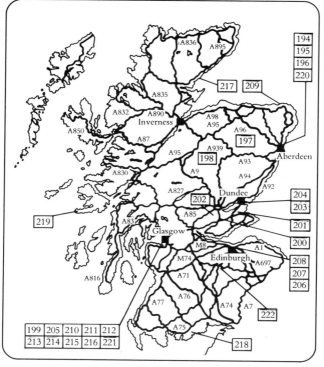

SCOTLAND

were built at the Alexander Hall shipyard for the modern Japanese navy. Two of these, the *Ho-Sho-Maru* and the *Wen-Yu-Maru*, were small gunboats and the third, the *Jho-Sho-Maru*, was a 1,500-ton steam ram armed with two 110-pounder guns and eight 64 pounders. The Glover brothers [209] who had various business interests in Scotland and Japan, were the agents for bringing these naval orders to Aberdeen. One of the Hall family died in Japan while training the Japanese seamen how to operate these ships. The Hall shipyard closed in 1958.

A number of sailing ships were built at Aberdeen for trade with Japan – the *Owari*, the *Kagoshima*, the *Helen Black* and the *Satzuma*. Also built in the city was a patent slip dock which was installed at Nagasaki and may have been part of the equipment used when Mitsubishi was set up.

(196) Duthie Park, between George VI and Queen Elizabeth Bridges, Aberdeen, Grampian

Duthie Park's Japanese garden was formally opened by the Japanese Ambassador to Britain, His Excellency Toshio Yamazaki, in June 1987. Designed by landscape architect Takashi Sawano, who was trained in Japan but is now based in London, the garden contains a man-made stream meandering between rock pools with stone bridges leading to a pond. Nearby is a *yukimi-doro* (a snow-viewing lantern). The wisteria trellis or *fuji-dana* and small fences have all been built the traditional way with bamboo tied with coarse sisal giving the garden an authentic look. The design and choice of plants is intended to foster peace as the garden is a memorial to the 210,873 people who died in Hiroshima and Nagasaki when atom bombs were dropped in 1945. The outline of the water's edge is the shape of the Chinese character *kokoro*, meaning 'heart' and according to Japanese symbolism the pine tree on the island and the camellia, wisteria and bamboo all speak of endless peace. All the plants and trees are of Japanese origin – Japanese maples, flowering cherries, bamboo, rhododendron, azalea – and give some colour all year round.

'The design and choice of plants are intended to foster peace':
Duthie Park's Japanese garden [196]

Inside the adjacent Winter Garden conservatories (the largest indoor garden in Europe) is a small dry landscape garden called *kare-sansui*, built mostly in stone and gravel and using only a few plants. The origin of such a garden lies in Zen Buddhism and its simplicity and symbolism is meant to encourage meditation. The composition of trees, pruned shrubs, rocks, and gravel symbolizes the natural scenery of mountains, valleys and islands. The gravel is raked into different patterns to represent the waves in their different aspects.

A feature of the garden is a *shishi-odoshi*, or deer frightener. This is a device invented many years ago by farmers to scare off animals and birds that damaged crops. Water flows along the short section of the bamboo pipe. When the section becomes full, the weight tips the open end down emptying the water. The closed end then swings quickly down and strikes a log or stone. The noise is supposed to startle the deer and they quickly depart. *Duthie Park is on the left (north) bank of the Dee between King George VI and Queen Elizabeth bridges. Open all year.*

ALFORD

(197) Japanese Water Garden, Kildrummy Castle, Alford, Grampian (Tel: 09755 71331)

Once Japan's self-imposed isolation had come to an end in the middle of the last century, Western visitors began arriving to trade, teach and look around. Writers of the time tended to eulogize the quaintness of Japan – the Fuji, fan and cherry blossom approach of Gilbert and Sullivan's *Mikado*. Even though the operetta hardly offered profound insights into the real Japan, it helped to foster an interest in Britain in all things Japanese. One of the ways that wealthy landowners could capture the 'mysterious and exotic East' was to create a Japanese garden and soon there were a number of Japanese gardeners arriving in Britain to give it an authentic touch.

This seems to have been the case at Kildrummy Castle where estate records show that Japanese landscape gardeners were hired to construct the Japanese Water Garden. Colonel James Ogston, a soap manufacturer, purchased the Kildrummy estate in 1898. Leaving the 13th century castle as a splendid ruin, he built an English Tudor-style house to live in and worked on the Water Garden between 1902 and 1904. *Kildrummy Gardens Trust is located in the grounds of Kildrummy Castle on the A97 just off the A994 from Aberdeen. 1 April–31 October open daily 9am–5pm.*

BLAIR ATHOLL

(198) Blair Castle, Atholl Estates Office, Blair Atholl, Pitlochry, Perthshire (Tel: 079681-355/6/7)

The ancestral home of the Dukes of Atholl has a number of Japanese connections. Among items on display in Blair Castle is a suit of 18th century Japanese horse soldier's armour and a number of matchlock guns made in Japan around 1800. The castle also has mementoes of various visits made to it by the Imperial family. In appreciation of the hospitality given to him and his party by the 8th Duke on his visit to Britain in 1921, Crown Prince Hirohito awarded him The Order of the Rising Sun (7th Class). The future emperor also planted a copper beech, which can be seen in the grounds, and went fishing. Writing to thank the Duke for showing the Crown Prince something of what life was like in the Highlands, the then Foreign Secretary Lord Curzon ended his letter to the Duke by saying: 'If I may say so I think that your biggest achievement was having a handy salmon in a handy pool which (if the newspaper reports are to be believed) impaled itself at the correct moment on the Crown Prince's fly'. Emperor Hirohito's son, Crown Prince Akihito (now Emperor Akihito) also enjoyed the hospitality of the Dukes of Atholl in 1953 and 1976 but the trees planted on these occasions failed to survive the harsh Scottish winter. *Blair Castle is seven miles north of Pitlochry, just outside Blair Atholl off the A9. Open Easter weekend and 1 May to second Sunday in October 10am–6pm, Sunday 2pm–6pm, July–August 12 noon–6pm.*

BOTHWELL

(199) Bothwell, near Hamilton, Strathclyde

Henry Dyer, the engineer, who was the first principal of

Tokyo Engineering College, was born in Bothwell. For main entry on Dyer, see: [216].

BRIDGE OF EARN

(200) Condie, Bridge of Earn, Tayside

At Condie was the ancestral home of the Oliphant family. Laurence Oliphant worked in the diplomatic service and was instrumental in setting up a trading agreement with Japan as secretary to Lord Elgin [205]. Although he never owned Condie, Oliphant often went there on holiday. For main entry on Oliphant, see: [60].

CUPAR

(201) Hill of Tarvit Mansion, Cupar, Fife (Tel: 0334 53127)

Owned by the National Trust, Hill of Tarvit Mansion has a museum with a handful of Japanese items – some 17th century Japanese chargers, 19th century porcelain and a few bronzes. *Located two and a half miles south of Cupar off the A916. 1 May–31 October 2pm–6pm. April weekends only 2pm–6pm.*

DOLLAR

(202) Cowden Castle, Dollar, Central; Muckhart Churchyard, Muckhart, Central

At one time Ella Christie's Japanese garden at Cowden was described as the best in the Western world but today, and sadly, it is uncared for and a number of the shrines and tea-houses have been vandalized.

The garden was the creation of the rich, eccentric, peripatetic Miss Ella Christie, the daughter of a Lanarkshire mineowner who had bought Cowden castle and estate in the middle of the 19th century. In 1906 Ella Christie embarked on a Far East tour which included Japan. 'Beyond my castle', Miss Christie wrote, 'was a marshy field, watered by a stream, with a backdrop of a misty mountain'. When

'Rich, eccentric, peripatetic': Ella Christie's garden at Cowden Castle [202]

visiting Kyoto and the famous temple gardens, the entranced Miss Christie decided there and then what she was going to do with her Scottish bog. She lost no time in commissioning Taki Honda, a lady graduate from the Imperial School of Garden Design in Nagoya, who arrived in Scotland in 1907 with her tools and equipment and began by damming the stream. In six weeks Taki Honda created the basic design. After she had returned to Japan, Miss Christie and her head forester continued to work on the garden; periodically a Professor Suzuki, an adviser to Kew Gardens, came to Cowden to oversee the project. It was this professor, who had the remarkable title, Eighteenth Hereditary Head of the Soami School of Imperial Design, who told Miss Christie that there wasn't a Japanese garden outside Japan to touch hers.

In 1925, Professor Suzuki found a Japanese gardener to work full time for Miss Christie. A small, gnome-like figure who had lost his family in an earthquake, he was known only as Matsuo and was to spend the rest of his life at Cowden. His presence in a rural Scottish community in the early years of this century was sufficient inspiration for a number of colourful stories.

After her treks in Tibet, India, Japan, China and elsewhere, Ella Christie was already referred to as the female Marco Polo of Scotland and was known to have an exotic circle of international friends. There was, therefore, little reason to doubt the rumour that the strange new Oriental face at Cowden was none other than the Japanese emperor himself. 'Incognito, of course!' it was whispered.

The Christie family's mausoleum, with gardener Matsuo's tomb in front (left of centre): Muckhart Churchyard [202]

Soon after visiting London to meet a Japanese embroideress with a view to marriage (Professor Suzuki was the matchmaker), Matsuo became ill and died in October 1937. The local paper, the *Alloa Advertiser*, said that with his death 'a kenspeckle figure has been removed from the Dollar district' ('kenspeckle' is a Scottish word meaning easily recognized or conspicuous). Matsuo is buried in Muckhart Churchyard, just to the left of the Christie family mausoleum where his employer, Miss Ella Christie, was laid to rest 11 years later.

The Cowden Japanese garden was very famous in its day – Queen Mary visited it in 1938 and it was periodically open to the public. But with Miss Christie gone, the garden lost its mentor. The Victorian and Edwardian age which had funded it had long disappeared and 20th century governments came to exact high taxes and higher death duties from owners of Scottish castles. In recent years the present owner, Robert Stewart, has been attempting to get planning permission and financial help to restore his great aunt's garden. So far he has been unsuccessful. Without support, one of the greatest Japanese gardens outside Japan must inexorably revert to

Scottish countryside. *Cowden is just off the A91 between Dollar and Muckhart.*

DUNDEE

(203) District Archive and Record Office, City Chambers, Dundee, Tayside

There are general references to Japanese trade in the records of Dundee Chamber of Commerce lodged in the District Archive and Record Office. In the correspondence of the Reid family are references to Ludwig Janson who became a POW when fighting against the Japanese in the Russo–Japanese War 1904–05.

(204) 17 Bright Street, Lochee, Dundee, Tayside

Neil Gordon Monro (1863–1942) was born in Woodbine Cottage (now 17 Bright Street) in 1863. He went to Japan as a medical missionary and studied Japanese archaeology in his spare time. In 1908 he wrote *Prehistoric Japan* and in the 1930s carried out important work among the Ainu. He donated his collection of Japanese prehistoric pottery vessels, stone implements and metal work to the Royal Scottish Museum [208].

DUNFERMLINE

(205) Dunfermline Abbey; Broomhall, Dunfermline, Fife (Tel: 0383-872222)

In Dunfermline Abbey, there is a memorial to the 8th Earl of Elgin in the Bruce Aisle. A direct descendant of Robert the Bruce, James Bruce was the second son of the Lord who gave his name to the Greek Marbles now in the British Museum. Like his father, James devoted his life to public service. Born in London in 1811, he went to Eton and Oxford and in 1841 was elected to the House of Commons. After serving as governor of Jamaica and governor-general of Canada, the 8th Earl of Elgin and 12th Earl of Kincardine was sent by the government as envoy to China in 1857. The following year he went to Japan and in less than a month of extraordinary diplomatic activity, secured a treaty which opened certain ports to British trade and admitted foreigners into the country. His secretary at this time was another Scotsman, Laurence Oliphant, whose ancestral home was Condie, near the Bridge of Earn on Tayside [200]. Lord Elgin conducted the negotiations through a third party – the only common language was Dutch so he borrowed American Consul-General Townsend Harris's secretary, a Dutchman called Heusken, to act as intermediary and the treaty itself was written in Dutch. Although he was in Japan in August, the hottest part of the year, he was impressed with the civility, good temper and cleanliness of the Japanese and concluded: 'My trip to Japan has been a green spot in the desert of my mission to the East'. Lord Elgin was offered the appointment of Viceroy and Governor-General of India (the highest diplomatic honour of that time) and died of a heart attack while crossing a makeshift bridge over a river in the foothills of the Himalayas. He is buried at the little Anglican church at Dharmasala, near Simla but there is a more elaborate memorial to him in the Anglican cathedral in Calcutta. A copy of that memorial is on the wall of a room at Broomhall, the family home which is not open to the public, but, within reason, a visiting party can be entertained.

EDINBURGH

(206) The Central Library, George IV Bridge, Edinburgh (Tel: 031-225 5584)

The Central Library has a Dyer Collection presented in 1945 by Miss M. Dyer, daughter of Henry. The collection includes Japanese prints and watercolours, scrolls and the two Orders given to him by the Japanese government with authorization to wear the same signed by Queen Victoria. For main Dyer entry, see: [216]. *Open Monday–Friday 9am–9pm, Saturday 9am–1pm. Written application to Mrs Norma Armstrong, Head of Information Services, to view the collection.*

(207) 18 Melville Street; Dean Cemetery, 63 Dean Path, Edinburgh

Unlike many who wrote about their experiences of Meiji Japan, Isabella Bird's account is not of the breathless,

'Only one thing could still her travels': the house in Melville Street where Isabella Bird died [207]

gushing isn't-it-quaint variety. *Unbeaten Tracks in Japan: An Account of Travels in the Interior including visits to the Aborigines of Yezo and the Shrine of Nikko* is an important record of what life was like off the beaten track in the late 19th century. The book has been reprinted by Charles E Tuttle. Isabella Bird died at 18 Melville Street and is buried in Dean Cemetery in Section M, number 22 in the old part of the cemetery. For main Isabella Bird entry, see: [133]. *The cemetery is at 63 Dean Path which is off the Queensferry Road, about a mile from Edinburgh's West End. The cemetery is open to visitors 9am–5pm (or dusk).*

(208) The Royal Museum of Scotland, Chambers Street, Edinburgh (Tel: 031–225 7534)

The Royal Museum of Scotland has some Japanese items of outstanding interest including some unique Japanese antiquities from the Munro Collection [204]. Artefacts from the pre-Buddhist age (before AD 538) include two Haniwa horses. Many of the best pieces – *netsuke*, swords and sword furniture, Ainu material, *cloisonné*, musical instruments – can be found on the second floor balcony of the Main Hall in the Oriental Gallery. *Open Monday–Saturday 10am–5pm, Sunday 2pm–5pm.*

A red earthenware horse, 4th–5th century AD – a Haniwa figure which was included in the grave furnishings of the early historic period: Royal Museum of Scotland [208]

FRASERBURGH

(209) Commerce Street, Fraserburgh, Grampian

Thomas Glover was born in Fraserburgh in 1838, the fifth son of Thomas Berry, a civilian chief officer to the Coast Guard, and Mary Glover – see also: [195]. He went to school in Saltoun Place and later attended Channonry House School in Old Aberdeen. Glover is best known as a merchant trader who first went to Japan in 1859. During the 1860s he was involved in a number of business ventures, mainly in Nagasaki. His much-visited residence there is believed to be the oldest Western-style house in Japan – known, somewhat enigmatically, as Madame Butterfly's house.

Kanagawa (now Yokohama), Nagasaki and Hakodate were the three treaty ports opened to trade in 1859 following Lord Elgin's visit [205] as a result of the commercial treaties with the United States, Holland, Britain, Russia and France.

Thomas Glover was one of a number of adventurous men who arrived at this time with little or no capital but a gambling spirit. He established his own company and his first major business was the export of Japanese tea to England using Jardine Matheson ships. By 1863 he was employing over 1,000 Japanese in the tea business.

From 1864 to 1867, Glover & Co, in which two of his brothers were now also involved, was the largest Western firm in Nagasaki. Thomas Glover was prospering through arms dealing. The domestic political tumult of Japan in the late Tokugawa period offered great opportunities for a firm of flexible independent merchants. Glover & Co sold ships, arms and ammunition to the Bakufu and those domains that supported the shogunate as well as to those domains like Satsuma, Choshu and Hizen which were anti–Bakufu and pressing for the reforms that eventually led to the Meiji Restoration.

Orders for ships were passed through Glover Brothers founded by his brother Charles. The *Ho-Sho-Maru* from the Alexander Hall shipyard in Aberdeen was a 350 ton gunboat launched in July 1868 destined for the Choshu domain. The much bigger *Jho-Sho-Maru* at 1,500 tons was constructed for the Higo domain and sold at a price of 360,000 Mexican dollars, the currency used for trading in Japan in those days.

Between 1868 and 1870 Glover & Co faced serious finan-

A wooden gong in the shape of a fish – from a collection of old musical instruments at the Royal Museum of Scotland [208]

cial difficulties. This was the result both of rapid expansion during the arms dealing period and changes in domestic Japanese politics. The stability of the Meiji Restoration had replaced the civil war.

In 1870 Thomas Glover was declared bankrupt. He stayed in Japan and worked at the Takashima coal mine until 1877 by which time all his debts had been paid off. He then went to work in Tokyo as consultant to Mitsubishi and died there of Bright's disease in December 1911 at the age of 73.

GLASGOW

(210) The Burrell Collection, Pollock Country Park, Glasgow, Strathclyde (Tel: 041-649 7151)

The Burrell Collection has a small collection of Japanese art – about 30 woodblock prints, mainly *surimono* and *bijin-e* including works by Utamaro and Hokusai. *Open Monday– Saturday 10am–5pm, Wednesday late opening till 9pm, Sunday 12 noon–6pm.*

(211) Glasgow Art Gallery and Museum, Kelvingrove, Glasgow, Strathclyde (Tel: 041-357 3929)

The Art Gallery and Museum has an outstanding collection of Japanese items. These include arms, armour and archery equipment; fine lacquerware of the 18th and 19th centuries; large pieces of furniture as well as boxes; Buddhist images in bronze and lacquer; pipes and all smoking utensils; musical instruments collected by Henry Dyer [216] and textiles, including clothes worn by *daimyo* (feudal lords).

Probably the most important collection historically is that sent by the Japanese government in 1878 [213]. Over 1,150 specimens represent every art and craft known in Japan at that date. It is a time capsule taken at the beginning of Japan's industrialization and could never be repeated. The name of the artist and the province from which the object comes has been entered in the records. The collection was an exchange for manufactures and paintings from Glasgow and the West of Scotland. The Japanese prints from the Edo era are not often on public display – visitors who wish to see them are advised to write or phone for an appointment. *Open Monday–Saturday 10am–5pm, Sunday 2pm–5pm.*

(212) Glasgow University Library and Hunterian Art Gallery, Hillhead Street, Glasgow, Strathclyde (Tel: 041–339 8855)

The University Library has a miscellaneous collection of Japanese material, including Engelbert Kaempfer's *History of Japan* translated by J. Scheuchzer, published London 1728, two volumes with 45 plates and an album of 48 Japanese

Girl Sealing a Loveletter from Tosei Bijin Awase – colour woodcut by Kunisada: Hunterian Art Gallery [212]

Fireworks over Bridge from 'Cinsen' – woodcut by Shuntosai: Hunterian Art Gallery [212]

lithographs illustrating the Russo–Japanese war. For more on Kaempfer's collection, see: [7]. Among the papers of the American artist James McNeil Whistler (the largest collection in existence) is correspondence, mainly from the 1860s, relating to the response of Whistler and his circle to Japanese art and artefacts.

The Hunterian Art Gallery at the university was bequeathed Whistler's significant collection of Japanese works of art by his sister–in–law Rosalind Birnie Philip. Whistler was one of the first artists working in Europe to collect Oriental art. During his time in Paris where he trained as a painter he was introduced to Japanese prints and porcelain. Whistler acquired a screen (now in the gallery) painted by the contemporary woman artist Nampo Jhoshi. On the back of this he stretched two pieces of paper on which he painted one of his first nocturnes *Blue and Silver: Screen, with Old Battersea Bridge* in 1872. Its composition is directly influenced by Japanese prints. Whistler's print collection included works by Shuncho, Hiroshige, Hokusai, Kiyonaga and Toyokuni and a book of woodcuts by Shuntosai. Of the over 300 pieces of blue and white porcelain in Whistler's collection dating from the 17th to the 19th century, a number of Japanese works are on permanent display.

The gallery also owns another small group of Japanese woodcuts from the Gilbert Innes Collection. These include works by Kunisada, Yeisen, Shunshi and Shunzan.

The gallery also has the largest collection anywhere of the furniture and designs of the celebrated Scottish architect Charles Rennie Mackintosh [213] and contains the reconstructed main rooms of his last residence in Glasgow at 74 Southpark Avenue. Japanese influence can immediately be recognized in his manipulation of space and light in interiors and his orchestration of contrasting visual and spatial effects. The Mackintosh Wing may be closed at certain times and parties must book in advance. *Open Monday–Friday 10am–11.30am and 12.30pm–5pm, Saturday 9.30am–1pm.*

(213) The Charles Rennie Mackintosh Society, Queens Cross, 870 Garscube Road, Glasgow, Strathclyde (Tel: 041-946 6600)

The society was established in 1973 to foster interest in the work of the great Glasgow-born architect. Mackintosh (1848–1928) grew up and received his architectural training in the city. He became interested in Japanese art and his

Ladies at a Picnic – colour woodcut by Kiyonaga: Hunterian Art Gallery [212]

architectural work and painting show considerable Japanese influence.

Mackintosh was particularly influenced by Christopher Dresser, another Glaswegian, who published his influential book *Japan, its Architecture, Art and Art Manufactures* in 1882 and lectured in the city. At the same time an exhibition of Japanese decorative arts took place and Dresser used items from there as illustration. As early as 1878 Glasgow had received a gift from the Japanese government of ceramics, textiles and paper, as a result of Dresser's own visit to Japan.

Mackintosh and his wife were very interested in flower arranging. An 1896 photo of their flat at 27 Regent Park Square shows an *ikebana* display and a number of Japanese prints. Every single item in the flat was designed by Mackintosh. Its spaciousness, and lightness, and calmness gives an impression of a Japanese interior. There is a Japanese branch of the Charles Rennie Mackintosh Society which regularly publishes a newsletter. The society's Glasgow headquarters are in a building designed by Mackintosh, the only major building for church purposes designed by him which was actually built. *Open Tuesday, Thursday and Friday 12 noon–5.30pm, Sunday 2.30pm–5pm or by arrangement with the Honorary Secretary.*

(214) The Mitchell Library, North Street, Glasgow, Strathclyde (Tel: 041–221 7030)

The Mitchell Library is the largest reference library in Scotland and it contains Japanese albums, some *kakemono* and a most important 18th century *e-makimono*, executed about 1710 and depicting the history of the 12th century Prince Yoshitsune. These three scrolls form part of the Dyer Bequest given in 1924 and 1927 – see: [216]. *Open Monday– Friday 9.30am–9pm, Saturday 9.30am–5pm.*

(215) The Museum of Transport, 25 Albert Drive, Glasgow, Strathclyde (Tel: 041-357 3929)

The museum has a number of model ships and one locomotive relating to Japan. The *Sazanami* was built in 1898 and 1899 by Yarrow & Co for the Imperial Japanese Navy and is one of 18 *Akebono* class TS destroyers built between 1898 and 1905. The ship took part in the Battle of the Sea of Japan during the war with Russia 1904–05 and captured the commander of the Russian fleet, Admiral Rodjesvenski. Another model is of the single screw cargo vessel *Saikio Maru* built in 1888 by the London & Glasgow S&E Co Ltd for Nippon Yusen Kaisha, today more usually known as the shipping company NYK. The model train is a 2-Co-Co-2 Express Passenger Locomotive built by the North British Locomotive Co, Glasgow. These locomotives had a top speed of 95 mph and eight were supplied to Japan in 1924. *Open all year 10am–5pm, Sunday 2pm–5pm, except 25 December, 1 January.*

(216) Strathclyde University Archives, McCance Building, 16 Richmond Street (Tel: 041-552 4400); 52 Highburgh Road; The Mitchell Library, North Street (Tel: 041-221 7030); The Necropolis, Glasgow, Strathclyde

Born at Bothwell, near Hamilton in Strathclyde in 1848 [199], Henry Dyer studied engineering in the evening at Anderson's College (later to become part of Strathclyde University) in Glasgow while serving an apprenticeship with a marine engineer in the daytime. Dyer later went to Glasgow University and graduated with an MA and DSc, the first student in Scotland to take a doctorate in engineering.

Dyer was at Anderson's College at the same time as a young Japanese named Yozo Yamao who was working in Napier's shipyard in the daytime and attending the college in the evening. Yamao and four other samurai of the Choshu clan (including Hirobumi Ito, later to become prime minister) first arrived in Britain in 1863 – see also: [34]. William Keswick, of the trading company Jardine Matheson, was a shipping agent in Yokohama at that time and had secretly arranged their trip. When they arrived in London, Hugh Matheson, the head of the company, met them and boarded three of them (including Ito) with Alexander Williamson, the Professor of Chemistry at University College [34].

The young Japanese were expected to learn as much as they could about British teaching institutions in which engineering and other applied sciences had a central place. In 1865, Ito returned to Japan where he played an important role in smoothing the way for the Meiji Restoration. Yamao stayed on and studied in Scotland before returning to Japan in early 1870 and joining the Ministry of Public Works, whose minister Ito had become.

In April 1871, Ito and Yamao drew up plans for an engineering school to train technicians for the execution of public works and the industrialization of Japan. Before his departure to America and Europe as a member of the Iwakura Mission, Ito was briefed to hire up to seven foreign teachers for the proposed college. When the mission arrived in London, Ito contacted Hugh Matheson, who was agent for the Japanese Ministry of Public Works in London. He in turn contacted the Professor of Engineering at Glasgow University, W.J.M. Rankine, who had no hesitation in recommending his most brilliant recent engineering graduate, the 24 year old Henry Dyer.

Dyer spent ten years in Japan as the Principal of the Engineering College. He was awarded the Order of the Rising Sun (third class) – the highest of its kind given to any foreign employee, the Order of the Sacred Treasure (second class) and the title of Honorary Principal for his special service to Japan. He published several books, the most notable being *Dai Nippon: The Britain of the East*, and became known as one of the leading authorities on Japan and its industrial and political development.

Dyer resettled with his family in Glasgow where he continued to act as an agent of the Japanese government and as a friend to the large numbers of Japanese students who came to study engineering in Glasgow. In 1915 he received an Honorary Degree of Doctor of Engineering from Japan and was made an Emeritus Professor of the Imperial University of Tokyo. He died in Glasgow in 1918 at his house 8 Highburgh Terrace (now known as 52 Highburgh Road).

The Mitchell Library houses the Henry Dyer Bequest given by his family in the 1920s. It consists of some 6,000 items with special emphasis on Glasgow and Scotland and on all aspects of Japanese life. There are numerous reading scrolls and *kakemono* or hanging scroll pictures, albums and examples of *ukiyo-e* [214]. Henry Dyer is buried in the Necropolis. Edinburgh's Central Library [206] contains a

Dyer Collection of Japanese prints and watercolours and the two Orders presented by the Japanese government.

GOLSPIE

(217) Dunrobin Castle, Golspie, Sutherland (Tel: 0408-633177)

Dunrobin Castle is the most northerly of Scotland's great houses and has been continuously inhabited since the early 1400s. It is the ancestral home of the Dukes of Sutherland.

In the Queen's Corridor is a painting by John Michael Wright similar to the one held in the Tate Gallery in London. Painted in 1680 and believed to be of Sir Neil O'Neil, 2nd Baronet of Killeleagh (?1658–90) there is a suit of Japanese armour in the foreground. Where did it come from and why was it included?

In 1614 Shogun Ieyasu's son, Hidetada, had sent two suits of Japanese armour to James I and VI, king of England and Scotland which are still in the Tower of London, but the armour in the painting is not identical with either of these. By 1680, when the portrait was painted, Japan had been, except for the small Dutch settlement at Nagasaki, closed to the West for 60 years.

One of Wright's friends was a Jesuit priest who had been sent 'a collection of rareties' including samurai armour from the Jesuits in Japan. This had been sent just prior to the Jesuits' expulsion and the persecution of all Christians in Japan. The painter Wright was also known to have two books from Japan in his own library; these were *A Description of Japan and Siam* published in 1663 and Ferdinando Mendez Pinto's *Voyages and Adventures*. Art historians surmise that O'Neil, the subject of the painting and a notably aggressive Catholic (he was killed at the Battle of the Boyne) may have insisted the armour be included. The savage persecution of Catholics was a notorious fact about contemporary Japan and the armour could show O'Neil as a defender of the Catholic faith, the arms of its persecutors lying like a trophy at his feet. *The castle is half a mile north of Golspie on the A9. Open mid-June–first week in September daily 10.30am–5.30pm.*

KIRKUDBRIGHT

(218) Broughton House, High Street, Kirkudbright, Dumfries and Galloway

This was the home of the artist E.A. Hornel, one of the 'Glasgow Boys' – artists of the Glasgow School of painting recognized as a group between 1880 and 1895 and much influenced by Japanese art – see: [212] and [213]. Hornel spent time in Japan from 1893 to 1894 and again in 1922. The garden at Broughton House was constructed by Hornel to remind him of his time there and a number of the plants were actually brought back from Japan by him.

Hornel went to Japan the first time with his artist friend George Henry. The art dealer Alexander Reid, who had a gallery in Glasgow at 227 West George Street, paid for their trip. Both artists were well established. Hornel described the reasons for their trip as: 'to go to see a reed shaken by the wind. For those acquainted even slightly with Japanese art the words express the spirit and the *motif* of its delicate achievements. Japanese art, rivalling in splendour the greatest art in Europe, the influence of which is now fortunately being felt in all the new movements in Europe, engenders in the artist the desire to see and study the environment out of which this great art sprung, to become personally in touch with the people, to live their life, and discover the source of their inspiration'.

Quite obviously both artists were making a pilgrimage. They consulted Murray's *Guide to Japan* which gave lists of necessary food and clothes viz 'pyjamas with short gaiters are strongly recommended for walking in' and they carried letters of introduction. When they arrived in Japan they tried to fulfil their stated hope of living in the Japanese manner but European visitors were still expected to reside within fixed areas called Concessions. To live among the Japanese, they resorted to the ruse of arranging to be in the employment of a Japanese. For a 'consideration' they went to work for a house agent, supposedly furnishing plans of houses to let. But after some time anti-foreigner feeling manifested itself – some Japanese newspapermen discovered them and conducted a campaign for their removal.

At first they were not worried. Henry wrote: 'Being used to newspaper slating at home, it didn't annoy us much at first. Besides it was in Japanese and that made it hurt less, although it looked dreadfully diagrammatic and scurrilous'. Eventually they were forced to move back, much to Hornel's discomfort, to the Concession 'where every second man you encounter is a missionary, and your rest is chronically broken by the uncongenial clang of the church bells, whose notes are as unmelodious and distressing as the music (so-called) of the Japanese'.

They found the other British people friendly, especially those at the legation. They met 'Earthquake' Milne [78] and experienced small earthquakes regularly. They engaged a cook who, next day, installed a wife, who took in a girl to help. The next week the girl brought her mother and several other dear relatives so that the services of a dozen domestics were obtained and 'Hornel hadn't even to tie his own bootlaces'.

They travelled by rickshaw, which prompted Hornel to worry about the danger of racing rickshaws (shades of Tokyo taxis today) getting their wheels locked and crashing which might have caused, according to Henry, 'a vacancy in the Associateship of the Royal Scottish Academy, and deprived Glasgow of one of its most notable painters'.

Hornel reported on visits to geisha and tea-houses which were particularly painful – at 5 feet 11 inches he could not kneel for long in the Japanese manner. He also found the music of the geisha painful but their dancing sedate and beautiful.

The two artists sought out and mixed with their Japanese counterparts, but this did not prevent them being highly critical of the work they saw. Hornel was saddened when he visited an exhibition of artists working in the traditional style – he saw clever brush strokes which did not express great ideas. Other Japanese artists had gone to study in Europe 'foolishly adopting the tricks of Paris and Munich'. Hornel's view was that these artists had learned their painting but lost their art.

Hornel summed up the situation in a paradox. Countries struggling to free art from the deadly embrace of Academies and Departments of Art and Science were turning to Japan for inspiration. But for their part, the Japanese were turning for inspiration to the Academies and Departments of Art and Science in Europe.

The Japanese print, although universally admired, was in

its death-throes because of the arrival of photography. It found a new subject, the impact of the West on the traditional Japanese way of life. Garish and grotesque works, using analine dyes, were produced showing Japanese sitting stiffly in Western clothes, walking in bustles or using sewing machines. This was not the Japan that Henry and Hornel had come all that distance to visit. In the work that they produced in Japan they scrupulously avoided all reference to Western influences.

The two artists left Japan in May 1894 and arrived back in Britain in July having been away 19 months. Based on his time in Japan, Hornel produced about 40 paintings for Reid's gallery in April 1895. The exhibition was a tremendous success with the *Glasgow Herald* describing it as 'daring, brilliant, original'.

Hornel's description of Japan also describes his pictures. 'I love to remember them as a large and happy family, clattering by in the sunshine with smiling faces and no thought of the morrow, to spend the day mid plum or cherry blossom . . .'. *House, garden and gallery open daily to visitors 11am–1pm and 2pm–5pm. Access to the library by prior arrangement with the Honorary Librarian.*

MULL

(219) Tobermory Memorial Clock; Torosay Castle Japanese Garden, Mull

Tobermory Memorial Clock has a pagoda-like look to it and was erected in 1905 in memory of Henrietta Amelia Bird with funds bequeathed by her sister Isabella. For the main entry on Isabella Bird, see: [133].

Torosay Castle Japanese Garden is a 1982 addition to the main garden which is about 11 acres, part Italian and part water garden. The Japanese part uses loose gravel and rocks and includes an arched red wooden bridge and a pagoda with other Japanese ornaments and lanterns. It was designed by Lt Col A.G. Miller DSO, a trustee of the Torosay estate, and based on his visit to Japan made in 1960 and, in particular, his visits to gardens in Kyoto. *Open all year round.*

MUCHALLS

(220) Muchalls, near Aberdeen, Grampian

Following the treaties that Lord Elgin and other representatives of Western powers secured from Japan, the government undertook 'to provide all ports to foreign trade with such lights, buoys and beacons as may be necessary to render secure navigation'. When the British Ambassador, Sir Harry Parkes [33] drew the attention of the Japanese government, in 1868, to this clause, which had not been fulfilled, he was informed that they were perfectly willing to carry out their obligations, but they lacked the necessary technical expertise in order to do so.

Two brothers of the Scottish Lighthouse Board, David and Thomas Stevenson were commissioned and drew up a scheme for lighting the entire coast of Japan. They designed and had manufactured the necessary lanterns and apparatus and had them shipped out to Japan. Another Scot, Richard Henry Brunton, who was born in Muchalls as his father was chief officer of the Coastguard there, was recommended by the British Board of Trade to supervise the scheme.

Brunton and two assistants, Blundell and McBean, arrived in Yokohama in August 1868. The Scottish engineer was to stay eight years in Japan and by the time he left 36 lighthouses, two lightships, 13 buoys and three beacons had been established under his guidance. Construction of the lighthouses was complicated by the threat of earthquakes but Brunton overcame this problem by combining solidity with strength, using stone, brick, wood or iron depending on the local suitability and availability.

Brunton worked closely with Hirobumi Ito [34], one of the first Japanese students to study in Britain and later to become prime minister, and struck up a firm friendship with him. In 1872, Ito accompanied the Iwakura Mission to Europe and Brunton acted as his guide in visits to industrial establishments in London, Birmingham, Manchester, Liverpool, Newcastle, Middlesbrough, Edinburgh and Sheffield. Two years later, Brunton's lighthouse headquarters in Yokohama (where he trained Japanese in lighthouse construction and keeping) were visited by the Emperor Meiji and Brunton was presented to the Emperor by Hirobumi Ito who was then the Minister of Public Works.

The Scottish engineer's work in Japan was not limited to lighthouses. He helped establish the first telegraph line from Yokohama to Tokyo and then from Tokyo to Nagasaki, thus making communication possible between Tokyo and London via the Great Northern Telegraph. He constructed one of Japan's first iron bridges on the road from Yokohama to Tokyo and he upgraded Ino Tadataka's fine survey of Japan (completed in the first quarter of the 19th century) by increasing the scale to 20 miles to the inch to show towns and villages, rivers, mountains, roads and paths in as great a detail as was possible.

Brunton was a man of principle and determination who earned respect for his civil engineering work despite being impatient and arrogant on occasion. The two assistants who arrived with him went back to England after a year. He candidly described the difficulties of his time in Japan when he wrote: 'The conscientious and efficient conduct of work in Japan was a task which presented the most perplexing difficulties. Their high pay, their different mode of living, their want of disciplinary power and the knowledge that foreigners were more or less indispensable to the Japanese rendered European assistants most intractable and difficult to deal with. Resignation, insubordination, absence from duty, drunkenness, and other aberrations of conduct among Europeans employed in the service of the Japanese government became frequent and distressing. On the other hand, the semi-ignorance of the native servants of the Emperor, and the self-esteem, untrustworthiness, craftiness and corruption of the Japanese underlings rendered co-operation by an honourable foreigner with them extremely irritating'.

Brunton decided he had two choices in order to get things done in Japan. 'The first choice, which promised quietude and repose, was to let things take their course, give advice when asked for, feeling undisturbed if it was neglected, and become imbued with the Oriental estimation of the valuelessness of time, allowing nothing that hinders progress to perturb or annoy. Such was the method in the 1870s, by which the European could become a favourite with his Japanese employer. The second choice was to insist on a due enforcement of his directions but this line is almost certain to create friction as the Japanese had made up their minds to make what use they could of their foreign servants, but in no case to have them become their masters, or to invest them with any power. They hold them in the position of advisers or instructors only, without the authority to direct'. Despite Brunton's assertive attitude he was personally commended for his significant contribution to the modernization of Japan by the emperor when he was received in audience in 1872.

PAISLEY

(221) Museum and Art Galleries, High Street, Paisley, Strathclyde (Tel: 041–889 3151)

The Museum and Art Galleries have a number of Japanese items (swords, porcelain, ivories) which were donated about 100 years ago. These are not on permanent display but genuine researchers are granted access. *Open all year Monday–Saturday 10am–5pm. Closed bank holidays and Sundays.*

STOBO

(222) Stobo Castle, Peebleshire (Tel: 07216–249)

The present Stobo Castle was completed in 1811 and is a famous health spa today. Guests have free access to the adjacent Japanese water gardens; otherwise the owner, Leo Seymour, opens them once a year to the public. The gardens were laid out 100 years ago when the estate was owned by Hylton 'Punch' Philipson, all-England rackets champion and test cricketer who played in two series against the Australians alongside the legendary Dr W.G. Grace. The Japanese plants, shrubs and trees are now in their maturity and the stone lanterns and bridges add to the authenticity.

14 | *Northern Ireland*

BELFAST

(223) Ulster Museum, Botanic Gardens, Belfast
(Tel: 0232-381 251/6)

Ancient China brought prayer and war to its Japanese neighbour – and the dating on the 10 foot high lantern normally outside the Ulster Museum commemorates both.

The dedication inscribed on the lantern is sacred. It is to Osaka's Shitennoji Temple (the Temple of the Four Saints). The temple was founded in 593 AD by Prince Shotoku, Japan's first great patron of Buddhism. Japanese Buddhism was then little more than half a century old, having been introduced from China and Korea in 538 AD.

The Ulster Museum's lantern is an excellent replica of the original lantern from the Temple of the Four Saints. The replica, dated and signed, was made during the Tokugawa Era (1600–1867) by the bronzesmith, Seibei Tanaka. However, it is the date of the *original* work – from which the Ulster replica was made – that is so interesting. For some time prior to his first invasion of 19 November 1274, China's Kubla Khan had been making clear signals to the Japanese that they too should become his vassals. The Kamakura samurai responded defiantly by decapitating Khan's emmisaries. In May of the same year (the date is clearly marked) the original Osaka lantern was dedicated to Buddha. The Japanese monks prayed for his protection. Before the end of 1274, Kubla Khan's ships and his invading armies had been drowned in the seas off Japan. That's the divine significance of the Ulster Museum's bell. (Just before going to press, it was learned that the lantern had been vandalized).

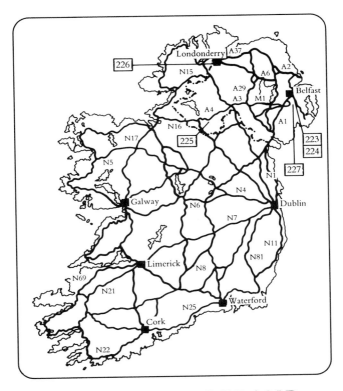

NORTHERN IRELAND

A few paces away, still outside the museum, is a nice four foot high temple bell of the Genroku era (1688–1704). Inside the museum, there is a fine lacquered palanquin from the mid 19th century, a few pieces of Japanese weaponry and some ceramics but nothing else of much general significance.

For the specialist, however, the geology department of the museum may have some surprises. Here there are over 100 specimens of Japanese origin. About 71 are minerals, some remarkably fine. The keeper especially notes a hand sphered crystal gazing-ball. There is also a rare and valuable 'Japan Twin' which occurs in mineral quartz – apparently exhibiting what is termed Japan Law. Technical enquiries to the Keeper of Geology please! *Open Monday to Friday 10am–5pm, Saturday 1pm–5pm, Sunday 2pm–5pm.*

(224) The Queen's University, Belfast, University Road; 13 St Ives Gardens, Stranmillis, Belfast

W.G. Aston (1841–1911), the translator, matriculated to Queen's College (now Queen's University) in 1859, took his BA in 1862 and his MA in 1863. In 1862, his scholastic achievements (he studied classics and modern languages) made him both general prizeman and class prizeman. In 1882, the college awarded him an Hon D Litt.

At one period of his life, Aston had a house at 13 St Ives Gardens, Stranmillis, about a quarter of a mile from Queen's. From a reference to the house's 'Japanese ornaments' and its owner's 'long flowing cloak' (a kimono?) it may well have been after Aston had been to Japan. For main Aston entry, see: [226].

FLORENCECOURT

(225) Maguire's Bridge; Moneen House, Moneen; St John's Churchyard, Florencecourt, Co Fermanagh

Before the glorious Meiji Restoration of 1868, there was the inglorious civil war. Off the battlefields, casualties spilled into temples already overflowing with the dying and the dead. It was here in the half light, through their pain and delirium, the Japanese soldiers saw a giant, built like a grizzly and were convinced they had joined their ancestors.

The god among the wounded was Ulsterman Dr William Willis (1837–94), broad, bearded and six foot four. He had joined Britain's new legation in Edo (Tokyo) in 1862, under Sir Rutherford Alcock [77] and was engaged as surgeon and assistant interpreter. However, it was as a medical man with compassion as great as his bulk that Willis would be remembered by both Japanese and British alike.

Japanese medical science, Willis soon discovered, was still in the dark ages and he laboured tirelessly to bring it into the light. Against the common practice of putting wounded prisoners to death, Willis constantly pointed out the value of human life. He insisted that he be given equal access to both sides in the civil war. Where there had been neglect, Willis brought care, new medical skills and the first use of the splint in Japan. Where there was filth and brutality, he introduced hygiene and painless septic surgery with chloroform.

'A medical man with compassion as great as his bulk', Dr William Willis [225]

William Willis was born on 1 May 1837, some 10 miles from Florencecourt, at Maguire's Bridge. For a man who grew up to earn the name of 'the gentle giant', Willis had a very different upbringing. His father, who worked in the Revenue Service, was a harsh, brutal man. It was only through his elder brother, James, that William was able to pursue his studies, at Glasgow and then Edinburgh to obtain a medical degree.

The house of James Willis, where his brother, Dr William Willis, died in 1894 [225]

Although William Willis spent much of his working life abroad – in Japan and Thailand, among other places – it was to the lakeland country of County Fermanagh that he always returned. William spent the Christmas of 1893 with his brother, James, at Lisdeevan House, now called Moneen House, Moneen, Florencecourt. He died there on Wednesday 14 February 1894, aged only 57. His well kept grave is in St John's Churchyard, Florencecourt (not in the old Killesher graveyard, with the earlier Willis burials). In 1985, Athlone Press published *Dr Willis in Japan: British Medical Pioneer, 1862–77* by Hugh Cortazzi.

Perhaps Dr William Willis's best epitaph should be that of Britain's second minister in Japan, Sir Harry Parkes [33] who had known Willis for some 16 years. 'The cause of humanity and the progress of scientific medicine in Japan', Parkes wrote, 'have been materially aided by his able and long sustained exertions'.

LONDONDERRY

(226) Londonderry

Just as the Bible has been the foundation of European culture, to understand the Japanese, it is necessary to have some idea of the early sacred texts. This was certainly the belief of William George Aston (1841–1911) who, in 1896, became the first man to translate the *Nihon Shoki* into English.

The *Nihon Shoki* (The Ancient Chronicles of Japan) originally appeared in 720 AD and are considered to be the final version of the slightly earlier *Kojiki* of 712 AD. Written in abstruse classical Chinese, the *Nihon Shoki* is part history, part myth, and part public relations. It gave the early Japanese the illusion that they belonged to an old, long established culture, to stand alongside ancient China. The book's pseudo-history supplied the Imperial family with a direct lineage to the gods and in the hands of ultra-nationalists, the myth-histories have been used to justify the superiority of the race.

Born in what is now Northern Ireland near Londonderry on 9 April 1841 and educated at Queen's University, Belfast, the young Aston showed early evidence of his linguistic skills by becoming a gold medalist in the classics and gaining honours in languages and literature.

When he arrived at the pioneer British legation in Japan as student interpreter in 1864, there were perhaps no more than half a dozen Europeans with any working knowledge of Japanese. There were no dictionaries, no grammars, not even any proper phrase books. In 1869 and 1872, Aston's own grammars were published, followed by a work on Japanese literature in 1899, and on the native Shinto religion in 1905.

Like Ernest Satow [98], a legation colleague, Aston's knowledge of the Japanese language and history enabled him to sound out grassroots support for the opposing royalist and shogunate camps – each battling for the future control of Japan. Based partly on this intelligence, the British were able to judiciously back the restoration of the emperor and reap the many trading benefits after this took place.

Aston retired from Japan in 1889, settling in Beer, Devon, where he is also buried [93]. His unique collection of some 9,500 Japanese books and manuscripts is held in the Cambridge University Library [121].

Aston's contributions cannot be overstated. His works on Japanese literature and religion were translated into Japanese and quoted by the country's leading scholars. According to a contemporary academic, Dr Haga of Tokyo University, the trinity of Aston, Satow [98] and Chamberlain [87] were the cultural interpreters who prepared both countries for the benefits of the Anglo–Japanese Alliance of 1902.

SAINTFIELD

(227) Academy Primary School; Ballyhalbert National School; 1 Ballynahinch Road, Saintfield, County Down

W.G. Aston (1841–1911), first translator of the *Nihon Shoki*, was born near Londonderry. His first school was Donagheady National School in Donagheady Parish near Strabane. (Donagheady is also spelt Donaghanie.) When the family moved to Saintfield (a small town south-east of Belfast) Aston became a pupil at the Saintfield National School, where his father was a teacher and his mother an assistant. (The present school, the Academy Primary School, built in 1976, is about half a mile away.)

On 31 August 1857, Aston became a teacher at Ballyhalbert National School, about 25 miles away. This only lasted until 31 May the following year, when he was dismissed for 'inefficiency'.

The Aston family lived in the nearby schoolhouse, then 10 Cow Market. There has been remarkably little change in the actual building but Aston's house is now a furniture store, the present address being 1 Ballynahinch Road. For main Aston entry, see: [226].

15 | *Ireland*

BANTRY

(228) Bantry House, Bantry, County Cork
(Tel: 027-50047)

When Bantry House was contacted it was discovered that their prize lacquered chest from the Momoyama Period (1586–1615) was where they kept the cleaning materials!

These wonderful chests, which are often described as Marriage Coffers, are examples of the best of Japanese lacquerware. They were inlaid with mother-of-pearl and specially tailored to European taste. Shape, function, even decoration would have been in scant demand in the home market. The Jesuits, who first came to Japan in 1542, used them to store their robes and altar cloths.

It may be of salutary interest that one of these rare Japanese treasures went under the hammer at Christie's in 1989. (Admittedly, it had more showroom gleam than the one at Bantry House.) The reserve price was of the order of £70,000–90,000.

Other Japanese items of interest are a scarlet lacquer table, the waved circular top decorated in shades of gilt with pheasants and flowering trees; also several baluster vases and some ginger pots. But it's the cleaning materials you should head for first. *Located about half a mile north from the town, overlooking the bay. Open daily 9am–6pm (until 8pm most summer evenings).*

CARRIGALINE

(229) Carrigaline, County Cork

Twin brothers John and Cornelius Collins were born in

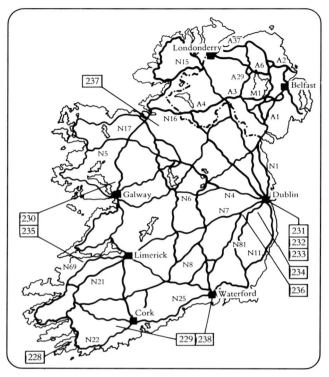

REPUBLIC OF IRELAND

Carrigaline in 1851 and both were instructors in the Imperial Japanese Navy. John went to Japan in 1873 and after 15 years service was rewarded with the Order of the Rising Sun and personally presented by the Emperor Meiji with another Order of Merit. He returned to Ireland in 1888 and was a local councillor and Justice of the Peace.

CONG

(230) Belwood House, Cong, County Mayo

As a boy, the author Lafcadio Hearn (1850–1904) spent holidays here at Belwood House with his cousins, the Elwoods, who owned 347 acres. Their once splendid house is now in ruins. For main Hearn entry, see: [232].

DUBLIN

(231) National Museum of Ireland, Kildare Street, Dublin (Tel: 01–618811)

About 1,700 years before the invention of the video camera, Japan's first picture stories were being produced in bronze. The artists were the shadowy bell-people, who lived in the area of present day Kyoto. They cast their images on strange bell-like objects called *dotaku*. The designs, in simple relief, give the first known images of Japan at the dawn of the metal age. Some depict fishing, hunting and everyday tasks. Others, such as the rare example in the National Museum of Ireland, have diagrammatic patterns. There are horizontal and vertical bands, diamonds, triangles and whirlpools. Dublin's *dotaku* is similar to the one designated a National Treasure in the National Museum of Tokyo. It belongs to the Yayoi period (c200 BC to 250 AD) and is about 16 inches high.

The characters *do* and *taku*, which make up the word *dotaku*, simply mean bronze bell. Bell ringing may thus have been the original purpose. With time, however, their clappers must have shrivelled in size until the 'bells' could no longer ring. Made principally of copper, a precious metal from China, it is reasonable to imagine the expensive non-functional *dotaku* advertising a rich man's riches. The *dotaku* may also have been considered sacred – revered in hunting or fertility rituals.

The *dotaku* is probably the National Museum of Ireland's most significant piece in an outstanding and varied Japanese collection of some 1,500 objects. The collection covers suits of armour, edged weapons, medicine boxes, combs, *netsuke*, carved wood and lacquer work, shrines, articles of bronze and brass, pottery and porcelain, textiles and wood block prints.

The 'Curator's choice' includes two other items of exceptional merit. One is a luxury palanquin, with the three-leaved hollyhock crest of the Tokugawas. The other is a gorgeous flower vase of the Meiji period (1868–1912), made by master craftsman Kume. Around it, brightly coloured carp ascend a pale blue waterfall.

The National Museum's Japanese collection was first opened in 1890 then, through lack of curatorial expertise, closed in 1960. However, in 1984, Professor Tomoyo Suzuki of the Tokyo National Research Institute of Cultural properties, selected the 200 most outstanding items. These are described and illustrated in a new colour catalogue. On 5 March 1985, the Museum's new Japanese Gallery was officially opened by the then Crown Prince Akihito and Princess Michiko. *Open Tuesday–Saturday 10am–5pm, Sunday 2pm–5pm.*

(232) 48 Lower Gardiner Street; 21 Leinster Square, the Rathmines; 73 Upper Leeson Street, the Rathmines, Dublin

They say that every young Western man who comes to Japan and falls in love with the country and its people is a Lafcadio Hearn (1850–1904). Hearn's romantic view of pre-industrial Japan is still that held by many an armchair traveller, even to this day.

Ireland's most famous Japanese link was born on the Ionian island of Lefkas, to Charles, an Irish staff surgeon in the British army, and a local Ionian girl, Rosa. At the age of two, while his father was stationed in the West Indies, Lafcadio's Uncle Richard escorted him and his mother to Dublin, where they arrived on 1 August 1852.

Lafcadio's first Irish address was in the then fashionable Lower Gardiner Street (now a guesthouse). Here Elizabeth Hearn, Lafcadio's great-aunt, was staying with her daughter and son-in-law, Jane Hearn and Henry Cloclough. Lafcadio's mother, Rosa, although from a family of proud local standing, was illiterate even in her own language and needed to speak English through an interpreter. Not only was she what the Hearns considered totally uneducated, there was something infinitely worse. To the staunch Protestant Hearns, Rosa's Catholicism was anathema.

It was probably the religious question more than any other that drew Rosa and Lafcadio away from Lower Gardiner Street to the wealthy home of Elizabeth Hearn's younger sister, the 60 year old Mrs Sarah Holmes Brenane, a convert to the Roman Catholic church. She lived at 21 Leinster Square, the Rathmines, a south Dublin suburb. Although long unrecognized, the house now has a commemorative plaque, unveiled at a ceremony held on 1 July 1988 and attended by the Japanese minister, Mr Kajiyama and the

'Ireland's most famous Japanese link', Lafcadio Hearn in kimono [232]

Lord Mayor. Lafcadio Hearn is similarly honoured with a plaque at the house occupied by him and Mrs Brenane, from 1856. This is 73 Upper Leeson Street, also in the Rathmines. In 1854, Rosa became mentally unbalanced and was sent back to Lefkas. Lafcadio was made an informal ward of Mrs Brenane. For a time, she doted on the child. The careless happiness of young childhood ended for Lafcadio, however, when Mrs Brenane sent him to a catholic seminary in France, by all accounts a bleak, harsh place. Then, at 13, he went to boarding school near Durham, at the Roman Catholic college of St Cuthbert's, Ushaw [137].

At the age of 19, in extreme poverty, short in stature and disfigured, Hearn sailed to America. The price of the fare was probably the last thing his family ever did for him. In America he obtained work as a journalist. His marriage to a black girl, which lasted three years, broke the miscegenation laws and lost him his job. His luck finally changed. He became editor of the *New Orleans Democrat*, contributed to other periodicals and had several books successfully published. In 1890, Hearn was sent to Japan on an assignment. After quarrelling with his editor, he began the happiest period of his life – freelancing, working as professor of literature, marrying a well placed Japanese girl and even taking a Japanese name, Yakumo Koizumi. It was during this time that Hearn produced much of his best work.

In *Japan – An Attempt at Interpretation*, one of his most widely read works, Hearn strives to reach inside the Japanese psyche. He wrote, 'the occidental mind appears to work in straight lines, the oriental in wonderful curves and circles'. His eulogies on Japanese women reach out to every male visitor to Japan before and since. His writing also found a direct response in medievalists like Algernon Mitford [103], who so regretted the extinction of Old Japan.

'It has required thousands of years to make her', Hearn wrote of all the Madam Butterflys who ever lived. 'Before this ethical creation, criticism should hold its breath. She is an ideal beyond occidental reach. Her delicacy, her child-like piety and trust, her exquisite tactful perception of all ways to make happiness about her . . . Perhaps no such woman will appear in this world again for a hundred thousand years: the conditions of industrial civilization will not permit of her existence'.

73 Upper Leeson Street, where Lafcadio Hearn lived as a child with Mrs Brenane [232]

Lafcadio Hearn had also long been fascinated by the macabre. His first book on Japan came out in 1894 with another ten during his lifetime. Much of his writings drew on Japanese folklore and fantasy. Hearn's ghosts were not European but Japanese – gentle creatures in harmony with nature, the living and the dead.

In Ghostly Japan appeared in 1899, *Shadowings* in 1900, *A Japanese Miscellany* in 1901 and *Kotto* in 1902. One of his most popular books *Kwaidan* (Weird Tales) came out in 1904, the year in which the author died. *Japanese Fairy Tales* was not published until 1918 and *Karma and Other Stories* not until 1921.

In 1988, a new shrine appeared in honour of the author – the Lafcadio Hearn Library in the Embassy of Ireland, Tokyo. For other Hearn entries, see: [81, 137, 230, 238].

(233) Chester Beatty Library and Gallery of Oriental Art, 20 Shrewsbury Road, Ballsbridge, Dublin (Tel: 01–269 2386/269 6581)

The millionaire founder of the Chester Beatty Library and Gallery of Oriental Art was perhaps the art world's most fastidious collector.

In 1954, Sir Alfred Chester Beatty gave Japanese art expert and author, Jack Hillier, an astounding commission. His immense Oriental collections, Beatty told Hillier, already included representative art from most Eastern countries but very little on Japan. Beatty commissioned Hillier to fill this gap with one overriding consideration. Every item must be *without flaw*.

Hillier's recently published book, *Japanese Masters of the Colour Print*, had made its author something of an authority. This included a close knowledge of the Japanese art market. Hillier advised that there seemed to be only one kind of Japanese print that fulfilled all the Chester Beatty criteria, including the notional limit of £125 per print. This was the *surimono* print, which at the time was neither fashionable nor expensive, often small, mounted on stout paper, usually well preserved and held by private Japanese families. Acting on Sir Chester Beatty's authority, Hillier then proceeded to cream the world *surimono* market. The word *surimono* simply means 'printed object'. It could be a picture, text, or both picture and text. The essential difference between *surimono* and the infinitely more common kind of print is that a *surimono* was privately commissioned.

The *surimono* art form dates from around the 1790s. It was frequently used to commemorate an event, in both words and pictures. An individual *surimono* could thus be the cooperative masterpiece of painter, calligrapher and poet. And as each *surimono* was made for a bespoke market, there was considerably more scope for innovation and experiment – in style, size, type or paper, or even in the colours used.

To suit Beatty's policy of perfection at a price, the choice of *surimono* could not have been bettered. Hillier found he never had to pay more than £25 for even the noblest work. However, to satisfy Beatty's extraordinary standards, the culling was savage. Even some of Hillier's own favourites didn't pass muster. However, the outcome meant that the Chester Beatty *surimono* collection is among the best ever assembled.

Another Chester Beatty Japanese treasure is probably even rarer than the *surimono*. It is a unique collection of *Nara ehon*. These beautiful hand painted scrolls and books are Japan's equivalent of the illuminated manuscripts of medieval Europe. At opposite ends of the earth, monks serving different gods, had copied and preserved the literature, calligraphy, learning, faith and decorative skills, each of their own culture. For years, the very existence of the *Nara ehon* collection in the Chester Beatty archives had been forgotten, its importance unknown. In 1963, it was a chance meeting in Japan that led to the rediscovery of these Chester Beatty masterpieces.

In that freezing winter, two off-season foreigners huddled for warmth in a little back-street Kyoto restaurant. One, an American student, Barbara Ruch, was preparing for her doctorate in medieval Japanese literature. The other, an Englishman, was a specialist in Japanese woodblock prints. They found they differed passionately over their evaluation of Japanese art – especially in Ms Ruch's specialist subject: *Nara ehon*. The Englishman's parting remark, Barbara Ruch later recalled, was like a map to a treasure hunter. He said, 'If you're ever in Dublin, Ireland, I remember seeing some *Nara ehon* there once – in a small library'.

Barbara Ruch took the long way home, via Dublin, to the 'small library' in Shrewsbury Road. Nobody at the Chester Beatty seemed to know what she was talking about but a kind old lady took her to a hallway cupboard where there were a lot of very large, dusty, cardboard boxes. It was here that Ms Ruch found the 'lost' *Nara ehon*.

The excitement ignited by this discovery rang around the Japanese art world like a temple gong. In 1978, the first international research conference on medieval Japanese texts held outside Japan was hosted by the Chester Beatty in Dublin. Following this week-long symposium of 25 of the world's most eminent scholars in the field, the museum's *Nara ehon* collection was generally held to be amongst the finest of its kind. The texts deal in all manner of subjects, religious and secular, with strong, graphic drawings and rich, bright colours.

During the first royal tour of Ireland by members of the Japanese Imperial family, in March 1985, Crown Prince Akihito and Princess Michiko paid a special visit to the Chester Beatty Library and Gallery of Oriental Art. Among the items they were shown was a 17th century manuscript of Japan's great, classic 11th century novel, *The Tale of Genji*. This manuscript was once part of the dowry of the daughter of a great *daimyo* (feudal lord). All 54 volumes are preserved here, in the original black lacquer cabinet, decorated in fine gold.

Sadly, there is insufficient space to describe the museum's entire Japanese banquet in detail. But after you've feasted on the above, do please go on to the subsequent courses of early Buddhist material, metalwork, lacquer, *inro* and *netsuke*. Sir Alfred Chester Beatty died in 1968 at the age of 93. *Open Tuesday–Friday 10am–5pm, Saturday 2pm–5pm.*

ENNISKERRY

(234) Powerscourt, Enniskerry, County Wicklow (Tel: 01-286 7676)

The vast, famous and beautiful Powerscourt has, in a complex of European gardens, a Japanese *style* garden. It is not authentic but has some exquisite corners, charm and peace.

At a point near the entrance, where the view of the Sugar

'Exquisite corners, charm and peace' are to be found in the Japanese style garden at Powerscourt [234]

Loaf reminds many of Mount Fuji, you will find some of the elements of Japan. There is a red hump-back bridge, a pagoda, rills and a pond. The Japanese garden was built around 1910 – the great period for building Japanese gardens in the British Isles. The theme of life, initially used at Tully [236], was also attempted here.

Here again is the allegorical span of life. Two paths enter from the east and meet at the 'marriage bridge'. Continue and the route brings you to a grotto or fernery where there is a grave. From the grave you rise again through the tortuous grotto route. Eternity is ahead of you. At least that is the theory. It is a charming experience.

The spring and autumn are also worth seeing here. Japanese Sika deer were introduced in Powerscourt in the 1860s and supplied to 30 other parks from here. Sadly, they have by now all interbred with the native red deer. *Open 1 March–31 October 9am–5.30pm.*

GLIN

(235) Glin Castle, Glin, County Limerick
(Tel: 068-34173/34112)

Nobody knows precisely when the first Japanese prints arrived in Europe but there are plenty of stories of Oriental imports with a Hokusai or a Hiroshige used as wrapping paper. In Paris, in 1856, the printmaker, Felix Bracquemond, made a chance discovery of a printed book of Hokusai's *Manga* (random sketches). Hokusai was not only one of Japan's most well known artists, the sheer volume of his output is thought to have never been equalled anywhere. The *Manga* seems to have been widely copied from and circulated amongst Paris artists, spreading interest in Japanese prints. In 1866, a year before the first exhibition of Japanese art in Paris, Eugene Rousseau commissioned Bracquemond to decorate a huge dinner service. Bracquemond borrowed heavily from Hokusai and also from Hiroshige and Isai. Etchings were made of birds, flowers, fishes and so on. These were then cut up and transferred to the ceramic blanks. In the firing, the paper would burn, leaving the printed images. These would then be hand-coloured before glazing. The service, of over 50 pieces, is the first known example of *Japonisme* in the decorative arts. The term itself,

Japonisme, however, is thought to have been first used in 1872, by the French critic Phillipe Burty. In 1890, according to the present Knight of Glin, his grandmother needed a large service for giving shooting lunches. Hokusai seemed to fit the bill nicely. It's in the family dining room in the old servants' wing. *On the Shannon shore, eight miles west of Foynes, the village adjoins the demesne. Open 1–31 May 10am–12 noon, 2pm–4pm and at other times.*

KILDARE

(236) Tully Japanese Gardens, Kildare, County Kildare (Tel: 045-21251)

When King Edward VII won the 2,000 Guineas at the 1909 Derby, one Japanese name was on everyone's lips. 'Minoru, Minoru!' they shouted. Few, however, knew that Minoru, the winning racehorse, was named after the man who had just helped bring about one of the most unusual and interesting Japanese-inspired gardens in Britain and Ireland.

Minoru was one of two sons of master-gardener Eida. The millionaire Scottish brewer, the later Lord Wavertree, founder of the National Stud (and lessor of race-horses to the Royal stables) had commissioned the Japanese family to create a unique garden out of an Irish bog. Using the

'Using the symbolism of the Japanese gardening tradition and the materials of stone, plant and water, the brief was nothing less than to show man's journey from womb to death': Tully Japanese Gardens [236]

symbolism of the Japanese gardening tradition and the materials of stone, plant and water, the brief was nothing less than to show man's journey from womb to death.

As anyone visiting the Tully Japanese Gardens can see, Eida and family succeeded brilliantly. So well has the idea been interpreted that when, for example, the middle-aged look back on their lives, the path physically blocks the view of childhood. It is a reminder that in real life, clear accurate memory has limitations.

The making of the garden took four years. Under the direction of Eida and Minoru 40 labourers shifted hundreds of tons of limestone from several miles away. Large Scots pines were lifted and transplanted. A ship was actually chartered to sail to Japan and returned loaded with massive stone lanterns, plants, bonsai, a tea-house and even an entire miniature Japanese village. And all for £38,000. Compared to some of the other gardens taking shape at that time, Lord Wavertree seems to have got a bargain.

Eida wasn't so lucky. Having played the creator so successfully, he must have made the gods jealous and he died in London on the way home to Japan in 1912. Many years have passed in the Tully Japanese gardens since then. After Wavertree presented farm and garden to the British National Stud in 1915, there was a period of serious neglect. Then in 1943, the Irish National Stud became the new owners and under their stewardship, the Tully Japanese Garden was reborn.

Like most Japanese gardens of its age, Eida's creation is basically a hill or water garden, incorporating an inner tea-garden. As more and more travellers have recently realized, there is another very important type of Japanese garden, apparently overlooked in the grand Japanese garden building period around the turn of the century. The Ryoanji garden in Kyoto, a 16th century masterpiece by Soami, is probably Japan's most famous example of the *other* type of garden – the dry garden. In recent years, the Ryoanji has been the inspiration for a number of Japanese gardens throughout the world, but nobody has yet been able to explain how this apparently simple arrangement of 15 rocks and sand has maintained its fascination over four centuries.

During the 1970s, two dry gardens were created at Tully, using the same basic ingredients of rock and sand. The first, designed in 1974, continues the theme of Eida's original garden and takes man beyond death into eternity. The second, intended as a Zen meditation garden, was made two years later very much in the style of Ryoanji. *Located one mile from Kildare Town and five miles from Newbridge. Easter–31 October Monday–Friday 10am–5pm, Sunday 2pm–5.30pm, Saturday and bank holidays 10am–5.30pm.*

COUNTY SLIGO

(237) County Sligo

William Stone was born in County Sligo in 1822 and went to Japan when he was 50 to help in the establishment of a telegraphic system. He spent the rest of his life there and ended up as Foreign Adviser to the Department of Communications. Stone received numerous Imperial decorations for his devoted work and died in his 95th year in 1917. He is buried in Aoyama Cemetery in Tokyo.

TRAMORE

(238) Tramore, County Waterford

The writer, Lafcadio Hearn (1850–1904) came to this seaside resort in July 1857, with Mrs Brenane, his great-aunt. The unhappy marriage of Lafcadio's parents, Rosa and Surgeon-Major Charles Hearn, had just been dissolved, for which Mrs Brenane heaped all the blame on Charles. Even worse in the eyes of Mrs Brenane, a Catholic convert, Charles had married again. These were unpardonable sins.

After Charles was assigned to a post in India, he came to Tramore to say goodbye. Mrs Brenane refused to let Charles into her house but could not deny him access to his son. Lafcadio was permitted to accompany his father for a walk along the Tramore beach. Although neither Charles nor Lafcadio knew it at the time, this was the last time that either would see the other again. For main Hearne entry, see: [232].

Bookshops with significant Japan sections

This is a very selective list of London bookshops which specialize in books about Japan. Many general bookchains (such as Waterstones and Pentos) stock books about Japan or by Japanese writers and larger museums and galleries keep Japanese artbooks.

Books Nippon
64–66 St Paul's Churchyard
London EC4
Tel: 071-248 4957

J. Burley & Co
Lot 49, Exchange Bookshop
Camden Lock Place
London NW1 8AF
Tel: 071-629 2813

Dillons University Bookshop
1 Malet Street
London WC1
Tel: 071-636 1577

East Asia Books & Arts Co
103 Camden High Street
London NW1
Tel: 071-388 5783

Han-Shan Tang Ltd
717 Fulham Road
London SW6
Tel: 071-731 2447

Japan Publications Centre
66 Brewer Street
London W1
Tel: 071-439 8035

Neal Street East
5 Neal Street
London WC2H 9PU
Tel: 071-240 0135

Nihon Token-Do
23 Museum Street
London WC1
Tel: 071-580 6511

Overseas Courier Service
2 Grosvenor Parade
Uxbridge Road
Ealing Common
London W5
Tel: 081-992 6335

Arthur Probsthain & Co
41 Great Russell Street
London WC1B 3PH
Tel: 071-636 1096

Books Nippon, St Paul's Churchyard, EC4 and The Japan Centre, Brewer Street, W1 – the two major bookshops in London for books from and about Japan

Index

Arabic numerals refer to
entry **numbers, not page**
numbers. Roman numerals
refer to *page* **numbers.**
Numbers in bold indicate
main entries.

Abbot Hall, 166
Aberdeen Art Gallery, 194
Aberystwyth Arts Centre, 191
Adams, William, xi, xiii-xiv,
    45, 55, **71**, 113, 127, 177
Aerospace Museum –
    Wolverhampton, xxvii
Ainu, xxvi, 89, 94, 121, 124,
    204, 208
Akihito, as Crown Prince, xx,
    xxviii, 15, 113, 130, 150,
    198, 231, 233
Albert Sloman Library –
    University of Essex, xxvii
Alcock, Sir Rutherford, 11, 17,
    25, 43, 44, 54, 60, **77**, 162,
    225
Anderson, William, 7
Anglo–Japanese alliances, xviii,
    2, 98
architecture, 32
archives, 7, 29, 30, 42, 50, 56,
    113, 121, 148, 171, 175, 192,
    203, 212, 214
Arita, *see* porcelain
armour, xxvii, xxviii, 26, 31,
    55, 61, 63, 67, 74, **82, 108,**
    134, 138, 142, **160,** 177, 178,
    194, 198, 211, 231
Armstrong, Sir William (Lord
    Armstrong), 98, 130, **150**
art galleries, 31, 35, 62, 94, 99,
    84, 105, 125, 134, 138, 147,
    156, 158, 159, 160, 161, 163,
    177, 179, 180, 182, 183, 191,
    194, 210, 212, 233
artillery, *see* guns
Ashmolean Museum, 111
Astley Hall, 164
Aston, W.G., 93, 121, 224,
    226, 227
Atishimo, Prince, 15
Atkinson, Professor R.W., 91

Bagshaw Museum, 132
Bai-itsu, 111
Bamburgh Castle, 130
Bantry House, 228
Batchelor, John, **89**, 124
Batsford Park, 13, 103
Beatty, Sir Alfred Chester, 233
Bethnal Green Museum of
    Childhood, 38
Bird, Isabella, 129, 106, **133**,
    189, 207, 219
Blackburn Museum and Art
    Gallery, 159
Birmingham Museum and Art
    Gallery, 105
Birmingham Reference
    Library, xxvii
Bladen, Douglas, 16
Blair Castle, 198
Blunden, Edmund, 127, 117
Bodleian Library, 113
Bolton Museum and Art
    Gallery, 160
books, collections, rare, 7, 76,
    113, 115, 121, 192, 212
Bower, Denys, 67
Bowes, James Lord, 174, 171

Bowes Museum, 131, 171
bows and arrows, 61, 82, 211
Bradford Art Galleries and
    Museums, 134
brass, *see* metalwork
Brighton Art Gallery and
    Museum, 63
Bristol Museum and Art
    Gallery, 94
British Library, 7, 121
British Museum, 6
bronze, *see* metalwork
Bruce, James (Lord Elgin), *see*
    Elgin, Lord
Brunton, Richard Henry, 220
Buddhism, 26, 46, 62, 110,
    113, 223, 233
Burrell Collection, 210
Buncho, Tani, 111
Bury Art Gallery and Museum,
    161

calligraphy, 136, 141
Cambridge – University
    Library, 121, 7
Cambridge – University
    Museum of Archaeology
    and Anthropology, 121
carving, wood, xxvii, 26, 61,
    138, 154, 208, *see also
    netsuke; inro; and okimono*
Castle Museum – Nottingham,
    xxviii
ceramics, xxvii, xxviii, 6, 21,
    26, 76, 84, 92, 94, 99, 100,
    108, 111, 132, 136, 156, 157,
    158, 178, 188, 191, 231
Chiddingstone Castle, 67
Canterbury Royal Museum
    and Art Gallery, 64
Carlisle Museum and Art
    Gallery, 163
Cavendish, Thomas, 99
Cecil Higgins Art Gallery and
    Museum – Bedford, xxviii
Chamberlain, Basil Hall, **87**, 94

Chatham Historic Dockyard,
    65
Chester Beatty Library and
    Gallery of Oriental Art, 233
Cheltenham Art Gallery and
    Museum, xxvii
Chokushi-mon, *see* Royal
    Botanic Gardens
Christie, Ella, 202
Christopher, xiii, 99
Clove, 55, 99
Collins, John and Cornelius,
    229
Compton Acres, 79
Conder, Josiah, 32, 118
Cosmos, xiii, 99
costume, 111, 142, 156, 187,
    211
Cowden Castle, *see* Christie,
    Ella
Cragside, 150
Croydon Airport, 49

Dallam Tower, 181
deer scarer, (*shishi-odoshi*), 170,
    196
Derby Museum, xxviii
Dogger Bank Incident, *see*
    Russo–Japanese War
dolls, Japanese, xxvi, 38, 140,
    156
Dorset College of Agriculture
    Garden, xxvii
dotaku, see temple bells
Douglas, Archibald, 73
Dover Museum, 68
Dundee District Archive and
    Record Office, 203
Dunfermline Abbey, 205
Dunrobin Castle, 217
Duthie Park Japanese Garden,
    196
Dyer, Henry, 78, 199, 206,
    211, 214, **216**

Earle, Joe, 26
East, Alfred, 125

Edinburgh Central Library, 206

Edo period, *see* Tokugawa period

Eisen, Keisai, 180

Elgin, Lord (James Bruce), 19, 60, 82, 200, **205**, 209, 220

Elswick Cemetery – Newcastle upon Tyne, 145

e-makimono, see paintings

Endo, Kinsuke, 34, 91

engineering, 34, 91, 216, 220

Exbury Gardens, 69

Fan Museum, 41

Fanhams Hall Japanese Garden, 128

fans, 41, 51

first British troops in Japan, 162

first Europeans in Japan, xii

first Japanese Mission to England (1862), 44, 68

first Japanese sailors (1614), 55, 99

first Japanese to reach British Isles, 99

Fitzwilliam Museum, 119

Fumihito, HIH Prince, 6, 113

Fushimi, Prince, 68

Gakutei, Yashima, 163, 194

gardens, Japanese, xi, xvii–xviii, xxvii, xxviii, 57, 58, 66, 69, 70, 72, 79, 102, 103, 122, 126, 128, 141, 143, 149, 151, 167, 170, 181, 184, 196, 197, 202, 219, 222, 234, 236

Genji Monogatari, *see Tale of Genji, The*

Gladstone Pottery Museum – Stoke-on-Trent, xxvii

Glasgow Art Gallery and Museum, 211

Glasgow Museum of Transport, 215

Glasgow University Library, 212

Glin Castle, 235

Glover, Thomas, 209

Glynn Vivian Art Gallery and Museum – Swansea, xxviii

gravestones, Japanese, curious, xxvi, 52, 155, 202

Gray Art Gallery and Museum, 138

Great Japan Exhibition, 1981/2, xx, 6

Grindon Museum, 156

guns, 43, 44, 67, 82, 150

Hall Park Japanese Garden, 141

Hamada, Shoji, 21, 84, 92, **100**, 158, 179, 191

Hammersmith and Fulham Central Library, 56

Hancock Museum, 146

Haniwa period artifacts, 67, 208

Hanley City Museum and Art Gallery, xxvii

Harris Museum and Art Gallery, 183

Harunobu, 159, 163

Hascombe Court Garden, 72

Hastings Museum and Art Gallery, 74

Hawes, Albert George, 97

Hill of Tarvit Mansion, 201

Heale House Gardens, 102

Hearn, Lafcadio, 81, 137, 193, 230, **232**, 238

Herbert Art Gallery and Museum, xxvii

Hereford City Museum and Art Gallery, xxvii

Hilditch, John, 132

Hillier, Jack, 233

Hirobumi, Ito Prince, *see* Ito, Prince Hirobumi

Hirohito, Emperor, xix, xx, 10, 58, 80, 113, 115, 116, 121, 162, 198

Hiroshige, Ando, 159, 163,
212, 235
Hokusai, Katsushika, 159, 163,
210, 212, 235
Holburne of Menstrie
Museum, 92
Hornel, E.A., 218
Horniman Museum and
Library, 51
Hunterian Art Gallery, 211

Ieyashu, Shogun, xiii–xiv, 55,
71, 177
Ilfracombe Museum, xxvii
Imari, *see* porcelain
Imperial Japanese Family, 6,
10, 15, 30, 58, 68, 80, 113,
115, 116, 121, 130, 150, 157,
198, 231, 233
Imperial War Museum, 50
Inoue, Kaoru, 34, 43, 91
Inoue, Masaru, 34, 91
inro, 51, 61, 74, 76, 105, 134,
136, 160, 178, 233
Ipswich Museum, xxvii
Ito, Prince Hirobumi, 5, **34**,
43, 91, 98, 216, 220
ivories, 134, 136, 139, 152, 178,
194, 221, *see also netsuke;
inro; and okimono*

Japan–British Exhibition
(1909–10), xviii, 56
Japan Festival 1991, 57
Japan Information and Cultural
Centre, 20
Japan Society, 62, 125
Japanese Artist in London, A, 9,
16
Japanese School, Acton
(*Monbusho*), xxvi
Japanese Village in London, 17
Japonisme, xvii, xxvii, xxvii,
158, 159, 235
Jardine Matheson, 34, 91, 121,
209

Kaempfer, Engelbert, 7, 212
kakemono, see paintings
Kamiaki, 190
kami-kaze, xxvii, 179
katana, see swords
Kew Gardens, *see* Royal
Botanic Gardens
Kildrummy Castle Garden, 197
Kiyonaga, Torii, 163, 212
Koizumi, Yakumo, *see* Hearn,
Lafcadio
Kojiki, 87, 226
Koryusai, Isoda, 163
Kunichika, 190, 194
Kunisada, 167, 190, 212
Kuniyoshi, Utagawa, 166, 167,
194
Kyoto Japanese Garden, 57

Lacquerware, 26, 61, 62, 67,
74, 76, 94, 108, 111, 121,
131, 132, 136, 143, 156, 172,
178, 183, 210, 211, 223, 228,
233
Lady Lever Art Gallery, 182
Laing Art Gallery, 147
Lambeth Palace, xxvi
Lancashire Fusiliers Museum,
162
Lancaster Museum, 169
lanterns – stone, *see* gardens
lanterns – temple, 136, 223
Leach, Bernard, 21, 84, **92,
100**, 158, 160, 191
Leeds City Museum, 142
letters, *see* archives
Leverhulme, Lord (William
Hesketh Lever), 182, 184
Liberty's, xvii, 21, 30
libraries, 7, 29, 30, 56, 63, 64,
74, 76, 80, 94, 113, 121, 145,
153, 175, 185, 190, 192, 206,
212, 214, 216, 233
Liefde, xiii, 71
Liverpool Botanic Gardens
(Calderstone Park), 170
Liverpool Museum of Science

and Industry, 176
Liverpool Record Office, 171
London Protocol, *see* first
    Japanese Mission (1862)
Lotherton Hall, 143

Maidstone Museum and Art
    Gallery, 76
Mackintosh, Charles Rennie,
    212, **213**
Manchester City Art Gallery,
    177
Manchester Museum, 178
manuscripts, *see* archives
Marine Society, 65
Markino, Yoshio, 9, **16**, 40
Maruyama, Okyo, 94
masks, 51, 112, 183
Matheson, Hugh, 34, 91
Matsuo, *see* Christie, Ella
medicine, 225
Meiji era (1868–1912), xvi, 21,
    33, 73, 98, 116, 153, 186, 209
Merseyside County Museum,
    172
metalwork, 111, 134, 154, 178,
    179, 188, 201, 211, 231, 233
Michiko, Princess, 231, 233
Mikado, xvii, 17
Milne, John, 27, 59, **78**, 168,
    172, 185, 218
minerals, Japanese, 223
Minton Factory Museum,
    xxvii
Mitchell Library, Glasgow, 214
Mitford, Algernon Bertie
    (Lord Redesdale), 7, 13, 22,
    103, 116
Monro, Neil Gordon, 204, 208
Mount Ephraim Gardens, 70
mountaineering, 123
Murasaki Shikibu (Lady
    Murasaki), 3, 35
Museum of Artillery, 43
Museum of Mankind, xxvi
museums, xxvi, xxvii, xxviii,
    1, 6, 18, 26, 27, 38, 41, 42,
43, 48, 50, 51, 61, 62, 63, 64,
68, 74, 76, 82, 92, 94, 99,
105, 111, 121, 131, 132, 134,
136, 138, 139, 142, 154, 156,
159, 160, 161, 162, 163, 169,
172, 176, 178, 179, 183, 187,
188, 208, 211, 223, 231, 233
musical instruments, 121, 208,
    211

Nara period (710–784), 7
National Library of Wales, 192
National Maritime Museum,
    42
National Museum of Ireland,
    231
National Portrait Gallery, 35
Natsume, Soseki, 4, 36, 47, **48**,
    53
Navy, Imperial Japanese,
    xxviii, 42, 65, 73, 80, 86, 97,
    109, 120, 139, 145, 148, 150,
    161, 171, 176, 195, 215
netsuke, 51, 61, 74, 76, 92, 94,
    105, 121, 134, 136, 138, 160,
    172, 183, 194, 208, 231, 233
Newcastle upon Tyne Central
    Library, 145
newspapers, *see* archives
Newstead Abbey Japanese
    Garden, 126
Nihon Shoki, 226
Nissan Institute of Japanese
    Studies, 113, 117
Noh, 183, 112, *see also* masks
norimono, see palanquins
Nottingham Museum of
    Costume and Textiles,
    xxviii
Nuruhito, Crown Prince, 57,
    113

Ogilvy, Lady Clementine, 8
Ogisu, Takanori, 130
okimono, 74, 94, 105
Okumura, Masanobu, 177

Oliphant, Laurence, 19, **60**, 77, 200, 205
Oldham Art Gallery and Museum, 179
Ono, Yoko, 24
Oriental Museum – Durham, 136

paintings, xxvii, 31, 94, 111, 125, 126, 130, 158, 164, 212, 214, 217, 218
Paisley Museum and Art Galleries, 221
palanquins, 223, 177
paper making, 121
Parkes, Lady Fanny, 11, **33**
Parkes, Sir Harry, 11, **33**, 104, 121, 153, 220, 225
periodicals, *see* archives
photographs, archival, xxvii, 80, 92, 111, 112, 136, 145, 153, 161, 164, 185, 186, *see also* archives
Plymouth City Museum and Art Gallery, 99
Pitt Rivers Museum, 1, **112**
porcelain, xiv–xv, 26, 61, 76, 94, 99, **101**, 111, 114, 131, 138, 143, 144, 157, 164, 166, 182, 183, 187, 201, 212, 221, 231, 235
Portsmouth Central Library, 80
pottery, *see* ceramics
Powell Cotton Museum, 61
Powerscourt, 234
puppets, 51
prints, Japanese, xxvi, xxviii, 63, 76, 94, 105, 119, 134, 136, 147, 158, 159, 163, 166, 167, 177, 180, 190, 194, 206, 210, 211, 212, 231, 233

railways, 34, 85, 91, 107, 153, 165, 169, 215
Redesdale, Lord, *see* Mitford, Algernon Bertie

Rivington Gardens, 184
Rochdale Library, 185
Rochester, Guildhall Museum, 82
Rokumeikan, 32, *see also* Conder, Josiah
Rossendale Museum, 187
Rothschild, Edmund De, 68, 114
Royal Albert Memorial Museum, xxvii
Royal Botanic Gardens, 58
Royal Museum of Scotland, 208
Russell–Cotes Art Gallery and Museum, 62
Russell–Cotes, Sir Merton, 62
Russo–Japanese War, 42, 65, 108, 139, 145, 161, 203, 212
ryak umanto-darani, *see* paper making
Ryoanji, 236

St Helens Museum and Art Gallery, 188
Saffron Walden Museum, xxvii
Salisbury and South Wiltshire Museum, xxvii
Saris, Captain John, xiv, 55, 99
Satow, Ernest, 7, 39, **98**, 113, 226
Satsuma ware, *see* porcelain
Schloss, Arthur David, *see* Waley, Arthur
Schools, Japanese, xxvi, xxvii, xxviii, 83, 110
Science Museum, 27
Sheffield Central Library, 153
Sheffield City Museum, 154
seismology, 78
Sherbourne Castle, 101
Shinto, 6, 23, 178, 226
shipbuilding, xvii, xxviii, 42, 65, 98, 109, 145, 148, 150, 161, 195, 209, 215
shogunate, *see* Tokugawa period

Shoji, Hamada, *see* Hamada, Shoji
Shotoku, Empress, 7
Shuncho, Katsukawa, 163, 212
Shunshi, 212
Shuntosai, 112
Shunzan, 212
Siebold, Philipp Franz von, 6, 7
Sika deer, xxvii, xxviii, 23, 114, 234
Smith, Lawrence, 6
Snowshill Manor, 108
Southampton Art Gallery, 84
Soseki Museum, *see* Soseki, Natsume
Soseki Natsume *see* Natsume, Soseki
Stobo Castle Gardens, 222
Stone, Benjamin (photographic collection), xxvii
Stone, William, 237
Storry, George Richard, 117, 135
Sumiyishi, 163
Sunderland Museum and Art Gallery, 156
surimono, 233, 210, *see also* prints
Suzuki, Professor Tomoyo, 231
swords, xxvii, xxviii, 43, 61, 63, 64, 67, 74, 76, 82, 94, **105**, 108, 130, 136, 142, 147, **154, 156**, 172, **178**, 179, 183, 190, 194, 208, 221

Taki, Minoru, 6
Teikyo School in UK, xxvii
Tower of London, 55
Taisho, Emperor, 30, 116
Tale of Genji, The, 3 ,26, 35, 65, 233, *see also* Waley, Arthur, *and* Murasaki Shikibu
Tales of Old Japan, see Mitford, Algernon Bertie
Takahama, Kyoshi, 58

Tanaka, Seibei, 223
Tate Gallery, 31
Tatton Park, 167
tea ceremony, 102
tea ceremony utensils, 76, 178
tea-house, 6, 102
temple bells, xxviii, 231
Temple Newsam House, 144
Terajima, Munenori, xvii
textiles, xxviii, 26, 94, 132, 188, 190, 211, 231
Thorpe Park, 66
Togo, Admiral Heihachiro, xvi, 42, **65**, 120, 145
Tokugawa period (1600–1867), xiv, 7, 76, 82, 108, 140, 156, 159, 160, 177, 209
Torin, 163
Torosay Castle Japanese Garden, 219
Town Docks Museum – Hull, 139
Toyokuni, Utagawa, 166, 167, 194, 212
toys, 172, *see also* dolls
Trevithick, Francis Henry, xvi, 107, 165
Trevithick, Richard Francis, xvi, 85, **96**, 165
tsuba, see swords
Tsunematsu, Sammy Ikuo, 48
Tsushima, battle of, 65, *see also* Russo–Japanese War *and* Togo
Tully Japanese Gardens, 236

ukiyo-e, 159, *see* prints
Ulster Museum, 14
Usher Gallery, xxviii
Utamaro, Kitagawa, 119, 159, 163, 167, 210

Victoria and Albert Museum, 26

Waddesdon Manor, 114
Waley, Arthur, xxvi, 3, 12, 35, 88
Wallace Collection, 18
Wallington Hall, 157
war, memorials and records, xxviii, 2, 29, 50, 162, 176
Warrington Library, 190
Warwick District Council Art Gallery and Museum, xxvii
weaponry, 130, 136, *see also* swords; guns; armour; *and* bows and arrows
Wellcome Institute for the History of Medicine, 27
Weston, Reverend Walter, 14, **123**

Whitworth Art Gallery, 180
Wilberforce House, 140
William Morris Gallery and Brangwyn Gift, xxvi
Williamson, Professor A.W., 5, **34**, 75, **91**
Willis, Dr William, 33, **225**
Wirgman, Charles, 28
woodblock prints, *see* prints

Yamao, Yozo, 34
Yashitori, 190
Yeisen, 166, 212
York City Art Gallery, 158
Yoshio Markino, *see* Markino, Yoshio

The Japan Society

Founded 1891

The Japan Society was founded in 1891 with the primary objective of promoting the study and understanding of Japan in Great Britain. It also aims to contribute to the further development of friendly relations between the two nations.

In pursuit of its aims the Society organizes in London regular lectures about Japan, its history and culture and periodic functions to support better understanding between the British and Japanese peoples.

From its early days the Society has had Royal Patrons, sometimes British, sometimes Japanese. HRH The Princess Margaret, Countess of Snowdon, became its British Royal Patron in 1986.

The Society has 250 corporate as well as more than 1000 individual members, including leading Japanese companies operating in the UK and British companies doing business with Japan. Leading universities and libraries worldwide are among subscribers to the Society's publications.

The Society has an extensive library on Japanese subjects housed in the Japanese Embassy in Piccadilly, London W1. The library is open to the public from Monday to Friday.

The Society publishes half yearly its 'Proceedings' covering lecture texts and other material of permanent interest, also books on Japanese subjects through its own publishing company.

The Japanese Ambassador is President of the Society, ex-officio. Sir Hugh Cortazzi GCMG is Chairman of the Council in the Society's Centenary Year.

For membership details please contact The Secretary, Room 331, 162–168 Regent Street, London W1R 5TB, Tel 071-434 4507.